Urbicide in Palestine

Exploring the way urbicide is used to un/re-make Palestine, as well as how it is employed as a tool of spatial dispossession and control, this book examines contemporary political violence and destruction in the context of colonial projects in Palestine.

The broader framework of the book is colonial and post-urban destruction urbanism; with a working hypothesis that there are links, gaps and blind spots in the understanding of urbicide discourse. Drawing on several examples from the Palestinian history of destruction and transformations, such as Jenin Refugee Camp, Hebron Old Town, and Nablus Old Town, a methodological framework to identify urbicidal episodes is also generated.

Advancing knowledge on one historical moment of the urban condition, the moment of its destruction, and enhancing the understanding of the Palestinian Israeli conflict from urbanistic/architectonic and urbicide/spacio-cide perspectives through the use of case studies, this book is essential reading for scholars and researchers with an interest in urban geography and Middle East politics more broadly.

Nurhan Abujidi received her PhD in architecture, urban design and regional planning from the Catholic University of Leuven, Belgium, where she is currently a visiting professor. She worked as Director, Research Director and International Relations Coordinator at the school of Architecture, San Jorge University, Spain. She is Associate Researcher with the COSMOPLIS research group on City, Culture and Society at the VUB, Brussels, Belgium, working on the areas of military urbanism and architecture of resistance.

Routledge Studies in Middle Eastern Politics

Urbicide in Palestine

Spaces of oppression
and resilience

Nurhan Abujidi

Routledge
Taylor & Francis Group

LONDON AND NEW YORK

First published 2014
by Routledge
2 Park Square, Milton Park, Abingdon, Oxon OX14 4RN

and by Routledge
711 Third Avenue, New York, NY 10017

Routledge is an imprint of the Taylor & Francis Group, an informa business

© 2014 Nurhan Abujidi

British Library Cataloguing in Publication Data
A catalogue record for this book is available from the British Library

Library of Congress Cataloging in Publication Data
Abujidi, Nurhan.
Urbicide in Palestine: spaces of oppression and resilience/Nurhan Abujidi.
    pages cm.—(Routledge studies in Middle Eastern politics; 63)
    Includes bibliographical references and index.
    1. Cities and towns—Political aspects—Palestine.
    2. Arab-Israeli conflict—Social aspects. 3. Urban policy—Palestine.
    4. Sociology, Urban—Palestine. 5. Refugee camps—Palestine.
    6. Cultural landscapes—Palestine. 7. Cultural property—Palestine.
    8. Nationalism—Palestine. 9. Palestinian Arabs—Ethnic identity.
    I. Title.
    HT147.P27A28 2014
    307.76095694—dc23   2013032384

ISBN: 978-0-415-62705-4 (hbk)
ISBN: 978-1-315-81909-9 (ebk)

Typeset in Times New Roman and Stone Sans
by Florence Production Ltd, Stoodleigh, Devon, UK

We Palestinians have a habit of dedicating our work to Palestine.
In a context such as urbicide, maybe it is a practice that we all need
—to reaffirm to ourselves first of all that Palestine still exists, will
remain and live on.

The practice of dedicating includes an act of coming to terms with what has been written. I have to confess, that I still have not, as it symbolizes far more than what is written. Not as a piece of literature—but as a lived experience of those who are Palestinians and still living in Palestine. An experience that projects also the condition of many nations and communities worldwide.

Maybe it would have been easier to dedicate something that is about a time, a place or a topic that was more cheerful. Not in this case.

Palestinians know what urbicide is. They use other terms, understand it differently . . . and are forced to live with it.

Thus, I chose not to dedicate this to Palestine. For it has enough.

I dedicate it—

To those who don't know,
To those who have forgotten,
Or to those who simply choose to disdain what they know,
Who chose to ignore what they had created.

Contents

Figures

xii *Figures*

Acknowledgments

This book has benefited from the efforts, support, advice, encouragement, assistance, faith and passion of many people without whom this book would not be in its current form.

The book is the product of ten years of research in different universities in Belgium and Spain in which I have met many interesting scholars. I have learned an immeasurable amount from working among them, and they have been immensely important to the genesis of this book. Many have been especially kind, commenting on drafts and providing ideas. Thanks, in particular, to Han Verschure, Jef Vanden Broeck, Luc Reychler, Andréa Bruno, Hamdan Taha, Ismael Sheik Hassan, Lieven De Cuater, Hilde Heynen, Ahmed Zaib Khan, Yehya Serag, Felix Arranz, Jose Antonio Turegano, Angel Comeras, and Patricia de Monte.

Further afield, I have received vital support from different institute and research funds, and my gratitude goes to the Belgian Technical Cooperation, Erasmus Mundus, and UNESCO. My sincere thanks to ASRO KU Leuven for hosting me during my PhD (2003–2007) research and for hosting me during the writing of this book in 2013; special thanks here to Hilde Heynen for here important support in this regard. I also thank my friends and colleagues at COSMPOLIS, City Culture and Society at the Vrije University of Brussels, especially to Eric Corijn for his support and friendship.

I have also benefited from a wide range of critical feedback, which is especially important to a book of this breadth. My debts here are too numerous to list in full, but include Elia Zurieq, Falah Ghazi, Sari Hanafi, Abdullah Lux, Yasmeen Abu Laban, David Lyon, Eyal Weizman, Berma klein Goldewijk, Martin Shaw, Martin Coward, and Benedikte Zitouni.

I must emphasize, of course, that all mistakes and weaknesses of the current work remain my own.

Sincere thanks go to my friends in Palestine and the students of the 5th year in the department of architecture, An-Najah University, 2004–2005 group, who helped me in the field work and data collection: Ala' Anatr, Mukaram Abbas, Allam Elkashef, Ruba Subuh and Hanan Masri. Special thanks go to Zahara Zawawi for her help in obtaining missing information, maps and photos from the site were of great help. I also thank my friend Hamdi Maqbul, the architect of Nablus Municipality, for his invaluable aid in obtaining many archived and classified documents about Nablus. I also thank the inhabitants of Nablus Old Town for their tremendous help and collaboration during the fieldwork.

The visual material in this book draws on the work of a large number of friends and colleagues. Many thanks to Yasser Qudih, Hani Murtaja, Abed Qusini, Basel Mansour, Fadi Aruri, Khaled Qamhieh, Nablus Municipality, Hamdi Maqboul, Mu'ath Taher, Mohammad Rojoub, and Amal Kaawsh.

I should note that previous versions of parts of this work have already been published as follows: Chapter 6 in *Arab World Geographer* (vol. 9, issue 2, 2006, pp. 26–154); Chapter 7 in *Surveillance and Control in Israeli Palestine*, edited by Elia Zurieq, David Lyon and Yasmeen Abuklaabn (2011), London and New York: Routledge, pp. 313–335), also in *Contemporary Arab Affairs Journal*, (vol. 2, issue 2, 2009); and, finally, parts of Chapter 8 as a chapter in *Cultural Emergency in Conflict and Disaster*, edited by G. Frerks and B. Goldewijk (2011), Rotterdam: NAi, pp. 322–344.

My thanks go to Peter Aeschabacher, Marilyn van de Weijer and Wouter Bervoets for our endless chats over the topic and many other interesting themes, for his important help in rethinking the book structure and the visual material.

My sincere gratitude goes to my friend Ismae'l Sheikh Hassan for the interesting discussions and debates about Palestine and the complexity of this theme, for being able to translate and express my thoughts, those that were hard to verbalize, and also for taking me to see Palestine in different eyes and from a different perspective.

My thanks go to Routledge for their support in publishing this book.

I am deeply grateful for my sisters, Jehan and Wijdan, and my Mom for their unconditional love and help. Their genial spirits and their enormous network helped me to access the unobtainable while I was outside Palestine.

My indebtedness goes to Noureddin and my children Amine and Lina. Noureddin was husband, friend and assistant, and came to terms with being the father and mother to our children during the several hectic periods this research went through. I thank him also for tolerating my stress, frustrations and the many setbacks.

Nurhan Abujidi, Leuven

Introduction

Experiencing spaces of oppression and resistance

*They utterly destroyed all in the city, both men and women, young and old, oxen,
sheep, and asses, with the edge of the sword . . . Then they burned the whole city
and everything in it, but they put the silver and gold and the articles of bronze
and iron into the treasury of the Lord's house.*

(Joshua 6: 24)

This passage, recorded in the Old Testament Book of Joshua, in reference to
an early incursion on Jericho by Israelites, is a chilling reminder that human history
has frequently witnessed war for, and in, cities. Numerous other examples attest
to this fact: from the sack of Carthage in the Third Punic War, through the savage
destruction of Magdeburg in the Thirty Years War, to the bloody siege of Stalingrad
in the Second World War. Cities symbolize human progress in architecture,
artistic culture and social organization. Their degeneration into the violence and
chaos through armed conflict thus strikes a deep chord in the popular imagination
(Evans, 2004: 287).

In the twenty-first century, political violence and war are being re-inscribed
into the micro-geographies and architectures of cities in ways that, while super-
ficially similar to historic defensive urbanism, inevitably reflect our contemporary
conditions as Graham (2007) concludes.

Cowen (2007) argues that even with the demise of the revolution in military
affairs, the conviction that warfare itself has radically changed from a clash of
national armies in non-urban theatres to a future of irregular warfare in city streets
is still to be witnessed in the world in the coming decades.

The contemporary military urbanism is about spatial engineering and reorganization via complex surveillance and control and in many cases via the lethal
devastation of cities. The latest developments in the Arab world, in what is con-
troversially called the Arab Spring, is an explicit example of how cities became
the very theater and spaces of oppression and resistance.

It is hoped that this book will be an important contribution and complementary to the growing body of research on political/military urbanism in general and on urbicide in the Occupied Palestinian Territories in particular. It is premised on a dialectical redefinition and methodological development of an integrated frame-work to analyze and understand the theme of city (place) identity in connection with urbicide and resistance meanings and conditions. The debate around the mutual link between these different paradigms is based on questioning the centrality of space and spatial dynamics in forming a common language between them. The research on city partly persisted to affirm the intimate relation and position of space and spatial dynamics with city (place) identity and the centrality of this city (place) identity with its spatial dimension to military urbanism/urbicide and resistance discourses and activities. The theoretical arguments complemented by the Palestin-ian case study challenge called for new operational definitions, methodologies and understanding of the underlined themes that on one hand went beyond the traditional classic view of these themes as theoretical paradigms. On the other hand, the use of a detailed case study adds a strong experimental tool that confronts the multitude of common interrelated theoretical rhetoric and assumptions with realities. In political violence and urban warfare studies, city (place) identity is often discussed and represented in the city's symbols of identity (public build-ings, cultural artifacts). This common rhetoric and limited perspective lacks the spatial, social and cultural considerations and dimensions of city (place) identity. Furthermore, the discussion on military urbanism/urbicide is connected to the deliberate destruction of the above mentioned form of identity. This constrained outlook normally marginalizes the widespread destruction of the urban built environment and undermines the potentials and discussion on urbicide discourse. The other rhetoric that this research addresses is the power relations in colonial contexts in which charting of different resistance techniques is meant to highlight how people in their daily life survival activities develop creative techniques of resistance in such extreme urban conditions.

The importance of studying urbicide as a theory supported by a case study is, first, to rationalize and unearth what is normally perceived as a dark spot of city history—a moment that is typically not well documented. War times are marginal in city/urban research. Academic research invests energies and time in post-war moment or in peace moment focusing on development, reconstruction, urban renewal, and urban design issues. Critical theorists Ryan Bishop and Gregory Clancey (2003: 64) clearly state that modern urban social science in general has shown marked tendencies since the Second World War to directly avoid tropes of catastrophism (especially in the West). They argue that this is because the complete annihilation of urban places conflicted with its under-lying, enlightenment-tinged notions of progress, order and modernization. In the post-war Cold War period, especially, "The City," they write, had a "heroic status in both capitalist and socialist storytelling" (Bishop and Clancey, 2002: 66). This worked against an analysis of the city as a scene of catastrophic death:

"The city-as-target remained, therefore, a reading long buried under layers of academic Modernism" (67).

Most research on urban destruction and urban warfare normally focuses on the geopolitical, economical, military techniques and other issues that are not directly connected to urban and social matters.

Second, it aspires to provide and formulate a document and elaborated methodology of registering, researching, and analyzing urbicide. This document can be used as a tool to investigate cases that can be included in urbicide discourse or not. Consequently, appropriate legal measures can be developed to alleviate urbicide to the level of war crimes against humanity, exactly like genocide. The protection of human life is as important as the protection of urban civilizations and cultural identity; the moral commitment of the architect activist is the deriving engine behind such concerns.

The narratives on urbicide advance the knowledge on one historical moment of city life, the moment of its destruction. Moreover, registering urbicidal activities generate a counter-narrative that reveals other perspectives, accounts and interpretations of city history. Normally the history of war and victory is written and promoted (through media) by the victorious party. The weak party's voices are silenced. It is therefore a way to empower devastated communities and let their voices be heard. It is a way of contrastive interpretation of writing historical facts and events.

The research focus is on the Occupied Palestinian Territories, a case that is already exhaustively researched in general but that at the same time lacks an in-depth analysis of actual urbicidal activities. The detailed documented urbicidal case study of Nablus Old Town and its devastation through four years of Israeli military invasions and operations is the first document to be produced on devastated cities in the Palestinian case—and may also be the first on the international level, as far as this research is aware. It operates on city biography narrative principles from urban, spatial, socio-economic and perception perspectives. Less detailed discussion on other cases from the Palestinian context has been included to give a more comprehensive insight into urbicide discourse and a closer look at the colonial space engineering practice for oppression via surveillance, control and destruction strategies in Israel/Palestine. Consequently, a different and complementary perspective of the Israeli colonial project in Palestine to the vast literature and research yet from urbanistic and architectonic perspective can be generated.

The other challenge that the research encountered is the limited number of references on urbicide discourse. Most of the presented resources in this research are from Anglo-Saxon literature because the author's limited knowledge of other languages meant that she could not investigate urbicidal episodes and theory that are available in French, German, or Slavic, for example. The discussions on urbicide are normally developed by Western scholars with the focus on the Balkan case. The Middle East and Palestine have been also discussed by scholars such as

Steven Graham and Martin Coward, but their limited knowledge, experience, and insights into the specificity of the Middle Eastern and Palestinian conflict and the nature of their cities, culture and social tissue generate a macro perspective of two elements of the urbicide process: its mechanisms and the military techniques for its implementation. This book is therefore important for its first-hand analysis, experience and extensive field work, which will consequently highlight detailed insights into the human and socio-spatial dimension of urbicidal process. The work of Stephen Graham in cities under siege gives a comprehensive view on military urbanism, and he should be credited for advancing the knowledge on this discourse. Though he articulates several interesting cases around the globe, his work did not succeed in digging into the level of the lived experience of people within cities targeted by the "new military urbanism"—a limit that he himself acknowledges. The books of the prominent Israeli researcher Eyal Weizman (2007, 2011) are considered to be key work on the Occupied Palestinian Territories; they do bring out the voices of people—but a very selective strata of the Israeli military elites, soldiers and humanitarian's workers, architects and activities are incorporated. At the same time it lacks the everyday experience of occupation, oppression and resistance that this book intends to highlight and complement with the existing literature on the colonial project in Palestine.

This book is divided into three main parts. In Part I—City, war and urbicide: inquiry—Chapter 1 presents the history of the intimate relationship between city, urbanity, and destruction in war events. It further highlights the development of warfare and differences in the pre-modern, modern and contemporary periods. Chapter 2 develops a dialectical reading of the body of theory and doctrines on urbicide discourse, constructing the different modus, patterns and mechanisms that urbicide might follow.

Part II—Urbicide in Palestine—explores the way urbicide is used as a tool to un/re-make the Palestinian territoriality/urbanity as well as a tool of spatial dispossession and control. Drawing on the long history of political urbanism in Palestine since 1948, Chapter 3 analyzes the history of urban/territorial destruction in Palestine and links it with the Zionist ideology and perception of land and people. Chapters 4, 5 and 6 focus on the contemporary destruction of Palestinian urbanity in the twenty-first century; a methodological framework to identify urbicidal episodes is also generated. Using the case of Nablus Old Town, the book unravels the complexities and ambivalences in the Palestinian space through capturing the impacts that urbicide generates over the material, spatial, and socio-cultural conditions of the city. As well as highlighting the impacts of urbicide on people's collective memory and their perceptions of self, other and place. The cases of the Jenin refugee camp destruction in 2002 and the Israeli attacks on Gaza in 2010 are briefly analyzed and accentuate the discussion on the similarities and shifts in the Israeli military doctrines in military urbanism and urbicide strategies.

In Part III—Revision—Chapter 7 analyzes the occupation apparatus of surveillance, destruction and construction in the Occupied Palestinian Territories; the book highlights other multilayered forms of states of exception that emerge in the Palestinian space that acknowledges the Palestinian resistance discourse and its role in shaping the contours of the territory. The book demonstrates how the dilution or negation of the Israeli colonial strategies of control, surveillance and destruction in the OPT potentially produces other modes of Palestinian resistance through everyday tactics, commemoration, and reconstruction projects, and also produces a Palestinian awareness of the Israeli military spatial practices that consequently shapes their spatial resistance strategies.

The interest in military urbanism and warfare destruction in the post-Cold War era has gained a momentum beyond the typical conception of the destruction as military necessity, as a new relationship between war and the city has emerged in the warfare military doctrines. The increasing number of armed conflicts and of urban violence such as the destruction of Grozny by the Russian Army, the Israeli bulldozing of Jenin refugee camp in 2002 and the lethal destruction of Aleppo in 2013 highlights the importance of examining both this interconnection of the city and conflict/war destruction and their link to resistance dynamics. The systematic targeting of urban areas and cities are often interpreted as targeting architecture based solely on the cultural and social value of buildings. Targeting architecture is a process of targeting symbols of city identity. This type of destruction has been given terms under several paradigms—warchitecture, cultural cleansing, cultural genocide, and identicide, for example. The misconception and interpretation of this phenomenon is due to the limited perspective of identity and urbanity. Consequently, abstracting city identity in the symbolic buildings and cultural artifacts undermines the fact that normally in urban warfare, a larger scale of destruction is witnessed in devastated cities—as, for example, in Sarajevo, Mostar, Nablus Old Town, and the latest Aleppo 2013 destruction. This typical interest and focus on the destruction of symbols of identity limit the opportunity to understand the global picture and the reality of urban destruction. A detailed documentation of this urban destruction is rarely found on the destruction of cities in history such as Dresden, Sarajevo and Mostar, and this handicaps this field of research.

Part I

City, war and urbicide

Inquiry

1

Cities and war

The destruction of man-made places has been a recurrent consequence of natural calamity and human violence. Graham (2005) argues that cities have played a strategic role in military campaigns throughout history, since the time of Trojan War. Whether because of their geo-strategic location, their concentration of wealth and power or their inherent symbolic value, be they fortified cities of ancient times or the urban metropolis of modern times, cities have always carried prominence in the strategy and execution of warfare between rival entities. Today's unprecedented worldwide urbanization is rendering this phenomenon ever more predominant than at any other time in history. The most significant causal relationship between warfare and the development of urban settlements is the protection that cities have afforded against external enemies. Walled cities offered the dual advantages of numbers and defendable boundaries. It is generally much safer to be in a city than living alone in the hinterland. Thus, cities arguably trace their initial *raison d'être* and the subsequent growth of their significance, above all other secondary benefits of the collective living, to the physical and psychological security that the collectivity afforded against uncertainties beyond the walls. Mumford (1961: 44) writes: "The power of massed numbers in itself gave the city superiority over the thinly populated widely scattered villages, and served as an incentive to further growth." Pirenne (1936: 21) sees the origins of European cities in "Fortified cities erected by the feudal princes to provide shelter for their men." Bloch (1961: 20) notes that "the disorders of the early Middle Ages had in many cases induced men to draw nearer to each other."

The advantages of a consolidated and fortified urban morphology against the external hostile forces are evident in the rise and fall of empires. Constantinople continued as a major city for centuries after the military strength of the Byzantine Empire had collapsed. The city's legendary wall structure kept its residents safe even in the absence of the imperial military might. Likewise, ancient cities such as Babylon, Jericho, Paris, London, and Rome all began as fortified places for collective safety.

Cities were not only self-contained spheres of daily lives for their residents but, later, also integral parts of a system of power projection by the larger political entity, be it an empire or a kingdom. Modern cities trace their origin to the city-states of the Greek polis. War of the Greek civilization was a struggle between the city-states, and although warfare often took place outside the city, the urban centers were always the ultimate spoils of war. The Roman Empire, based in the greatest city-state of all, built fortified cities as centers of its gradually far-flung power. Cities were the bulwarks of the empire's power projection, defended against the barbarian hordes. The sack of Rome itself symbolized the end of the Empire's territorial cohesion and the descent into fractured political authority and social uncertainty.

Urban settlements have grown fatalistically indifferent toward defense by neglecting their fortifications and strategic layout. While cities have always been closely interwoven with military technologies, concerns and strategies, as Steven Graham (2003) argues, the intensification of global urbanization, growing population pressures, resource shortages and resultant inequalities in distribution are further deepening the significance of urban terrain as the strategic site of military, socio-economic and representational symbolic struggles.

City, urbanity and war: historical perspective

> *Warfare, like everything else is being urbanized.*
>
> (Graham, 2005: 4)

Pre-modern period: first urban settlements

Eduardo Mendieta (2004: 6) argues that cities are the jewels of empires with their own sets of logics deriving from the various dialectics of the imperial design. Cities are the maelstrom from which the storms of war surge. Cities have been the locus and the pivot of war. They are the fundamental physical, political, and economic setting in which conditions toward war develop. Lewis Mumford (1961) highlights that the institutionalization of war—and, in fact, the modernization of the means of waging war—was made possible by the emergence of cities (as early as the civilizations of Mesopotamia and Egyptian dynasties, between 3,000 and 6,000 years ago). The sacrificial rituals of the ancient times to the totemic and blood-thirsty gods were transformed into rationalized and regimented projects of "mass extermination and mass destruction" through the organizing of societal institutions and the accumulation of the military power bestowed upon a king (Mumford, 1961: 42). The rituals—once exercised to ensure fertility and abundant crops, an irrational act to promote rational purposes—were transformed into a rational execution of physical power by one community over another in order to eliminate uncertainties from the continuity of the power structure. Mumford demonstrated how the historic development of kingship was accompanied by a shift in the socio-religious practice from the sacrificial rites of the fertility god to the cult of sheer physical power. During the development of the early prototype urban communities of the Neolithic times, the king sought to attribute his earthly authority with the divine origin in order to legitimize his absolute rule. As urbanity took on its ever-increasing complexities, the king came to replace god as the very source of divine protection, and his words were the law. The king found it necessary to consolidate, maintain and project his ever-increasing power and to reaffirm his divinity through deliberate acts of destruction and killing:

> If anything were needed to make the magical origins of war plausible, it is the fact that war, even when it is disguised by seemingly hard-headed economic demands, uniformly turns into religious performance; nothing than a whole sale ritual sacrifices.
>
> (Mumford 1961: 42)

Royal power came to measure its strength and divine favor by its capacities not merely for creation but even more through pillage, destruction and extermination. Mumford (1961) observes that the establishment of law within the urban civilizations has been accompanied by laws regarding warfare: "Plato declared 'in the Law', every city is a natural state of war with every other."

As the city transformed the waging of war into a legitimate means of acquiring power, hegemony and wealth, in turn the city itself became the target of war; its developing economy, power and resources: "As soon as war had become one of the reasons for the city's existence, the city's own wealth and power made it a natural target" (Mumford 1961: 46). The city with its accumulated tools and equipments, and its hoards of gold, silver and jewelry heaped in palaces and temples, became the legitimate end target of military campaigns. Historians date the rise of organized warfare to the establishment of cities; the chief enemy of the city was a rival city under another god that claimed equal power. Mumford argues that the city became the means and ends of war, thus perpetuating the institution of war. If we have superseded war, it is partly because we are urbane, grounded in the city that gave birth to war and that war parented. When war became fully established and institutionalized, it started to spread beyond its original urban centers. Violence thus became normalized and spread away from the urban centers where the collective manhunts and sacrifices were first instituted. Throughout the greater part of history, enslavement, forced labor, and destruction have accompanied and penalized the growth of urban civilization. Thus, the sacking and killing of fortified cities and their inhabitants were the central events in pre-modern war (Graham 2004a, after Weber: 58).

For more than a thousand years afterwards, state power remained fragmentary and its borders uncertain, and the city retained a special role in the state. The city in medieval Europe was a fortified space, the only relatively certain territory wherein the writ of rulers ran. Graham (2004a) explains how during the fifteenth and sixteenth centuries modern nation-states emerged in Europe as "bordered power containers," and started to seek monopoly on political violence. He further argues that these cities that lay at the core of nation-states were no longer the organizers of their own armies and defense. They maintained political and economic power; it was the elite of these cities who directed violence, control, repression, and the colonial acquisition of territory, raw materials, wealth and labor power from afar (Driver and Gilbert, 2003).

The pre-modern war is essentially social rather than technological in character; it is an expression of the existential rather than the instrumental aspect of warfare. Pre-modern conflict merges unconventional—to use the term *du jour*, asymmetric —warfare methods with the conventional or semi-conventional military activities of failed states. The pre-modern model of conflict also tends to exploit the rise of non-state actors, cultural identity politics, and ethno-political conflict. In many respects, pre-modern war represents what Evans (2002) describes as a cultural revolt against the philosophy of Western liberal globalism; it is a conscious rejection of the universal values based on cosmopolitan democracy that followed Western victory in the Cold War. Evans argues that pre-modern struggles embrace aspects of sub-state or intrastate civil conflict and ethnic cleansing ranging from Bosnia through Somalia to East Timor. Evans (2002) argues that those who wage such struggles may choose to sport middle-class suits and exploit the spread of advanced technology, but their mind-sets are mixtures of the anti-modern, the millenarian, and the tribal. Such radicals embody what Pierre Hassner (2000: 205) has called "the dialectic of the bourgeois and the barbarian."

Modern war: unconventional place annihilation

Paul Virilio (2002) contends that military projects and technologies drive history and that the transition from feudalism to capitalism was driven not primarily by the politics of wealth and production techniques but by the mechanics of war. Virilio highlights how the traditional feudal fortified city disappeared because of the increasing sophistication of weapons and possibilities for warfare. For him, the concept of siege warfare became rather a war of movement. In *Speed and Politics* (1968), Virilio suggests "history progresses at the speed of its weapons systems." Graham (2004a: 165) sees that the deliberate destruction and targeting of cities has been a re-occurring event throughout 8,000 years of urban history. He stresses the fact that there is a strong link between urbanization and the prosecution of political violence to modernity, as the infusion of cities and warfare is becoming a de facto. He further refers to Pieterse's (2002: 3) account of this strong connection between city, war and modernity: "After all, modernity, through most of its career, has been modernity at war."

Modern wars are strongly represented in First and Second World Wars. Although the two wars are not similar in terms of the type of weapons, military strategy and scale of destruction they produced, they are classified as modern in terms of the scale of international engagement in these wars.

The First World War is considered the last classical war in a period that witnessed an increase in cities' sizes, especially Berlin. The technology for bombing civilian targets in the First World War was so weak that only Paris was really in danger. As such, the dominant effect of war on city growth was the rise of war-related industries and government in these capitals, and this tended to stimulate city growth. This war was the last classical war of a symmetrical engagement between state armies in the open field. Until this moment of history no specific term or discourse was developed to define or reflect on the urban destruction that results from war fighting.

The Second World War announced the rise of place annihilation. It was a completely different war to the First World War; it marked a shift in war techniques and approaches in the twentieth century—a shift to "total war." Total war meant that cities and their population overwhelmingly became the actual target of war where, as Martin Shaw (2003) suggests, bombing moved from the selective destruction of key sites within cities to extensive attacks on urban areas and, finally, to instantaneous annihilation of entire urban spaces and population. Hewitt argued that the Second World War was "a warfare that strove towards, it did not always achieve, an end of the settled historic places that have been the heart of civilian life" (1987: 446). Only Paris—which saw little bombing—escaped unscathed. London, and particularly Berlin and Dresden, lost substantial numbers from their population during the war. The destruction of housing was massive and, unsurprisingly, the population also fell. Hewitt coined "place annihilation" to describe the massive and, in many cases, total destruction that occurred in many major cities around the globe, such as Hiroshima, Nagasaki, Berlin, and Dresden. The industrial city thus became "in its entirety" a space for war. But this literature is overwhelmingly concerned with the destruction wrought by aerial bombing during the Second World War.

Graham (2005) argues that in modern war there is a direct connection with and a concentration on city destruction and sometimes on the city's total annihilation. He further suggests that historically urbanity in its deepest meaning and essence was the target of war destruction:

> In an urbanizing world, cities provide much more than just the backdrop and environment for war and terror. Rather, their buildings, assets, institutions, industries and infrastructure; their cultural diversities and symbolic meanings, have long actually themselves been the explicit target for a wide range deliberate, orchestrated attacks.
>
> (Graham 2005: 32)

Kaldor (1999) recognizes the historicity of Clausewitz's ideas on war as the articulation of Napoleonic Wars experiences—its pre-dating of the industrialization of warfare, modern alliances and the codification of the laws of war. In particular, she recognizes that "Clausewitz could not possibly have envisaged the awesome combination of mass production, mass politics and mass communications when harnessed to mass production." Kaldor (2001) argues that in twentieth-century wars there is a parallel with the pre-modern period, which was also characterized by a diversity of military forces—feudal levies, citizens militias, mercenaries, pirates, for example—and by a corresponding variety of types of war. While cities have always been closely interwoven with military technologies, concerns and strategies, it is now clear that the intensification of global urbanization, resource shortages, inequalities and population pressures are further deepening the role of urban terrain as the strategic site of military, social and representational struggles.

Two interlinked developments have been critical for Kaldor (2001) in bringing about these changes. One is the sheer destructiveness of modern warfare. As all types of weapons have become more lethal and/or more accurate, decisive military victory has become more and more difficult. The scale of destruction in the Second World War (some 50 million dead) is almost unbearable to contemplate. The Cold War could be understood as a way of evading or psychologically suppressing the implications of that destructiveness. Modern wars are seen as modern because they reflect the key distinctions of modernity: between public and private, internal and external, economic and political, civil and military, combatant and non-combatant. In many of the areas where new wars take place, it is possible to observe a process that is almost the reverse of the process through which modern states were constructed.

Post-modern wars are based on high-tech aerospace power, casualty limitation, and cautious exit strategies, such as we saw during the Kosovo conflict of 1999. In many key respects, the war over Kosovo was the model of a post-modern conflict. It was, to borrow David Halberstam's ironic phrase, "war in a time of peace"—a conflict carefully calibrated, enabled by high-tech weaponry. However, post-modern conflict based around high-technology aerospace power has created its own antithesis—asymmetric warfare, including the threat of weapons of mass destruction. In the West's public consciousness, modern war is based on high technology and the conventional force-on-force warfare of the kind associated with the two world wars, Korea, and the Gulf. In contrast, post-modern war is mainly characterized by the extremes of Western risk aversion, since for the Western powers the stakes seldom involve issues of vital security or national survival.

Michael Evans (2002) maintains that the new world order with globalization and new trends of international security contributed to the major shift of war engagements. He further argues that by 2001 the contemporary international security system had bifurcated, that is, it had split between a traditional twentieth-century state-centered paradigm and new twenty-first-century sub-state and trans-state strata. The great change in the early twenty-first century international system from that of the last quarter of the twentieth century is the transition away from a dominant state-centered structure towards one marked by a greater number of sub-state and trans-state actors.

Graham (2002b) suggests three types of struggle and destruction that characterize the post-modern war. The first concerns the urbanization of war itself, in which there is an intensifying interest in the role of the city as a strategic site for military and geopolitics fighting. Graham gives examples of this concern in the Cold War doctrine, even more evident in post-Cold War conflicts such as those in Chechnya, Somalia, the Balkans and Palestine. For his second characterization, Graham links the adaptation of urban terrorism to the networked city as the central terrain of contemporary life. Conflicts are no longer state vs state; they involve a growing number of groups, which he calls anti-modernization, ethnic, religious, etc, fighting for various reasons ranging from self-determination to anti-global-ization, for drug mafia wars and so on. Graham argues that these struggles take the form of bloody internecine urban warfare as well as cyber-terror attacks aimed at undermining the functioning of global and corporate information systems. The example that Graham uses to demonstrate best the adaptation of urban terror to the new urban technological age is 11 September in New York City. The third struggle concern in Graham's description is the militarization of civil societies themselves. It is clear, as Graham mentions, that the civil fabric of cities is being saturated with techniques and technologies only recently developed in the military domain. He gives the example of GPS and mobile phone systems that helped to develop a city-saturating culture of control driven by the spiraling incidence and fear of crime, a growing social polarization, and the proliferation of major civil unrest in cities.

Yet, while modern, post-modern and pre-modern forms of war overlap with each other, each mode has distinctive features. Modern war remains symbolized by, in the words of Evans (2002), a classical philosophy of encounter battles on land, air and sea between the armed forces of rival states. This is a mode of classical warfare that can be traced back to the first properly recorded battle in history when the Egyptians defeated the Hittites in the chariot and infantry battle at Kadesh in 1285 BC. The most recent model of armed conflict by encounter battle was the 2003 Iraq invasion by the United States army, when American and Iraqi forces— employing missiles, tanks and mechanized infantry—clashed at the doors of Baghdad. The Israeli military invasion of south Lebanon in July 2006 and the recent Israeli military operation in Gaza, 2009–2013, are other examples.

From the end of twentieth century onwards there is no longer a "theater" of war; it is no longer possible to define the spatial limits of destruction. Con-comitantly, it has become increasingly difficult to demarcate the temporal limits of war. Declarations of war, ceasefires, and so-called peace treaties are increasingly irrelevant—in some cases, in fact, conceptually incoherent (most obviously, perhaps, in what is called a "war on terrorism"). War is no longer conceived to be a spatially or temporally finite phenomenon.

Urbanity and urban destruction: the emergence of urbicide

There are competing ways of conceptualizing the different forms of urban destruction and naming them under different discourses. For example, in the Second World War the physical and material destruction of cities is termed "place annihilation" by Kenneth Hewitt, and was extended to ethnic cleansing in Kosovo by Hugh Clout. The urban destruction that occurred in Palestine in 1948 and Bosnia in the 1990 was identified by scholars such as Ilan Pappé (2006) as ethnic cleansing discussed as spatial violence. In these historical cases the focus of academic research and theoretical discourses was on the mass displacement of inhabitants in which the physical destruction was marginalized and considered as a consequence of such displacement.

Other terms emerged during these wars. Urbicide[1] was elaborated to describe the bombing and mass destruction of cities such as Mostar Sarajevo in Bosnia and Herzegovina, Jenin camp and Nablus in Palestine, the destruction of Fallujah Iraq, and the devastation of the southern Lebanese villages. Cultural cleansing or cultural genocide, and identicide were used to indicate the fate of mosques, churches, museums, archives, libraries, schools, and other symbolic buildings.

Inevitably, these terms were part of a propaganda war, but all too often they reflected the new landscapes of Croatia, Bosnia and Herzegovina, Palestine, Afghanistan, Iraq and more recently the destruction of the southern Lebanese villages in summer 2006. The above mentioned definitions of urban destruction are perceived in this research as limiting the focused perspective of urban destruction to a specific type of destruction and armed conflict. It is argued that they cannot be used as a holistic approach to define urban destruction.

It is likely that an event is defined and described in the literature by several of the terms mentioned above; the Bosnian and Palestinian cases are examples. This highlights the need to synthesize a holistic approach that can accommodate the characteristics of any urban destruction taking place in armed conflicts and war. In this context urbicide is articulated to be a strong discourse that represents a comprehensive discussion of urban destruction in its totality regardless of the nature of conflict or type of urban destruction.

These discourses are discussed and classified according to their connotation and their approach to urban destruction—the discourses that discuss a similar concept are combined. For example, discourses that approach urban destruction from the type and nature of destruction are articulated together—the themes of cultural cleansing together with cultural genocide, for instance. Concepts that discuss the consequences of urban destruction are assembled together— so identicide is combined with the debate on memoricide. Themes that question the logic and motives behind destruction are grouped together—such as the assertion of collateral damage with the discussion of damage for security reasons. On the other hand, theoretical discourses that project special significance are articulated separately as they hold unique signification—place annihilation is an example.

Collateral damage and damage for security reasons

The conventional interpretation of the plunder of the urban environment illustrates destruction as either collateral damage or the result of militarily necessary actions. "'Collateral damage' refers to 'incidental casualties and . . . property damage' that result from military action" (Rogers, 1996: 15). Collateral damage as defined by Wikipedia is a military euphemism that was made popular during the Vietnam War. The euphemism has now been in use so long that it is an accepted term within military forces, meaning:

> Unintentional damage or incidental damage affecting facilities, equipment or personnel, occurring as a result of military actions directed against targeted enemy forces or facilities. Such damage can occur to friendly, neutral, and even enemy forces.
>
> (USAF, 1998)

Collateral damage "occurs when attacks targeted at military objectives cause civilian casualties and damage to civilian objects" (Fischer, 1999). The main principle of collateral damage is that it is an unintentional (or incidental) development of military action. Thus the damage is the consequence of munitions either missing their targets, or hitting other buildings on the way to their intended targets. A more complex interpretation might argue that the destruction of the urban environment is incidental to attempts to achieve certain military objectives. The conventional international law definition of collateral damage and the concept of proportionality to investigate collateral damage incidents is set out in the 1977 Protocol I to the 1949 Geneva Conventions (Protocol I) at Article 52 (2). For all practical purposes, the customary international law definition of proportionality is the same as the conventional definition. That definition has also become the customary international law definition of military objective.

Military necessity can be broadly defined as "those measures which are indispensable for securing the ends of the war, and which are lawful according to the modern laws and usages of war" (Lieber quoted in Rogers, 1996: 4). As such, certain buildings are lawfully destroyed in order to achieve certain military ends; the destruction of a building (a bridge) that might seem to have only incidental military use, can, therefore, be justified as militarily necessary. The main implication of this linkage is that at least significant military input will be necessary in determinations of military objective, collateral damage and proportionality. The major challenge of this implication is ensuring that the resulting decisions achieve the proper balance in the basic dynamic of the law of armed conflict, i.e. they satisfy both military and the humanitarian factors, neither of which has primacy. Infrastructure (bridges, roads and trains network) is the typical example of logistic strategic targets that are commonly taken to constitute a military (as opposed to civilian) object.

Air Commodore Wilby justified the destruction taking place in Serbia during the NATO bombardment in 1999 as militarily necessary, noting that:

> Every target we have struck has been one that has been considered to have great military significance to affect the Serbian military or the MUP [Serbian special police units] . . . bridges . . . have been selected because they are major lines of communication and . . . affect re supply of those troops . . . So . . . I would say . . . that all our targets have been justifiably . . . military targets.
>
> (NATO, 6 April, cited in Coward, 2009a: 21)

Thus, if the destruction of the urban environment is more widespread than the typical selected key buildings, and if the devastation covers a wide variety of buildings: housing, public institutions, cultural monuments, utility buildings, open spaces, then the destruction cannot be justified as collateral damage or damage for security reasons. Such damage is then a deliberate destruction of the built environment that qualifies as urbicide.

Ethnic cleansing

Ethnic cleansing is a distinctive politico-geographic problem that has been used in major urban warfare around the globe, for example in Bosnia, Palestine, and Armenia. Naimark (2001) argues that ethnic cleansing is not equivalent to genocide though both can and are found together. Genocide, in his usage (not that of the Genocide Convention), is an exterminate activity aimed at the destruction of part or the whole of a population, whereas ethnic cleansing is "to remove a people and often all traces of them from a concrete territory" (Naimark, 2001: 3). As well as the removal of a population, ethnic cleansing also targets the cultural and material landscape of the victims—what Porteous and Smith (2001) term "domicide" or the destruction of homes, communities, and sites meaningful to the former residents. C. Dahlman and G. O. Tuathai (2006) argue that the erasure of Palestine by Israel in the 1948 war has relevance in underscoring how ethnic cleansing is a politico-geographic problem involving place and community destruction, the erasure of the "Other" cultural landscapes, the renaming of locales and the repopulation of the land by a new group; Falah terms this place de-signification (Falah, 1996; Slyomovics, 1998; Benvenisti, 2000). Ethnic cleansing relies on an extremist discourse of political geography, defined by an aspirant power structure that maps an exclusionary and idealized political identity onto a particular territory. Put into practice, elements of this aspirant power structure use terror and violence to clear all "others" from the territory in order to realize an idealized convergence of identity and space. For its perpetrators, ethnic cleansing is a means to realize a political geography of security through separation and distinct borders.

Confusion materializes when overlapping two different phenomena and forms of political violence within the same discourse. Combining urban destruction with inhabitance displacement by force is not useful: it marginalizes the importance of urban destruction and its momentous impact on any place and its inhabitants. It also addresses the need to discuss urban destruction as a phenomenon of its own. It does not mean to separate them but to discuss them as two types of political violence on their own, as Coward (2005) suggests.

Place annihilation

Kenneth Hewitt (1983) coined the term "place annihilation" to describe the devastation of many cities during the Second World War. Hewitt defines war as the occasion of highly organized, premeditated, and collective acts of devastation and killing, he further states that warfare has the intentional aim of disorganizing enemy space. The process of place annihilation and immolation for Hewitt "is the combined destruction of resident civilians, residential communities, their neighbor-hoods, and major features of the urban environment and civil ecology" (Hewitt, 1983: 258).

Hewitt discusses in his thesis on war the link between war campaigns and the dehumanization process of the enemy as the "other": the perceived antithesis of "our" places or homeland and "theirs" are mobilized during war. Hewitt argues that place annihilation produces "placelessness." It is further used as a tool by targeting places indiscriminately, whether they are human settlements, political groupings or whole nations, to achieve the politico-biological crime of genocide. De-housing the population as a strategy of war was the second motive behind this total devastation. Hewitt further describes the main characteristics of place annihilation as the total devastation or razing of complete cities, such as Tripoli, Stalingrad, Wesel and Julich, Dresden, Hiroshima, and Nagasaki. Carpet bombing from the air was the main reason behind the scale of place devastation in the Second World War and caused many European cities to burn down completely.

Hewitt discusses place annihilation as representative strategies of immolation, sacrificing civilians and urban areas for other purposes. His argument about using place annihilation as a tool to achieve genocide or ethnic cleansing is rather convincing, as there is historical evidence. Hewitt's arguments are limited to the Second World War and its carpet bombing and total war characteristics.

Cultural cleansing: cultural genocide

The deliberate destruction in wartime of cultural heritage is no historical novelty. Sometimes destruction has been used to pillage for profit; at other time it has been part of the widely recognized right to annihilate the enemy. During the First World War, churches and old town centers were reduced to rubble, justified as damage of military necessity. During the Second World War, large German urban centers disappeared as part of strategic "area bombing" by Commonwealth air forces. Coward (2001b) argues that certain buildings are destroyed because they represent ethnic/cultural heterogeneity. Such interpretations have been offered in the case of the destruction of the Stari Most—Old Bridge—mosques and churches in the old center of Mostar. Croatian paramilitary leader Mate Boban remarked: "It is not enough to cleanse Mostar of the Muslims, the relics must also be destroyed" (cited in Riedlmayer, 1995). Riedlmayer (1994: 16) argues that the ruins of symbolic buildings in Bosnia signifies more than the ordinary atrocities of war: "Rubble in Bosnia and Herzegovina signifies nationalist extremists hard at work to eliminate not only the human beings and living cities, but also the memory of the past." This elimination of the memory of the past, argues Riedlmayer, is an integral element of ethnic cleansing. Riedlmayer argues:

> Though [w]e are . . . told that "ancient hatreds" are what fuel the destruc-
> tion . . . this is not true: the museums, libraries, mosques, churches and
> monuments speak eloquently of centuries of pluralism . . . in Bosnia . . . [i]t
> is this evidence of a successfully shared past that the nationalists seek to
> destroy.
>
> (Riedlmayer, 1994: 16)

UNESCO's draft declaration concerning the intentional destruction of cultural heritage states:

> Cultural heritage is a component of cultural identity and social cohesion so
> that its intentional destruction may have adverse consequences on human
> dignity, and human material culture makes up symbolic and cultural
> landscapes which create a particularity of place, they also act as narratives
> of collective memory that underpin the cohesion and identity of groups.
>
> (UNESCO, 2003)

The Bosnian war was characterized by the deliberate targeting and destruction of (among others) cultural, religious and historic landmarks. Targets included: the National Library at Sarajevo, the Regional Archives in Mostar, local and national museums, the Academy of Music, the National Gallery, entire historic districts, Muslim and Jewish cemeteries, and particularly places of worship. It is important to point out that the heritage of all ethnicities were damaged, but by far the worst damage was inflicted on Muslim heritage.

Non-sacred structures were also targeted for their symbolic significance; these include the Ottoman-era bridge in Mostar, Roman ruins, archives, libraries, and medieval and archaeological sites. The strong element addressed in the dis-courses on cultural genocide is that it reflects the systematic destruction of culture, so the rites, rituals, and places are no longer available to enact culture, and the people themselves have been killed or moved (if it happens with ethnic cleansing).

Either way, identity is defective, collective memory is rendered useless, and social fabric is destroyed.

These discourses of cultural cleansing and cultural genocide suffer from their focus upon the symbolic cultural heritage, which solely refers to one layer of urban destruction, the deliberate destruction of cultural artifacts. In other words, it focuses only upon the buildings whose loss is judged to be a cultural loss. However, the urban environment normally experiences more widespread destruction than these symbolic buildings. From the Bosnian history of cultural destruction it is evident that hundreds of other types of buildings were subject to destruction—for example, houses in Mostar Old Town and in many of the villages in Bosnia. The same can be noted in the Palestinian history of urban destruction—for example, Nablus old town (more details on Nablus are analyzed in Chapter 6). Indeed, urban destruction encompasses buildings that have no distinctive cultural value, or are of indistinct cultural provenance. Thus the interpretation of urban destruction as an attack on cultural heritage provides only a partial (though striking) account of the destruction of the urban environment in Bosnia among other cases; it does not account for the scale of the destruction or targeting of buildings that are not recognizable as such symbols of culture. Thus, cultural cleansing and cultural genocide are only partially reflecting the process of urban destruction; they reflect the destruction of cultural artifacts, but this destruction does not take place in a pure form or apart from the destruction of other types of the urban environment. The term "cultural" represents culture in its widest scope—language, arts and so on—so its focus is not solely on the urban environment and cultural artefact. Thus cultural cleansing does not provide concrete discussion on the urban environment—a separate discourse to discuss its devastation is needed.

Identicide—memoricide

The intentional destruction of landscapes of identity, "identicide," is a diagnostic feature of warfare deliberately employed during armed conflict in an attempt to damage the connection between people and the places with which they identify (Fentress and Wickham, 1992; Halbwachs, 1992; Hutton, 1993; Gillis, 1994; Nora, 1996; Mehrag, 2001, cf. Connerton, 1989). According to Sarah Mehrag (1999), identicide is the act of destroying vernacular and symbolic places during war with the intention of erasing cultural identity and a sense of social belonging. Identicide occurs when groups contest and aim to destroy one another's places of identity. Destruction or debasement of such landscapes has the power to revise memory to the point where group identity is itself endangered. Mehrag (2001) argues that the localization of memory on the material is what negotiates its survival, and by removing the material we begin to erase memory, which constitutes memoricide. Without landscape to trigger memory, there is no link with the past, and it recedes beyond our collective memory. Such acts of identicide subject people to periods of meaninglessness, forgetting, and loss of identity (memoricide) when their bond with place is broken.

However, Douglas Porteous and Sandra Smith (2001: 198) bring a different view of memory and memoricide in their discussion of the impact of domicide on urban destruction victims. They argue that memory cannot be totally erased while there are rememberers who can pass on stories to future generations, but it can be mortally wounded when these stories cannot be backed up by accessible documents or physical structures on the ground.

The interesting dimension of identicide is its link to the place of identity of the "other"; the difficulty, however, lies in limiting place identity solely to cultural identity.

The problems with these discourses are these: first, identity and memory cannot literally be killed physically—thus it is a metaphor; second, the killing of identity and thus memory is a consequence of another action of killing, which is the killing of the material evidence that is important for collective memory and people's sense of identity. These discourses are therefore strong connotations to define the consequences of urban destruction rather than the phenomenon of destruction itself.

Domicide

Porteous and Smith (2001) use the term "domicide" to describe the deliberate destruction of home by human agency in pursuit of specific goals, which causes suffering to the victims. They define the concept of home as "a hierarchy of physical places . . . may also be seen as a clustering at various levels." "The spatial concept of home is conceived as a series of concentric zones ranging from one's own room, dwelling, neighbourhood, village, town, or city, region, nation or country and finally the whole world." Two main categories are recognized: "extreme domicide"— brought about by overt violence, mainly war and other armed actions—and "everyday domicide." The latter is associated with development projects, large public facilities such as highways and airports, and urban renewal, and is often justified as being for "the public good." The argument focuses on the victim's suffering of the act of destruction, which adds an important stress on the human side of domicide. Two points that are interesting in their discussion and would use in the urbicide redefinition. First, domicide involves the erasure of the perspective and opinion of its victims; it is a relationship with "otherness" that proceeds through domination and attempted annihilation. Second, domicide is the devastation of the life world of places—and not simply of buildings, landscapes, ecologies and infrastructure.

On the other hand, Porteous and Smith's use of the theme domicide is quite confusing in several ways. First, the concept encompasses too much, losing force in a multiplicity of unrelated processes—national parks planning and the bombing of cities; strip mining and gentrification. Second, the exaggeration and extension of the term *domus*—which means the house or place to live in—to include all scales of the built environment is not convincing, and it evacuates the term domus from its essential meaning "the home." *Domus* refers to the physical house and

the household, including the wife, ancestors and descendants; it referred to แเ๛
places where the *pater familias* exerted his authority or acted as *dominus*.[2]
The concept and definition of domicide to describe the intentional destruction
of the urban environment is therefore redundant because it limits the intentional
exercise of violence to destroy a particular type of spatiality—homes—and not
all urban spatial forms.

Urbicide

The killing of cities or the destruction of the urban is a concept that has been
articulated to describe the intentional destruction of cities, although limiting the
notion of the urban within the geographic setting of cities is misleading. Still, it
is argued that this concept is the discourse with the capacity to define urban
destruction in all its forms. The powerful dimensions of urbicide rest in its reference to the destruction of the urban and urbanity. The problem of the urban and
urbanity arises in the different perspectives of the definition of this notion that
need to be further elaborated in linking urbicide and place identity. This theme is
discussed in details in Chapter 2.

Spacio-cide

The term "spacio-cide" was coined by Sari Hanafi in his article, "The Spacio-cide
of Palestine" (2006). Hanafi uses spacio-cide to describe two levels of destruction, the micro level of the urban and the macro level of the territory, in linking
it to the Occupied Palestinian Territories (OPT). On the micro level he claims
that spacio-cide not only targets cities but also the whole landscape and built
environment—from the rubble of devastated buildings and leveled hillsides to the
flattened vegetation that has been devastated not only by bombs but by
"industrious, vigorous destruction, which has toppled properties like a vicious tax
assessor" (Hanafi, 2006: 93), which he claims to be spacio-cidal and not urbicidal
activities.

On the macro level, which is the level of the whole territory, spacio-cide,
according to Hanafi, entails several characteristics:

- It is a strategic Israeli colonial ideology vis-à-vis Palestinian territories.
  According to Hanafi, spacio-cide is a colonial strategy aimed at territorial
  expansion.
- Spacio-cide is the deliberate denial and purposive ignorance of the demo-
  graphic development occurring in the territory in question.
- Spacio-cide is associated with not only the reshaping of a place but also the
  reshaping of borders, which Hanafi describes as "borders in motion."
- Hanafi argues that another characteristic of spacio-cide is its "three-
  dimensional nature," which complicates unsettled questions pertaining to the
  Israeli–Palestinian peace process.

Hanafi argues that the main objectives of applying spacio-cide strategies in the OPT is to pursue the Palestinian "voluntary transfer," to transfer the Palestinian *topos* to *atopia*, by turning territory to a mere land.

Hence spacio-cide presents a very important concept to define the devastation, manipulation and transformation of territorial spatial structure. Yet some ambiguities can be observed in the definition of this discourse.

The difficulty of the process that spacio-cide follows in Hanafi's definition rests in the combining of different processes of devastation on different levels and scales of resolution in one discourse. This is evident in the overlapping of the devastation at the micro urban scale with the destruction and transformation at the macro territorial scale. They are seen in this book as different but complementary processes. Hanafi explains, correctly, the macro spacio-cidal activities and mechanisms that target the territorial spatial networks, but at the micro urban scale he does not elaborate how the devastation of the urban is spacio-cide and not urbicide—the mechanism is not there. The other difficulty in Hanafi's definition and perspective of spacio-cide lies in being very specific to the Palestinian context. By limiting spacio-cide to colonial activities, he did not elaborate the discourse to include other cases from other contexts.

The devastation at the urban level should be treated as urbicide because it seeks the destruction of the urban per se; it follows different mechanisms to the devastation on the territorial scale. Urbicide aims at destroying the material components of these urbanities, by destroying the shared spatiality that constitutes the urban identity. The destruction of Jenin refugee camp aimed at the destruction and nihilism of the Palestinian political and military resistance represented by camps in general. It is the destruction of the Palestinian national identity imbedded in its national cause to resist occupation. Similar reasons can be seen in the destruction of Nablus Old Town, in that Nablus represents an important feature of the Palestinian cultural identity. Destroying the city entails wreaking this form of identity. The agency of territorial/spatial devastation, on the other hand, seen as a strong sign of spacio-cide, follows different rhythms and mechanisms. It entails the destruction of larger spatial relations and links—for example, the enclaving of the Palestinian communities from developments and urbanization. The devastation of the Palestinian infrastructure aims to hinder mobility between different urban areas that disrupt the territorial contiguity enforced by the erasing of the Palestinian traditional landscape and agriculture. It further aims at transforming the image of the Palestinian landscaper to project the colonial landscape and architecture through the constructing of settlements over the high summits of topography. This is spacio-cide. The difference between the two concepts is fragile, and they project similar hostile attitudes towards the built environment as needing reorganization and purification. The difference is about geographic spatial scale. In spacio-cide the material destruction is negligible; the important issue is the relations that have been destroyed and the impact that can result. For example, the destruction and erasing of 418 Palestinian villages in 1948 can be seen as a case of spacio-cide if combined with the rapid transformation process of the whole territory from Palestine to Israel. The physical reality of these villages is marginal in comparison to the overall process, because what is destroyed is the spatial network that connects these physical nodes and whatever exists between them (landscape, infrastructure, industries, and others). In urbicide the destruction of buildings on the urban scale counts very much as the link between the buildings that are the shared spatiality is destroyed by the destruction of buildings. Spaciocide aims at destroying larger territorial and national identity; urbicide aims at destroying urban collective identity.

Notes

1   The term "urbicide" was coined by Marshall Berman in the 1980s.
2   http://ancienthistory.about.com/od/familyanddailylife/p/RomanFamily.htm.

2

Urbicide
Theoretical inquiry

Dialectics of urbicide

It is inherent and natural for human settlements to change and transform through various trends of growth, decline, conflict, adaptation, and so on. With every change some aspects of the city will be lost, destroyed, erased, or removed, to be replaced by the new established reality. It was during the Balkan armed conflict of the 1990s that the deliberate destruction of the city as an act of military strategy began to be defined and singled out as urbicide (among other definitions used in the Bosnian case, as we saw in the previous chapter). This highlighted the need for addressing urban destruction as a conceptual problem in its own right, rather than merely treating it as an eventuality of other forms of political violence, such as ethnic cleansing and genocide. Stephen Graham (2004b) argues that urbicide is constructed from organized strategies that destroy specific social and physical aspects of urbanity.

At the beginning of the twenty-first century, research attempted to describe similar types of destruction and to link them to the Israeli destruction of the Palestinian built environment in Jenin, Nablus, and Hebron and to the destruction of Iraqi cities such as Fallujah by US armed forces. In other events, the term "urbicide" refers to different modes of urban destruction that appear to have driving forces similar to the above-mentioned examples. The events of 11 September 2001 in New York is one instance.[1]

This chapter attempts to illustrate the problem and dilemmas of establishing, researching, and defining the urbicidical discourse. It will look at urbicide as a type of political violence and mode of urban planning; the concern of this chapter is to focus on urbicide literature and discussion of the event of warfare. It further aims to link the concepts of urbicide, urbanity and identity. At the same time, its main objective is to elaborate the urbicide definition that is seen as the deliberate destruction of shared spaces/places, social networks, and political resistance to efface place identity that at the end generates placelessness.

Urbicide—murdering the city or the destruction of the urban—has been re-inscribed as an emergent scholarly discourse. Its focus was urban devastation in post-Balkan war at the end of the 1990s. The most forceful aspects of the urbicide literature have concentrated their efforts on the urban dimensions of this discourse, as well as on analyzing the prerequisites or the politics of this phenomenon. This chapter further aims to build upon and strengthen some conceptual aspects of the literature on urbicide by connecting this research field to discussions about the relationship between urbicide, and urbanity.

Urbicide literature can be classified into three main streams:

1   urbicide as "anti-urban, anti-city" violence (Berman, 1987a, 1996; Simmons, 2001; Graham, 2004a; Shaw, 2004; Heathcote, 2005);
2   urbicide as politics of exclusion, "anti-heterogeneity" (Coward, 2001b, 2004, 2005);
3   urbicide as war of (or against) terror (Graham 2003, 2004a; Gregory 2003, 2004).

Urbicide as anti-urban, anti-city violence

Scholars such as Marshal Berman (1987a, 1996), Martin Shaw (2004), Cynthia Simmons (2001), Stephen Graham (2004a) and Edwin Heathcote (2005) discuss urbicide as targeting cities for what they represent—spaces of cosmopolitan life and tolerance, ranging from their buildings, assets, and institutions to their industries and infrastructure, and extending to their symbolic meanings—both in acts of organized war and through bureaucratic and urban planning policies. Thus, urbicide can be seen as the destruction of homogeneous/plural culture/ethnic or economic centers that are deemed undesirable by urban development policies, with a view to achieving a more superior form and content for the city, or, indeed, its progressive erasure.

Urbicide in the context of urban renewal projects

The first perspective on urbicide is that of Marshall Berman, who was the first to coin and discuss this discourse in his article "Life in the Shadows: The Underside of New York City" published in 1987 (Berman, 1987a) and his chapter "Falling Towers: City Life After Urbicide" (Berman, 1996). Berman's reasoning of "urbicide," which he calls "the murder of a city," is linked with violence against urbanization, of which he says: "The anti-urbanism of the highway program is ultramodern." His focus was on the city as the pinpoint of destruction in the process of modernization (the infrastructure construction projects).[2] He claims that the American urban policy in the 1950s and 1960s was a successful plot to destroy cities. The erasing of many suburbs, neighborhoods (in reference to the Bronx's destruction to construct the Cross Bronx Express) and streets in New York City and their inhabitants were for Berman "victims of our post-war urbicide policy." He explains that what has been destroyed in realizing these giant national projects is not only the city's physical fabric but also its street life, which has disappeared to give space to highway junctions and traffic lights. Referring again to the Bronx's destruction, Berman parades the human dimension of what he considers a catastrophe, by reflecting on the indirect impacts of urbicide, such as the human sense of loss and violation of personal memories that have been obscured, in addition to the loss of an essential part of people's identity, the feeling of "home":

> Their vibrant cities were largely destroyed. When they woke up at their new addresses, it was often green and pleasant. But you can trust Robert Moses's sadistic genius to seize the *mot just* on their new lives: the big fact of life was that they were "subdivided," their suburban identity reduced and constricted their being.
>
> (Berman, 2006: 6)

Marshall Berman's arguments on urbicide introduced urbicide's contours exhaustively. He highlighted the socio-economic and aesthetic transformations that were brought about in this context—something that is not clearly present in other scholars' work, as we will see later. "Life in the Shadows" was a descriptive and sort of personal reflection about the destruction of his neighborhood, the place of his childhood memories and the sense of home. The reformulation of the social psychological impacts of the theme he had described earlier in the Bronx destruction was later elaborated to critique the general American urban policy. Berman's perspectives of urbicide project it as "the destruction of places, sights, sounds, activities, institutions (of building)" (1996: 1). Urbicide for Berman is thus about the destruction of the physical built environment as well as the elimination of particular forms of social life, which Berman variously describes as "places to rest, home," social relations of community and neighborliness, and, finally, the visibility of others and the presence of poor people. Together, the destruction of built and social environments means the end of sensory experiences —"sights" and "sounds" that may provide the affective foundations of socio-spatial identity, "home," and emancipation "freedom." In the context of modern urban projects, for example, the destruction of complete neighborhoods in the United States in the 1960s to make way for the construction of highway networks was perceived as a pre-emptive strike on certain social groups in favor of the capitalist elite. Berman (1996: 18) points out this link between capitalism and urbicide:

> One of the achievements of the great wave of modernization that began in the late eighteenth century was to incorporate urbicide into the process of urban developer [sic] . . . Its victims, along with their neighborhoods and towns vanish without a trace.

The difficulty of Berman's description of urbicide as anti-city lies is in his clarification or justification of the motives and driving forces behind planning policies in what he calls city haters: "Antipathy towards the city" is due to the pastoral nostalgia for a lost or disappearing rural life (2006: 3). The link between Robert Moses' national infrastructure projects and this nostalgia is not clear. Modernization by urbanization and destruction is a concept that was being used long before Robert Moses. Haussman's Paris urban renewal project is a good representative example. His project is interesting not only for the urban planning, in which the grand special boulevards connect two main nodes in the city, but also for the massive destruction of many Parisian neighborhoods, which gave Haussmann the reputation of "*artiste démolisseur.*" The destruction targeted the working class quarters, which were depopulated and razed to the ground. The destruction in the name of modernization here was used to secure Paris against a workers' uprising—a sort of preventive war, which is, in the end, a mode of spatial re-configuration. "Here urban destruction was not anti-urban, but it was one of the modern urbanity's very manifestations," argues Herscher (2005). Similar ideology can also be seen in nationalist modernist projects such as the Zionist discourse in colonizing Palestine. Thus, Berman's link between moderation, development projects and the concept of urbicide is confusing, as it will lead us to consider every act of destruction for the sake of development as an urbicidal activity.

Urbicide for genocide in the context of armed conflict

In his chapter "New Wars of the City: Urbicide and Genocide," Shaw (2004) situates the city as the main target in war and political violence. He describes war and its destructive machine as a tool and form of spatial organization. The chapter projects many historical examples of urbicide, from the strategic bombing of Dresden and Hamburg to Tokyo, Hiroshima and Nagasaki. Urbicide in this context is an attempt to "cleanse" a city that was perceived as morally polluted. Shaw's historical review stresses the anti-urban to be an essential element of the modern new war (in the period after the Second World War); even where they mobilized urban discontents, he claims that the ethnic national leaders in the Balkan wars depended mainly on the rural and small town hatred of the city, and were often led by urban elites who originated from villages. Similar arguments have been raised by Cynthia Simmons (2001), who stressed that "During the Yugoslav wars of succession, hatred of the city as a concept and the urge to destroy it (urbicide) were real." Hence, urbicide for Shaw describes a distinct form of anti-urban violence; this refers to the distinctive destruction of urban communities and values, driven by the aim of wiping out the cosmopolitan cultural heritage and intellectual life, as well as the ethnic plurality that characterizes urbanity. The powerful side of Shaw's scholarly work on urbicide is its link with other types of violence—that urbicide can interrelate with other types of "-cides" such as genocide. The link between what is destroyed and the meaning of destruction is very interesting as "it is what the city represents that is at stake, as much as the existence of its inhabitants and their physical surroundings."

Another important point that Shaw raises is the parallel violence against the rural—the anti-rural campaign that goes hand in hand with the anti-urban campaign, which emphasizes the multi-objectives of war and destruction. The attack on urban values is only one dimension of each phase of war. Shaw gives many historical examples, such as the Nazi destruction of the Soviet Union's cities and villages in 1941. As he explains, the motive behind the anti-rural campaign is to erase the roots of resistance that peasants represent and attempt to destroy all ways of life and values (the urban and the rural as well).

In Cambodia, too, the Khmer Rouge did not just empty the cities and destroy the intelligentsia: in their attempt to remake the people they also systematically relocated the rural population and wiped out the kin networks of the peasants. Peasants' ways of life and beliefs were just as much a target as urban ways and beliefs. The party aimed to destroy the pre-existing social organization and values (after Kiernan, Shaw, 2003: 147).

The difficulty of Shaw's link between the anti-urban and the anti-rural is not in combining them as phases of war destruction, but in considering the anti-urban as urbicide and the anti-rural as outside urbicide. urbanity for him is manifested in the geographic setting of cities

Urbicide as politics of exclusion

Martin Coward (2001b, 2004, 2005, 2009b) describes urbicide as a politics of exclusion, of "anti-heterogeneity." Urbicide, for this stream, entails destroying heterogeneous plurality as manifested in the spatial configuration of the urban environment. The destruction of the urban fabric is therefore the destruction of buildings that establish common/shared spaces in which plural communities can live their lives. It is the quality, nature, and values of the urban realm that are at stake in this conceptualization of urbicide. The aim is to destroy plurality, diversity, and heterogeneity in order to inscribe a more preferable homogeneity.[3]

Such politics is evident in ethnic nationalism. In Bosnia, for example, urbicide was used to eradicate the possibility of difference inherent in the public, shared spatiality of the built environment to create homogeneous territorial entities (Coward, 2005). This politics of exclusion can also be seen in other types of conflict. One striking example is the contemporary Israeli Wall of Separation, and Israeli house demolition policies have been discussed as rooted in a politics of exclusion that attempts to inscribe homogeneity by transferring the Palestinian built environment into separated enclaves to create a Jewish state more accurately defined as an "ethnocracy." Martin Coward (2001a:18) argues that:

> The Israeli urbicide comprises the transformation of agonistic heterogeneity into an antagonism. This destruction establishes zones of separation which naturalize the perception that Arabs and Jews are distinct and separate.

[On the establishment of zones of separation see Hass *et al.* (2001).] This consolidates Israel as a homogeneous entity predicated on a claim to an origin distinct from that of the Arabs. These zones of separation thus naturalize the exclusion of Arabs who are regarded as both heterogeneous to, and thus not welcome within, the Israeli state.

Of the "urban" at stake in "urbicide," Coward (2002a) draws on Louis Wirth's urban sociology to buttress the original arguments on urbicide. He suggests that:

> If we identify urbanity as entailing, principally, heterogeneous existence, we can say that the destruction of urban life is the destruction of hetero-geneity. The destruction of urban fabric is, therefore, the destruction of the conditions of possibility of heterogeneity. What is at stake in urbicide—the destruction of buildings which establish common/shared spaces in which plural communities live their lives—is thus the destruction of the conditions of possibility of heterogeneity
>
> (Coward, 2002a: 45)

Urbicide for Coward is the destruction of shared spaces and diverse identities. Its politics is in the denial of the agonistic heterogeneity that characterizes urbanity in order to inscribe homogeneity. In describing the destruction of Bosnian cities, Coward asserts another important point on urbicide characteristics: that it should be a widespread, and yet intentional, destruction of the urban environment. He emphasizes the point that the destruction of the heritage artifact (churches, mosques, libraries) happened to attract scholars' attentions in the Balkan wars while the place/space of everyday life—the habitat—was ignored. It is not only symbolic buildings and significant elements of Bosnian cultural heritage that were targeted for destruction. The urban tissue of Bosnia came under a relentless assault. As Nicholas Adams notes, along with mosques, churches and synagogues, "markets, museums, libraries, cafes, in short, the places where people gather to live out their collective life, have been the focus of . . . attacks. The widespread destruction of urban tissue is the destruction of a *common, shared* space" (Coward, 2004: 157 after Adams, 1993).

Coward, in contrast to Shaw, projects urbicide as a distinct form of violence; he claims that the destruction of buildings and urban spaces were intentionally planned for what they represented as symbols of ethnic heterogeneity. The importance of Coward's thesis is in its differentiation between urbicide as an event that stands for itself and urbicide as a tool. In his extensive discussions on the main characteristics of urbicide Coward draws attention to the destruction of buildings that compromise the shared spaces and are the symbols around which different ways of life are lived. Coward's main contribution to develop the theme of urbicide lies in his assertion of the necessity of understanding the destruction of the built environment beyond the anthropocentric political imaginary who studies political violence through human loss considerations. Urbicide for Coward refers to the destruction of buildings in order to destroy shared places, spaces, and heterogeneity rather than limiting it to the destruction of urbanity conceived as specific ways of life in particular cities. He argues that it is the politics of exclusion of how we see the "other" that is at stake in urbicide, in an attempt to inscribe homogenous enclaves.

This line of theory is of significant interest, and this research attempts to build upon this interesting argument. This plural/heterogeneous culture was not just represented in mixed marriages, neighbors of different ethnic origin, or those who declared themselves Yugoslavs rather than Bosnian-Serb/Croat/Muslim It was represented in the material cultures within which everyday lives were lived (Coward, 2004: 165).

The problem of Coward's interesting arguments about the characteristics and the logic behind urbicide, which is heterogeneity, rests on its link to the Bosnian case and the limit of this heterogeneity to ethnic religious difference. The difficulty in this point is that, first, urbicide is not only about anti-heterogeneity (hetero-geneity as Coward defines it). If, however, one submits that the relationship between urban form/tissue and content is more complicated, then not all strategies to destroy built environments would qualify as urbicide. In situations where built form and social life combine to produce homogeneous form of life and antagonistic relations among spatially differentiated social groups it might be the target of urbicide as well. Along these lines, for example, is Gregory's (2004) argument that the Jenin refugee camp or Fallujah may have been under vicious attack precisely because they represent coherently hostile communities of resistance that are further homogenized with spatial imaginaries of the Oriental "other." Therefore, for me, urbicide can be perceived in this context as the destruction of shared spaces/places to destroy their heterogeneity, which is seen in the existence of plural identities (that go beyond ethnic or religious identities, intellectual, professional, personal, and others) that qualify urbanity.

Urbicide as war of (or on) terror

Urbicide is also defined as war of, or against, terror (including state terror in colonial projects) and anti-terrorism, as described in the work of Stephen Graham (2003, 2004a) and Derek Gregory (2003, 2004). This thesis relies mainly on the insep-arability of war, terror, place annihilation, and modern urbanism (here within a very proactive colonization process). In such cases, cities are perceived, in the geopolitical imaginary of the political elite, as places of unrest that need to be regularized and reorganized, either by war or through urban-planning policies in colonized cities. Thus, urbicide is a product or element of armed conflict, war, pre-emptive strikes and anti-terror campaigns.

In his reading and analysis of urbicide Graham (2003, 2004a, 2005) stresses the urban dimensions of the neo-imperial warfare in places such as Palestine and Iraq. He articulates the increasing urbanization of warfare in the twentieth and the twenty-first centuries in which the intensifying military interest is in the role of cities as the key sites in which military and geopolitical conflicts are being fought. They do so in a context of intensifying global urbanization, the growth of urban terrorism, the implosion of many nation states and the efforts of the US and its allies to maintain and strengthen global political, economic, and military hegemony. Graham's contribution to urbicide involves a deployment of warfare, militarized urban planning and discourses of "anti-terrorism" to undermine the fact that "as throughout urban history, in these times of intensifying globalization urban areas are crucial centers of heterogeneous mixing" (Graham, 2004b: 332). This argument re-directs the notion of heterogeneity in Coward (2005) towards a combination of ethno-cultural group pluralism and post-colonial views on hybridity.

The second interesting point in Graham (2004b) is his suggestion that urbicide is a coordination of military strategies to destroy conditions of resistance and independence. For example, the contemporary Israeli military campaign in Occupied Palestine has been justified as "war on terrorism." Graham (2004b) has argued that in the OPT there are many Israeli strategies that constitute urbicide. This is readily manifest in the demolition of homes and urban living spaces, the intensive destruction of infrastructure, and the systematic undermining of the urbanization and modernization of Palestinian society by the construction of Jewish settlements, bypass roads, and the Wall of Separation. These strategies are "designed to fragment and undermine the contiguity and coherence of the enemy's territory" (2004b: 643) and construct instead an environment that maximizes the capacity of occupying forces to survey, surround and control occupied lands and populations. Graham further suggests that urbicide refers to the destruction of "the urban, civil, and infrastructural foundations" of Iraqi independence or the "proto-Palestinian state." Thus urbicide for him is a strategy for control and military surveillance that might be true for most cases of urbicide worldwide.

Major characteristics of urbicide

In the three categories above, urbicide has been discussed mainly with respect to military strategies, tactics, and objectives. Yet, at the same time, these authors stress the impacts of urbicide on the physical structure of the environment, ignoring or marginalizing the human experience of that destruction (apart from Marshal Berman).

Across and within these three categories of urbicide, various similarities and contradictions exist. The complementariness over certain issues related to urbicide can highlight some general characteristics of this discourse:

1   The setting is always an urban inhabited built environment (urban that is abstracted in the city).
2   There is always widespread or total damage and destruction inflicted on that setting.

3   The place of destruction is demonized or dehumanized—before it is destroyed.
4   The destruction is exercised to achieve spatial reconfiguration and control.
5   The destruction is always premeditated, intentional and planned.

Contradictions and contested issues in urbicide discourse

The three schools of thought on urbicide present conflicting positions on some of the issues that play an important role in defining what urbicide is about. These contradictory arguments are mainly about the meaning of the urban and urbanity that strongly presented itself in these discourses. The contradictions have led to confusion about which cases can be included and considered under urbicide and which should be excluded. This confusion is due to the limited conventional approach to the notion of the urban in its link to the geographic city settings, excluding other interesting cases from the discourse. Variations emerge in establishing what is urban:

1   by size—which is different from country to country;[4]
2   by legal status, e.g. the United Kingdom's cities;[5]
3   by new categorizations, such as the camp—a form of Palestinian urbanity defined by Graham[6] when he describes urbicide in Jenin refugee camp. Although the Palestinian camps exist in or near cities, they do not follow urban rules. They are places outside the *nomos* as Agamben (1998) has defined it. Sheik Hassan (forthcoming) redefines the camp as a new urban setting with special spatial, socio-cultural, economic and legal settings;
4   by cultural and discourse variation that excludes villages from the discourse while indirectly inscribing them in discussing other forms of urbicide. For example, the systematic Israeli housing demolition in Palestine is discussed as a form of urbicide although many of these houses lie in villages; an example is the Jerusalem area. The same can be said of the Israeli Separation Wall, which can be seen as an element of urbicidal activities. See Coward (2001a, 2005) and Graham (2002a, 2004b);
5   by etymological definitions: *urbanus* (*urbs*—Latin) as reference to Rome, implying that urbanity is a form of civilization parallel to that city as well as implying citizenship[7] (vs) *polis* (Greek), which places the city, town and village under the same urban categorization;
6   by the tools used to inflict destruction from planning policies, military assault war and "terrorism" activities; or
7   by the scale of the inflicted damage (in reference to the World Trade Center and Sarajevo).

These contradictions can best be presented first in the inclusion and exclusion of villages and camps from the discourse depending on the form of urbicide under discussion. For example, the hundreds of devastated villages in Bosnia and Palestine (during the 1948 war) are not discussed as urbicide. It is controversial enough to consider the Israeli home demolition policies as urbicide (Coward 2004) although they mainly take place in villages—in the Jerusalem area, for instance. Another example is the inclusion of the destruction of Palestinian refugee camps under the urbicide discourse although by definition camps do not belong to the notion of urbanity and the urban. It is therefore important to elaborate and regenerate a broader insight in the meaning of the urban and urbanity that satisfies and complies with this specific phenomenon of urbicide.

The second conflicting issue rests in the incorporation and mixing of two types of destruction: the destruction emerging out of developing projects with the destruction that materializes in the context of urban warfare. We find this misleading, confusing and undermining the power of urbicide. This mixing overlaps what is assumed to be the "normal" episode of urban transformations through development and urban renewal projects with the deviant rupture to all normalized place/city dynamics through radical devastation and transformation of urbanity through an exceptional event, the event of war. These two totally different approaches to urban destruction through development (excluding development projects in the context of colonial projects in colonized cities) versus urban warfare do not have the same energy nor do they have similar mechanisms or impacts to be included under the umbrella of the same theoretical discourse.

Redefining urbicide

There is an increase in urban destruction by urbanization, capitalistic speculation, terrorism, state backed violence and warfare. Urbicide has frequently been used to describe any of these episodes without being specific or captious about using this term. It is true that the term is newly researched and is not fully developed in terms of definition and characteristics that can be used to call an act of urban destruction urbicide. Calling every incident of urban destruction urbicide is not useful; it mitigates and weakens the power of this term, and it is the intention of the following section to develop this.

I suggest applying few limitations to the urbicide discourse and then reopening it for new possibilities to solidify its definition. First, there is a need to separate urban destruction resulting from urban renewal and development projects from urban destruction resulting from warfare. The destruction that result from urbanization and development process might be qualified as surgical urbanism or as Isabelle Verhaert (2006) calls it urbicidal urbanism. Thus, it is crucial to limit urbicide exclusively to the destruction resulting from urban fights and warfare. Second, there is an urgent need to redefine the notion of the urban and urbanity in order to clarify and strengthen other dimensions of this discourse such as its link to identity. Finally, investigating what is destroyed and what has been produced by urbicide (using different cases) can help in defining the common characteristics of urbicidal episodes, which will make easier distinguishing cases of urbicide from other cases of political violence such as ethnic cleansing and collateral damage. This redefinition entails the necessity to develop a proper analytical tool (using the case study) to read, analyze and synthesize urbicidal activities that the general literature and research on urbicide has not systematically developed or presented.

The urban and urbanity

The arguments of the three schools of thought on urbicide evolved around the meaning of the urban as vital for defining urbicide. This section demonstrates that correlating the term urban and thus urbicide only to the geographic settings of cities is not useful. It will not give a comprehensive understanding to the phenomenon of urbicide, which tends to target the built environment in general. More often, urbanity is limited and associated with the city, although it constitutes only one pole of it. The urban that is the main part of the etymology of urbicide originated in Western theories from the Latin word *urbanus*, meaning "of the *urbs*," where *urbs* essentially referred to Rome. Being like Rome might mean being sophisticated in manner but also being Roman in terms of citizenship and civilization.[8] In this abstraction of the world into a single citizenship by belonging to one particular city, the city itself was ceasing to be a word of its own, for which the status of *urbs* was known as a city-state system. On the other hand, the city in Greek is the *polis*; one of its synonyms is village or town; that means that the popular juxtaposition of villages with rurality, in turn excluding their destruction from the connotation of urbicide, is not always correct. It should be noted that the differentiation between the urban and the rural is still under debate. Geographers and governments have tended to define rurality by population per unit of area.[9] At the same time there are no international standards to clarify this dichotomy if it exists. The United Nations stated in a report that "given the variety of situations in the countries of the world, it is not possible or desirable to adopt uniform criteria to distinguish urban areas from rural ones" (United Nations, 2012). Robinson cites three principal reasons for the difficulties of differentiating between urban and rural on a continuum.[10]

In some countries city status is not always granted to urban areas. For example, in the United Kingdom, city status is granted to local government areas such as civil parishes and boroughs. Another difficulty in the differentiation of this process arises when rural and urban modes of life co-exist, as is the case with villages that become contained by urban area expansion and city sprawl thus consti- tuting two different entities in one geographic place—Chinese cities are a good example. The emergence of refugee camps in city centers or peripheries is another example. Finally, the world in the twenty-first century is in a growing urbaniza- tion process: borders will be eliminated with globalization and development of informatics system, and remoteness, which was once a characteristic of rurality, will disappear in the new world order as Tehranian describes it: "in a wired global village, where the new centres and peripheries are not territorial but information- bound" (1998: 423).

Any discussion of urban destruction and urbicide should therefore be liberated from restricted notions of urbanity such as size, number of inhabitants and so on. These measures are important for other fields of research; they are not relevant to discussions on urbicide. The urban should be approached from a different perspective in urbicide discourse, by empowering its hidden but major characteristics, the political dimension and its link with shared places/spaces and its bond with identity.

The urban as a political body and place of identity

Using the definition of the urban discussed earlier might help in extracting the link between the urban and the political. *Urbs* or urban refers to the notion of being Roman in terms of having the right of citizenship. In Liddell and Scott's *Greek-English Lexicon*, the meaning of *politeia* is linked with civility and citizen as polities, and is "the conditions and rights of the citizen, or *citizenship*, analogous to the Latin *civitas*—the politai–cives–citizens (–civilis–civil (civilized, civilization)) (–politics)."

The *Oxford English Dictionary* lists as the first meaning of civility "the art of government, politics" and as the second "courteousness, politeness." When we add the root of "civility"—"city"—we see why and how city, government, and a code of behavior are closely related. The Latin word for city is *civitas* and the Greek word is *polis*; both terms have become part of the English language as our words for city and politics respectively. As countless commentators have pointed out (e.g. Woolf, 1992), this conception of citizenship presupposes an imaginary, yet nonetheless rigid and real, boundary between the *polis* and the *oikos*, between the public space of political life and the material world of the household. Neither the Latin nor the Greek term meant a place but "the body of citizens of the community." Only in later Roman times did *civitas* become "*urbs*—the town or place occupied by the community."

The urban based on Hobbs's theory derives the word politics from the Greek word *polis*, which, literally, denotes the organization of daily life in the city. Hobbs's definition of urbanity and the city perceives the community as both the natural body and the political body of the city: "Man is not only a natural body, but also a body of the city, that is, a so-called political part" (Hobbes, 1998: 2).

For Coward (2001b) the political is understood as a fundamentally agonistic moment in which limits are established based on the inclusion and/or exclusion of the human being through which identity is constituted. He looks at urbanity that qualifies the sharing of existential spatiality that always implies existence in community that is not confined only to cities but also occurs in all those conditions in which the things with which we engage on an everyday basis intimate an ineluctable altering in our world. It is insofar as buildings constitute shared spaces in which specific instances of heterogeneity occur that they comprise the conditions for the possibility of agonistic relations of identity/difference, the networks of self and other, that we designate politics. (Connolly, 2002) If the urban environment consists of shared spatiality on which the existence of such plural identities (heterogeneities) is predicated, then it is the constitution of such spatiality that lies at the heart of the political. Destroying shared/heterogeneous spaces, contesting such spatiality, is a way of destroying or contesting certain agonistic/heterogeneous existences and as such comprises a fundamentally political event according to Coward (2001b).

The concept of place identity is a theoretical necessity for understanding the impact of the urban environment on the individual. Place identity refers to clusters of perceptions in the form of images, memories, facts, ideas, beliefs, values, and behavior tendencies relevant to the individual's existence in the physical world (Proshansky *et al.*, 1983). Proshansky argues that these clusters are related to the development of self-identity, which is largely a product of socialization. Coping in an urban setting requires socialization in the physical world at any number of periods during the life cycle. The urban environment comprises diverse physical settings, and place identity associated with different settings provides norms and values that regulate behavior patterns in given milieus. Thus, the individual behaves and interacts in certain ways in settings that involve crowding, privacy, and territoriality.

Mehrag explains how human being develop attachment to place which becomes their place of identity. Landscape (environment in general) provides a context within which humans live, and also provides the boundaries, quite complexly, within which people remake themselves and are "worked" upon by the landscape they have constructed. So framed, "place becomes like personality—unique and particular." Further, landscape is seen as a "prop" of memory and identity and may be contested because it holds significance for people, situating a "sense of place" and "genus loci." This emotional bonding of people with place is psychic in nature and resides in the "realm of memory" (Mehrag, 2001: 89).

The urban experience can develop what we call relational identity—what we are. Our identity is determined by the links we create when we live and act in the world. In Martin Heidegger's terms (Heidegger, 1997: 32–34), there are differences in our experiences of natural environments, small-scale built environments and urban environments. These differences are based on the simple fact that the objects to which we relate in these various milieus are different.

Harvey (1998) argues that the public arena can be seen as the body politic; he further states that "we must realize that both body and urban are intimately tied up in the means by which we forge and relate our identities." Identity and particularly group identity are relational phenomena; one defines oneself in relation to the "other." Communities are symbolically constituted at the boundaries (Cohen, 1993).

Thus, the political is seen as the main condition of the urban and identity; the main question in urbicide is not what destruction of shared spaces discloses. The main essence of urbicide lies in what has been destroyed and what has been produced by this phenomenon that reveals the political entailments of urbanity.

Buildings, not in their individual capacity but in their spatial relations and network, create a specifically heterogeneous spatiality that generates what we know as urbanity. These buildings are a fundamentally political event, since such hetero-geneous spatiality is precisely what comprises the condition of possibility of the network of identity/difference on which the political is predicated. It is in this sense that Heidegger sees physical space—space that can be understood as the volume inside an empty container—as being derived from existential spatiality.

Analyzing the phenomenon of urbicide is, then, an exploration into the com-position of shared spatiality that constitutes the essence of the experience of the political. Only if there is such shared space is the heterogeneity that urbanity comprises possible. Only if it can be shown that buildings are indeed constitutive of shared space is the term "urbicide" (defined as killing what characterizes urbanity—heterogeneity) appropriate for such destruction, as Coward (2001a) rightly explains.

The shared spatiality that constitutes urbanity at the same time embodies place/city identity as a medium for politics. Urbanity then is understood as a special form of identity; every place has its special form of urbanity that makes it differ-entiated from other urbanities. This uniqueness at the same time does not hinder the existence of other plural identities that constitute any community. It is the existence and confrontations of these plural identities in any given spatial setting that generates heterogeneity. The celebration of urbanity materializes in shared spatiality that fosters heterogeneous identities of the community and embodies them in a particular urban identity. In short urbanity is identified as the place and medium where different political debates take place; it is the place where different tensions and confrontations are absorbed and negotiated, and that in effect create particular identity out of plural identities and differences. Accordingly, urbicide can be defined as *the assault on urbanity that attempts to destroy shared spatiality as a political and social body and as a place of identity.*

Urbicidal episodes: forms and patterns

The condition that qualifies any given urban destruction as urbicide or not is highlighted in this section, with the aim of consolidating, opening up and enriching the discourse and discussion on urbicide rather than of finding a definite definition.

The previous sections have demonstrated how the political body constitutes the urban and how buildings are political in their heterogeneous spatial configura-tion. This leads to highlight urbicide as a holistic discourse that encompasses the destruction of the entire urban setting (fabric, tissue, infrastructure, landscape and so) and its entire built and spatial network and that also conceals different levels of destruction. It renders redundant terms such as domicide and cultural cleansing, and other terms that deal with the destruction of specific cultural buildings or types of building. Urbicide is therefore assumed to have the capacity to absorb other discussions and definitions of urban destruction.

Two forms of urbicide can be elaborated: direct urbicide and indirect urbicide. The discussion will treat destruction in terms of nature of destruction, level/scale of destruction, and typology of destroyed buildings.

Direct urbicide: urbicide by destruction

Direct urbicide is the direct deliberate material/spatial destruction of the urban environment. This form is the typical form known in many cases all over the world, for example at Mostar, Fallujah/Iraq, and the Southern Lebanon villages devastation in 2006.

This form can be projected in three cases:

1   Extreme urbicide: the complete annihilation of the urban, on the condition that the destruction of this urbanity is an attempt to destroy the collective or national identity, or on the condition that the annihilated place/space constitutes an important feature of national or collective identity. This case is much discussed and takes place in parallel with other forms of political violence such as genocide and ethnic cleansing. The infamous case of the annihilation of Dresden in the Second World War is a representative example.
2   The deliberate destruction of buildings of a specific building typology according to their symbolic meaning to the "other" (the assault on the urban as place of identity), such as the destruction of religious, national, and cultural buildings with high historical and symbolic value. Examples are Mostar Bridge, Sarajevo library, and Bosnian mosques and churches. This type of urbicide is normally discussed under terms such as cultural cleansing, cultural genocide, and identicide. This destruction normally takes place to efface the material evidence or the strong material/spatial representation of the other's identity, in order to erase or alter the other's collective memory embodied in historic buildings. This destruction does not take place separately from the devastation of other building typologies. The issue is that the destruction is widespread and more evident in particular building typology.
3   The wanton destruction of the urban environment (the urban as political body and place of identity at the same time). This destruction is a massive destruction of the built and spatial representation of the other. It entails the destruction of all typologies of building. The whole built environment is under assault, as happened in the destruction of Jenin refugee camp, a place and symbol of Palestinian political and military resistance. The massive destruction of Nablus Old Town and of Fallujah in Iraq are representative examples.

Indirect urbicide: urbicide by construction and control

Indirect urbicide involves measures that lead to undermine urbanity with slow and less visible physical/material destruction. It can involve laws, measure and actions that cause indirect destruction to the urban. The Israeli settlements in the

Occupied Palestinian Territories are a strong example. The construction of these settlements is described by Graham (2003) as urbicidal activities to subjugate the Palestinian natural urbanity, and this is seen by this research as urbicide by construction. The Apartheid Wall and the Israeli military checkpoints, are other examples that are described by Coward (2002a) as established zones of separation that naturalize the perception that Arabs and Jews are distinct and separate and consolidates Israel as a homogeneous entity predicated on a claim to an origin distinct from that of the Arabs. These zones of separation thus naturalize the exclusion of Arabs, who are regarded as both heterogeneous to, and thus not welcome within, the Israeli state. This form of urbicide is perceived by this research as a strong form of urbicide by control.

Urbicide as process

Seeing urbicide as a process of three stages of politics, action and effects is crucial to understand any urbicidal episode and might be applicable to any urbicidal case. The *planning* (politics) stage is what eventually allows the action of urbicide to materialize. This stage consists of a state of ignorance and denial of the "other," manifested in their dehumanization and the demonization of their urbanity/ spatiality. This is combined with the mechanisms by which this "Other" is controlled, a typical complex in colonial subjugation. From contemporary cases of urbicide, it is clear that the planning of the military assaults on a region is often accompanied by a powerful propaganda campaign to legitimize both the assault and the destruction of the enemy and the enemy's place/space. A strong example is the US campaign "War on Terror" and the American war on Iraq in which, according to Graham (2005), the American media promoted the war as the war on "Alqaeda fighters." In the assault on Fallujah (2004), which was a strong urbicidal episode promoted as an assault on "terrorist resistance," "Saddam loyal" or "foreign insurgents," Fallujah was dehumanized as "rat's nest" or "hornet's nest." Marine Colonel Gareth Brandel told the BBC before the second assault: "The enemy has got a face, he is called SATAN, he lives in Fallujah" (Wood, 2004).

This statement reflects the "othering" of the enemy who is considered inhuman, with a Satan-like nature that will never change. At the same time the home of the enemy is the incubator of the terrorist whose Satan-like nature is extended to his habitat, which is also deemed to be the producer of "other" terrorist Satans. These types of depiction construct and cast the enemy and the enemy's habitat beyond any juridical, legal and humanitarian considerations as they do not belong to this category. Consequently, the nihilism of the Satan "terrorist" and their habitat is justified and needed as an act of purification and cleansing of the cancerous danger. Similar attitudes are present in the Israeli urbicidal activities in the OPT.

The stage of *action* is embodied in the urban warfare and military operations that target and destroy various aspects of urbanity and identity.

The planning, control dynamics and destructive urbicidal episodes are manifest in the *effects* that urbicide generates within the new reality of the city. This is revealed in the resulting new physical/spatial condition of the city, which becomes a place, space, and state of exception,[11] a state that alters the human perception and experience of self and place.

It must be pointed out that studying urbicide as a separate form of political violence does not mean that it exists in pure form. Many forms of political violence can overlap in the process of urbicide, as with genocide and ethnic cleansing. The other point to emphasize is that different forms of urbicide can also overlap or lead to each other, or can happen individually.

This can be true also for the objectives and motives behind urbicide; they can be multiple, i.e. with more than one objective for destroying an urban environment. Urbicide can be seen both as a tool and as an end: it can be used to achieve other political violence or it can be an end in itself. What is important here is not only the logic behind urbicide, which was the main concern of the reviewed schools of thought on this concept. My argument is based on the challenge to treat urbicide as a holistic theme and to discuss it as a form of political violence and not be concealed within other types of political violence. The chapter has developed a tool to read, analyze, and highlight the reasons and logic behind this destruction, based on the Palestinian condition. It has then elaborated a methodology to analyze the nature and pattern of this destruction and, finally, argued for investigation into the impacts of this destruction on both the material/spatial environment and the human experience of this event of urbicide. Thus, seeing urbicide as a process of three stages of politics, action and effects is crucial to understanding any urbicidal episode and might be applicable to any urbicidal case. The specificity of the Palestinian context is seen in the occurrence of two forms of urbicide—the direct material destruction of urbanity (urbicide by destruction) overlapping with indirect urbicide through laws and other measurement seen as urbicide by construction and control.

Notes

1 Scholars stressed that the motives behind these incidents are anti-modernization and anti-civilization. See, for example, Heathcote (2005).

2 He describes these projects thus: "The 1960s began a prolonged horror show. The prime monster was the ever expanding Federal Highway System."

3 An example is the Zionist ambition in Palestine that wished to replace a diverse Muslim, Christian, and Jewish form of urbanity with an exclusively homogeneous Jewish urban and "modern agricultural" rural civilization.

4 For example, national variation results in enormous disparity between the definitions of rural communities. At one extreme, Switzerland regards communities of 10,000 inhabitants or less as being rural, whereas in Norway communities of 200 inhabitants are defined as the rural limit (Sayer, 1989).

5 City status is not always granted to urban areas. In the United Kingdom, city status is granted to local government areas such as civil parishes and boroughs. Cited in www.wikipedia.org, status of cities in the United Kingdom, accessed on 22 March 2006.

6 In Stephen's Graham article on Jenin Refugee Camp, "Constructing Urbicide by Bulldozer," he extensively discusses the Camp's devastation as part of urbicidal process. More likely he considered the refugee camp to be part of the urban discourse.
7 Proceedings of the British Academy, vol. 86; British Academy publications accessed on 15 January 2006.
8 Proceedings of the British Academy, vol. 86; British Academy publications accessed on 15 January 2006.
9 National variation results in enormous disparity between the definitions of rural communities. At one extreme, Switzerland regards communities of 10,000 inhabitants or fewer as being rural, whereas in Norway communities of 200 inhabitants are defined as the rural limit (Sayer, 1989).
10 The three reasons Robinson gives are: (1) The settlement continuum. There is no point in the continuum where urbanity disappears and rurality begins—the division between urban and rural populations is necessarily arbitrary; (2) The changing character of settlements. Changes in the nature of settlements have produced the phenomenon of urban sprawl. Suburbs and other changes have destroyed close networks of market towns and villages by transferring market functions to larger centers and attaching urban characteristics to settlements with only small populations; (3) Inadequacy of official designation. Arbitrary population limits employed by governments do not adequately or consistently define rurality. Problems of definition have resulted in added factors of land use characteristics, occupational, demographic, ecological, social organization, and cultural characteristics all being used as defining attributes. The plethora of definitions becomes unwieldy. (See Robinson, 1990.)
11 This concept was introduced by Giorgio Agamben, an Italian philosopher whose work focuses on bio-politics and on theories of post-sovereign power. His book *Homo Sacre: Sovereign Power and Bare Life* (1998) is the main source used to elaborate some of the arguments presented here.

Part II
Urbicide in Palestine

3

History of urban/territorial destruction in Palestine 1948–2002

After more than sixty years of contestation, the "Question of Palestine" arises as the iconic model of geopolitical spatial dilemmas that have marked both the twentieth and the twenty-first centuries. Even now, over sixty years later, it is difficult to comprehend how, between 1947 and 1948, over 400 Palestinian villages were systematically emptied and bulldozed, and an entire territory was confiscated in creating the new state of Israel (Sheik Hassan and Hanafi, 2009). Not only is this a conflict over space, and not only has it created new and extreme spatial configurations within historic Palestine; its impact has extended beyond these borders. The Nakba of 1948 and the Naksah of 1967 generated the largest and longest-lasting refugee problems in the world: currently more than four million Palestinians are refugees. As the late Edward Said (Said and Mohr, 1999: 11) observed, the paradox of living in exile has remained a major element for Palestinians both outside and within the Occupied Palestinian Territories (OPT) since 1948.

The destruction of the Palestinian urbanity/territoriality has a long history. These patterns of destruction were largely intensified after the emergence of the Israeli Palestinian issue in the beginning of the twentieth century. Scholars such as Weizman (2004b) and Graham (2003) connected the recent deliberate destruction of 2002 with the one of 1948 as part of the same process.

> The deliberate bulldozing of whole districts of cities by Israeli defense forces in spring 2002 is an intensification of an old policy. Bulldozing has been used as a weapon of collective and individual punishment and intimidation and as a means of shaping the geopolitical configuration of territory, since Israel's independence in 1948.
>
> (Weizman, 2004b: 197)

Territoriality emerges as a concept when discussions over the larger scale destruction of many cities, villages, and towns take place. This association is crucial in understanding and conceptualizing the destruction of larger spatial networks and structures on the scale of a whole territory. This type of destruction is perceived as an exaggerated phenomenon that exceeds urbicide and its capacity to explain this territorial destruction episode. The spacio-cide discourse is scale-specific, so it is suggested that this discourse explains intentional destruction and transformation on a territorial scale. Questioning the ideology, perception and mechanism that the Zionist movement adopted, followed and implemented to achieve territorial acquisition and transformation through destruction and appropriation is also examined. Three patterns of destruction in Palestine can be traced through history. These forms are constructed from: first, the actual *material/spatial destruction* of the Palestinian urbanity/territoriality that composes respectively urbicide/spacio-cide; second, *destruction by construction/reconstruction* of an Israeli urbanity/territoriality in the OPT, such as the Israeli policies and development of the Jewish settlements project and the Israeli-only bypass roads; third, *destruction by control*, which materializes in the establishment of control agencies through Israeli military laws, surveillance and the control network of military checkpoints, military bases and the Apartheid Wall. It is argued that these three forms generate urbicide on the level of urban settlement and creates spacio-cide when they dominate the regional and territorial scale.[1]

Territoriality, identity and spatiality: a theoretical discourse

There are two issues that are of interest on territoriality: its link to identity and its connections to spatiality.

Territoriality is defined by Robert Sack (1983: 55) as "a strategy for influence and control." He argues that human territoriality is the attempt to affect, influence, or control actions and interactions (of people, things, and affinities) by asserting and attempting to force control over geographic area. Sack (1983: 55) articulates that all human activities have a spatial component; political control may be absolute and precisely bounded. He links through territorial dimensions territoriality with power and sovereignty in his classification of territorial tendencies,[2] by pointing out that the territorial form of power is "a strategy for establishing differential access to things and people."

Some scholars disagree and define territoriality rather as only a cultural need of human cognition for reforming and solidifying individual and group identity (Altman, 1975; Cashdan, 1983). Others emphasize social processes that crystallize patterns of control over and within bounded units of space (Sack, 1986). Sack's definition appears to be somewhat unsatisfactory since the use of power for its own sake may not fully exploit the idea behind the concept. Rather, territorial control may be needed for the sake of identity and/or wealth. The cultural definition is deficient with reference to culture as "super organic" and with the difficulty of explaining how cultural patterns in society develop (Duncan, 1998). In contrast, the social definition reveals the possibility of re-examining social, cultural, and political restructuring of society in the defined space of daily life.

Territoriality and identity

One may perceive space either in the context of giving structure to a territorial strategy as an active factor that is able to influence human behavior, or in the context of a neutral framework in which human beings act. In the first context, one engages in controversial relations with environmental challenges in one's living space. Schnell (2001a) relates territoriality to the sense of attachment that human beings feel towards units of space as part of the arrangement of complementary relations that they effect with their surroundings.

There are three themes that are central to territorial strategies in the construction of national identities: territorial differentiation, territorial bonding, and territorial script. Narrating the national identity is not only a linguistic construct but is also constituted in concrete socio-historical and spatial contexts, as Jones and Natter (1999) argue. These sensibilities and patterns of territorial activity form during the social processes of structuring and restructuring. The restructuring occurs in three combined dimensions of reality. These dimensions demonstrate the strong link between the territorial construct with the spatial network of a given place as well as its impacts and role in establishing national and collective identities as argued by May (1983), Giddens (1984) and Schnell (1994). Looking first at the physical dimension, territoriality can appear as the material presence, which is the material culture of a population group, together with the structural mechanisms that represent its character and needs. This dimension articulates the collective identity that surfaces in bonding certain groups with the physical/spatial reality of a given territoriality. With the second—the social—dimension, mutual inter-action and power relations in the community manifest themselves, together with the arrangement of patterns of control over territory or over others by using territory. In the third dimension, the perception dimension, three issues find expression: the affinity of members of the community towards the territory; the group or individual identity in relation to the identity of the territory; and the myths[3] about territory that have become established in the public discourse.

Herb and Kablan (1999: 2) articulate the importance of territorial identity in the shaping of national and collective identity: that "territory is so inextricably linked to national identity that it cannot be separated out." There is no doubt that territory impinges upon the construction of national and state based forms of identity, but the way and extent of its impacts are open to question. Kablan and Herbs believe that the territorial dimension has not been well examined in the major studies of nationalism, and one of the goals of their research is to understand how national identity is connected to the territory and how it coexists and competes with other identities at different geographic scales. This strong link is evident in their argument that "the territory creates a collective consciousness by reinventing itself as a homeland" (Herb and Kablan, 1999: 17).

Territoriality as spatial construct

Collinge (1999) notes that territoriality refers to the socially mediated spatiality of political relations, producing formations that are interpreted as units such as nations, regions, and localities. As with any social relation, territoriality is an abstract principle for creating and reproducing social order, but at the same time, it has to be regarded as historically constructed and historically evolving. Territory plays a central role as the main—though by no means the sole—shaper of the nation. As Yiftachel (2002) argues, this shaping is incongruent with the thrust of leading theories on nationalism, which generally privilege national time, culture, or economy over the dynamics and intricacies of collective space. In other words, territoriality is much shaped and molded as a collective space.

Space for Sack refers to the medium in which we imbed identity. The interesting articulation of Sack's point of view on spaces resides in the association between space, war, and identity, in which he argues that places created out of space are the target of war; they are razed to destroy identities. Place (here in reference to any scale—urban, regional, even territorial) and its spatial components play essential roles in directing human behavior, and are capable of fomenting territoriality that is also the target of war destruction. He states:

> Space is something in which we embed our identity. Out of space, we create places that we choose, order, design, and make mean something. We target it and raze it to destroy identities. And we reclaim it in the name of science, or nationalism, or religion to establish identity. Place directs our actions and behaviors and it is capable of fomenting territoriality. We train professionals to design it, plan it, and make it mean something; we train our militaries to take it, hold it, and strategically mould it. Place becomes significant as we load it with memory, culture, and identity. In fact, identity is defined and supported by place, and in turn, places become part of one's identity and one's memory.
>
> (Sack, 1997: 135)

The previous argument on spatiality and its link to social, cultural, and political dynamics present space as an active structure that is in no way neutral.

To gain better insights into territoriality discourse in the Palestinian–Israeli discourse this study will use three major categorizations and characteristics of territoriality tendencies set out by Sack. Sack (1983: 59) formulates ten tendencies[4] of territoriality; for this book we will illustrate those that are strongly connected to our scope of discussion. The scale of territoriality in this discussion is limited to the scale of territory. This is generated from the understanding that territoriality occurs at all scales, from the room to the nation-state. Territoriality, as Sack argues, is not an object but a dynamic relationship between entities. The selected tendencies for discussion are:

1   *Classification.* As Sack explains, in this tendency territoriality involves:

> a form of classification that is extremely efficient under certain circumstances. Territoriality classifies at least in part by the area, rather by type. When we say that anything in this area . . . Is ours . . . were are classifying or assigning things to a category . . . according to their location in space.
>
> (Sack, 1986: 32)

2   *Enforcement.* Territoriality can be the most efficient strategy for enforcing control, if the distribution in space and time of the resources or things can be situated in unpredictable situations (Sack, 1986:32)

3   *Emptiness.* "When the things to be contained are not present, the territory is conceptually 'empty'. Territoriality in fact helps create the idea of a socially empty space . . . Not physically empty . . . Empty because it is devoid of socially or economically valuable artefacts" (Sack, 1986: 33).[5]

In general, space is perceived as the key factor in the generation and reproduction of collective identities. Group "spatiality" may include according to Murphy (2002) the degree of ethnic homogeneity or heterogeneity, the proximity of inter-state brethren, the degree of its peripherality, the level of its ideological territoriality, and the process of "territorial legitimization" involved in its identity construction.

Analysis of territorial spaces must hinge on the understanding of "active space," which is not merely a backdrop or a container of social change but something that exerts a vital influence on group identities and relations. The links between space, development, collective identities, and group relations are thus reciprocal; that is, while political processes create spatial outcome, these outcomes, in turn, create new political dynamics and impact national and collective identities. Hence, urbicide entails the destruction of urbanity that constitutes shared spatiality as a form of identity. The destruction of larger spatial networks and connections that constitute the national collective space and identity entails spacio-cide. This is how these forms of destruction are presented in this chapter.

The Zionist aspiration of "territorial/spatial construct"

Izhak Schnell (2001b) argues that in the early days of conceptualizing a Jewish state for all Jews in the world, Zionism made the territory the focus of Zionist activity. This focus implies concomitant actions of seizing territory, controlling it, and creating an affinity, an attachment, and a bond of identity between a constructed Jewish nationalism and a desired territory. Schnell further points out how pure colonization was a central strategy for realizing these "Zionist" national goals. According to Schnell, the Zionist territorial vision led to the Palestinian–Jewish conflict that concentrated on the control of territory. The aims and energies of the Zionist movement therefore became territorial *par excellence*: purchase the land, attract immigrants, build cities, develop agriculture, establish industries, settle colonies and launch an international struggle for Jewish political sovereignty. From an early period, then, space, place, and territory became the grains and core of the Zionist project in historic Palestine.

Following Schnell's view, during the stage of a mobilized society Zionism was based on a firm establishment of its territoriality, where conception of territoriality was based on three major actions: defining their national ideology from an ethno-nationalism perspective that will sustain only one tribe with a place in the territory; adopting a pure colonizing strategy consistent with its ethno-national logic; and developing a national economy that served these national and territorial interests (Schnell, 2001b: 194).

Zionist forefathers such as Theodor Hertzel (the founder of the Zionist movement in 1897) believed that the national ideology of Jewish territorial control in historic Palestine should be carried out by the Jews with the assistance of major European powers. Said explains how Zionism reinforced their national ideology in the way they presented their territorial vision.

Zionism will restore "a lost fatherland," and in doing so, it mediates between the various civilizations: that present-day Palestine was in need of cultivation, civilization, and reconstitution; that Zionism would finally bring enlightenment and progress where at present there was neither (Said, 1979b: 22).

Said (1979b) further articulates the Zionism doctrine by referring to three ideas or principles that, he says, dominated almost every Zionist thinker or ideologue that are presented in (a) the non-existent Arab inhabitants, (b) the complementary Western-Jewish attitude to an "empty" territory, and (c) the restorative Zionist project, which would repeat by rebuilding a vanished Jewish state and combine it with modern elements such as disciplined, separate colonies, a special agency for land acquisition, etc.

On the way to establish a Jewish state in historic Palestine, promoting and constructing territorial emptiness was important and essential for Zionism (to guarantee Jewish migration from Europe to historic Palestine).[6] We would suggest at least two dimensions of territorial emptiness as a Zionist construction: first, the denial of the existence of indigenous inhabitants of the desired promised land; second, practical measures implemented to accomplish this physical emptiness through war, destruction, land purchase, and confiscation.

In what follows we articulate the three main characteristics and tendencies defined by Sack and test them in reference to the Zionist territorial ambition in historic Palestine and the mechanisms they followed to achieve their territorial agenda.

Territorial emptiness: promoting territorial metaphorical emptiness, ignorance, and denial

Zionism began to stress the need to settle purchased land in the belief that only a Jewish spatial presence could lead to the creation of genuine territorial links between the Jewish nation and its homeland. Therefore, the plan to establish the desired or imagined "Land of Israel" began with land purchase. It is in this context according to Schnell (2001b) that one Zionist design developed to expand the frontier by the extensive spatial distribution of settlements and the simultaneous effort to ensure a Jewish majority wherever possible. Hence, one may describe the history of land settlement in Israel as consisting of waves of efforts to expand borders and ensure a Jewish majority.

Shafir (1989) observes that Zionist space was to be "pure," attempting to maximize both Jewish control and exclusivity—in terms of territorial, economic, and social perspectives. A double move was to represent historic Palestine or, as Zionists promoted it (Eretz Yisrael, the Jewish homeland) *"terra nullus"*—an empty land. This goal of Zionist ignorance or denial of the Palestinian people's existence is realized through the contestation of both the physical existence and also of the signification, or "symbolic," existence of the *other* (the Palestinians) in time and space. Norman Finkelstein (1995: 99) points out that the aim of Zionism has always been to create a Jewish state by establishing a Jewish majority in Palestine irrespective of the rights of the indigenous Palestinian Arabs. But at the beginning of the twentieth century, as Finkelstein explains, the sizable Palestinian population already living there made a Jewish majority seem impossible to achieve. For example, according to Finkelstein (1995: 99), in 1917, the year of the Balfour Declaration in which the British government promised to aid in the establishment of a Jewish homeland in Palestine, the Palestinian Arab population of 600,000 outnumbered the Jews by more than ten to one, as shown in Figure 3.1.

In this context, space becomes paramount, because it provides a concrete, achievable goal, and at the same time distances rivaling groups from realizing their competing national–territorial agendas. Khalidi (1997) explains the Zionist construct of territorial emptiness by seizing and claiming sovereignty over contested space on one hand and by denying and rejecting the other claims, history, and political aspirations to that space.

The first pattern and action to restrict and disregard the Palestinian spatial existence in Palestine occurred as early as the end of the nineteenth century. Then the "Zionist leaders and settlers denied (or at very least ignored) the presence of other inhabitants in the various areas of Palestine" (Morris, 1998: 226). This aim was achieved by projecting Palestine as an empty land in the Zionist propaganda of the Promised Land, a land without inhabitants—even sometimes without any physical, material or spatial reality.[7]

As Nassar (2006) explains, the Zionist geographical imaginary used earlier European photographs and descriptions by travelers and pilgrims who portrayed

**Palestinian cities
and villages**

○ **Jewish settlements**

0   20 25   30 Km

FIGURE 3.1 Location of Jewish settlements in comparison to Palestinian villages in
Historic Palestine before 1948

Source: Author adapted from PASSIA.org

a selective biblical story and history of the Holy Land. Their interest was to portray the link between the Jewish presence with nature and the land as natural and mutual between two complementary partners. At the same time, the Palestinian's relationship with the land is portrayed as one in which the Palestinian is seen as inferior, stranger and rejected by the land that (as they claim) he never cultivated—a controversial portrayal of attachment with the Jewish and estrangement with the Palestinian.

Thus in the Zionists' indoctrination, Palestine was reproduced and represented as an empty, neglected, abandoned, desolate land, fallen into ruins, to help justify the Zionist geopolitical vision of "a land without people for a people without land" as Said (1979a) explains. Eitan Bronstein (2004) argues that the Palestinian material culture (specifically, the rural—the urban was perceived and appreciated as part of biblical heritage) was of no importance to Zionists, as it was not regarded as an authentic component of the romantic biblical image of Palestine. He further states that the Zionist identity is built on a twofold negation of time and space by Jews outside Zion: "a negation of exile" and a negation of the existence of those indigenous to the territory of Zion. In the imaginary and in the perception of Zionist leaders, the Palestinians were "temporary guards or holders of the territory," on the one hand, and, on the other, their essential non-existence (or eventual disappearance) was seen as a relevant factor (Bronstein, 2004). Thus, the denial of the people extended to the denial of production in terms of their material culture and even of their physical destruction in the 1948 war.

Said (1979a) points out the fact that this denial policy has been consistent over the years, with all the constitutive energies of Zionism premised on the excluded presence, a form of territorial classification (a major territorial tendency described by Sack), in terms of "othering."

There was a functional absence of "native people" in Palestine: institutions were built that deliberately shut out the natives; laws were drafted when Israel came into being that made sure the natives would remain in their "nonplace"—Jews in theirs, and so on (Said, 1979a: 29).

Finkelstein (1995) confirms this point: "Until World War I, Israel Zangwill's slogan 'A land without a people for a people without a land' typified Zionist propaganda in Palestine." He continues by saying that "After the establishment of the state, Zionist literature systematically, and with considerable effect, rewrote the history of Palestine—in particular, by writing the Arabs . . . out" (Finkelstein, 1995: 95).

To promote territorial emptiness, special language and (using Sack's notions) a territorial classification were manipulated and used, in terms of territory versus theirs (us versus them). This classification was most likely used to justify the intensive use of power over territory by projecting the "other" as different, inhumane, backward, and uncivilized, in order to justify this oppression and cleansing.[8] The language that dehumanizes the Palestinians was elaborated by Zionism to address the Western and Jewish European communities and, interestingly enough, forces itself and reappears during any urban destruction in Palestine—a fact observed in the 2002 destruction in the OPT. (Here the three major territorial tendencies were employed: emptiness, classification and enforcement.)

In 1948 the conception of the "other" differed in the Palestinian Arab perspective in comparison with the Zionist Jewish one. Ben-Gurion summarizes this difference in the Palestinian/Zionist perception of the Jews and of Palestine and of each other in his book *My Talks with Arab Leaders* telling George Antonius:

> Although we were an Oriental people, we had been Europeanized and we wished to return to Palestine in the geographical sense only. We intended to establish a European culture here and we were linked to the greatest cultural force in the world.
>
> (1973: 133).

Ben-Gurion's attitude of "superiority" even made it possible for him to admit that in 1938:

> When we say that the Arabs are the aggressors and we defend ourselves— this is only half the truth . . . Politically we are the aggressors and they defend themselves . . . The country is theirs because they inhabit it, whereas we want to come here and settle down, and in their view we want to take away from them their country.
>
> (Quoted in Falpan, 1979: 141–142, citing a 1938 speech)

Simha Falpan (1979) outlined these conflicting views of the "other" in the Palestinian–Israeli conflict. He asserts that for the Palestinians, Zionism has meant utter devastation of a homeland coupled to a rebirth as the most radical (or progressive) political force throughout the Arab Middle East.

Said (1979a: 29) articulates this point and discusses it as part of general Oriental attitude towards the East and the "Orient." He states that:

> All the transformative projects for Palestine, including Zionism, naturally, have rationalized the eradication of present reality in Palestine with some argument about a "higher" (or better, more worthy, more modern, more fitting: the comparatives are almost infinite) interest, cause, or mission. These "higher" things entitle their proponents not only to claim that the natives of Palestine such as they are, are not worth considering and therefore non-existent but also to claim that the natives of Palestine, and Palestine itself, have been superseded definitively, transformed completely and beyond recall, and this even while those same natives have been demonstrating exactly the opposite.
>
> (Said, 1979a: 21)

Territorial "physical" construct versus "de-territorialization"

The United Nations Partition Resolution was adopted in 29 November 1947, granting European Jews the right to establish their state in the western part of historic Palestine (see Figure 3.2).

Ilan Pappé (2006) argues that this is exactly the date the ethnic cleansing of Palestine began as in early December 1947 there was a series of Jewish attacks on Palestinian villages and neighborhoods in retaliation for the buses and shopping centers that had been vandalized in the Palestinian protest against the UN Resolution during the first few days after its adoption. Though sporadic, these early Jewish assaults were severe enough to cause the exodus of a substantial number of people (almost 75,000).

To establish both territorial physical, material, and spatial emptiness and territorial control/sovereignty, the Zionist leaders commanded by Ben-Gurion drafted Plan D[9] (*Dalet* in Hebrew) in the second half of February 1948 (Masalha, 1992; Morris, 1998; Pappé, 2006). This plan contained direct references both to the geographical parameters of the future Jewish state (78 percent by Ben-Gurion) and to the fate of the one million Palestinian living within that space:

> The essence of the D [Dalet] plan was the clearing of hostile and potentially hostile forces out of the interior of the prospective territory of the Jewish State, establishing territorial continuity between the major concentrations of Jewish population and securing the Jewish State's future borders.
>
> (Morris, 1998: 62)

Ilan Pappé (1994) demonstrates how the deliberate expulsion of the Palestinian people took place:

> Plan D can be regarded in many respects as a master plan for expulsion. The plan was not conceived out of the blue—expulsion was considered as one of many means for retaliation against Arab attacks on Jewish convoys and settlements; nevertheless, it was also regarded as one of the best means of ensuring the domination of the Jews in the areas captured by the Israeli army.
>
> (Pappé, 1994: 98)

Pappé (2006) further points out that to achieve this goal, military operations were designed in the infamous Plan D following plans A, B, and C, in which territory was seized beyond the UN Partition Plan (see Figure 3.3).

As Pappé (1994, 2006) points out, Plan D included forced expulsions of hundreds of thousands of Palestinians from urban and rural areas, action accompanied by an unknown number of mass slaughters to get it done. The goal, according to Pappé (1994), was simple and straightforward—to create an exclusive Jewish state without an Arab presence. Pappé states that these operations were executed:

FIGURE 3.2 United Nations Partition Plan for Historic Palestine in 1947

Source: Author adapted from PASSIA.org

FIGURE 3.3 Areas seized and controlled by Israel beyond the UN Partition Plan in the 1948 war

Source: Author

> Either by destroying villages (by setting fire to them, by blowing them up, and by planting mines in their debris), and especially of those population centres which are difficult to control continuously; or by mounting combing and control operations according to the following guidelines: encirclement of the village, conducting a search inside it. In case of resistance, the armed force must be wiped out and the population expelled outside the borders of the state.
>
> (Pappé, 1994: 92)

This double territorial strategy that created a new Zionist nation while denying the existence of Palestinian nationalism remained effective until the early 1990, as Yiftachel (2002) points out. It illustrated both the prevalence of spatial control as a major national goal and the effective use of nation-state imagery of ethnic self-determination (Jewish State in Ertz Yisrael), to seize a contested territory and marginalize—or even deny—the indigenous population.

Territorial expansion-dis/contiguity

After the 1967 war, Israel occupied the rest of Palestine and put under its control the West Bank and Gaza Strip. Said (1979a) argues that the Israeli territorial ambition and expansion was more solidified after the Israeli occupation of the West Bank and Gaza in 1967. The same policy of destruction was carried out there: By the end of 1969, 7,554 Arab houses were razed, and by August 1971, 16,212 houses had been demolished. Efrat (2003) and Falah (2003) highlight that this process of territorial expansion, control and sovereignty continued rapidly in the Occupied Palestinian Territories (OPT) after the Likude party came to government in 1977, with the huge settlement project in the OPT known as the Sharon plan (Efrat, 2003; Falah, 2003).

The Palestinian perception of "Palestine"

For the purpose of the discussion in this chapter on the notion of urban/territorial destruction the focus is pretty much on the Zionist Israeli side of the story, as the main actor (in causing destruction) in this historical episode taking place in Palestine. This does not mean that the Palestinians were passive while watching their cities, villages, territory being destroyed or dismantled; their role has been embodied in a resistance movement from 1948 to the present.[10] During the first years of the British Mandate in Palestine, the Zionist ambition to establish a Jewish state in historic Palestine was not yet threatening. In the absence of active Jewish immigration to the land, the Palestinians would likely have formed, as Yiftachel (2002) argues, a typical anti-colonial national movement similar to other movements in other Arab states such as Egypt or Syria. The Palestinian ambition then was focused on ending colonialism in their country and establishing the State of Palestine. However, this nationalism was markedly different than the Zionist engagement with territory: whereas the Palestinians saw their collective territorial identity as inclusive, that all people residing in Palestine were considered Palestinians, including "pre-Zionist" Jews, The Zionists regarded only Jewish newcomers as part of the nation. Palestinian nationalism was, then, on course to develop incrementally as a modernizing territorial political organization typical to in situ collectiveness.

According to Said (1999), before 1948 Palestine had a central agonistic meaning for both Arab Nationalism and the Zionist movement. After 1948, the parts of Palestine still inhabited by Arabs were labeled as non-Jewish and do not belong to the Jewish state.

He further points out the fact that no Palestinian, regardless of political stripe, has been able to reconcile themselves to Zionism. After the 1948 Nakbah and the Palestinian deposition, and exile, the Palestinian collective identity began at this stage to form several distinct characteristics, centering on dispassion, the land, and the struggle for its protection and liberation. Here, the national identity is reshaped through territorial conflict; it is laden with signs of active space, vis-à-vis a frozen notion of national time to be recaptured only if space is fully controlled.

Quoting a survey in the OPT, Neta Oren, Daniel Bar-Tal, and Ohad David (2004) indicate the fact that the Palestinian ethos presents the Palestinians as the true native inhabitants of the same territory claimed by the Israeli Jews. They argue that the Palestinian goal, as opposed to the Israeli goal, is to establish a Palestinian state in this territory. Another goal declared by the Palestinians is the right of Palestinian refugees to return to their land, a goal that contradicts the Israelis' aspirations to have a Jewish state with a Jewish majority. The Palestinians employ their own historical, legal, demographical, societal, and cultural arguments to justify these goals. From the historical point of view, they argue that they have been living in the contested territory a long time before, struggling and resisting the several occupations of the country. From a social and cultural point of view, according to Oren *et al.*, during those years a Palestinian identity was created, a nation with its own language (Palestinian dialect of Arabic) and folklore, with villages and cities, intellectual and professional classes, and a highly developed national consciousness. Demographically, until the creation of Israel in 1948, there was an Arab majority in Palestine (Said, 1979a). Oren *et al.* (2004) conclude in their survey findings that the societal beliefs about the justness in having the whole country (pre-1948 historic Palestine) as a national homeland are central in the Jewish and Palestinian ethos and give meaning to their respective national identities.

Charting urban/territorial destruction and transformation in Palestine 1948–2002

The *first pattern* follows the actual material destruction of urbanity/territoriality, and is manifest in *two speeds/rhythms and three scales*.

The rhythms are either massive quick destruction or *slow* long-term systematic destruction. The three scales of destruction follow the rhythms. For example, the massive quick destruction can be found on the scale of whole territory such as the devastation of hundred of Palestinian cities, towns and villages in the 1948 war. Or it can be recognized on the scale of an urban area, such as the destruction of Nablus, Jenin refugee camp, and others in the 2002 Israeli military invasions of the OPT, or the Gaza destruction in 2009–2010. The slow rhythm of destruction is longer; in terms of time span, it targets single houses, and this pattern is represented in the systematic Israeli policy of house demolition in the OPT. The first pattern of destruction is generally motivated by the ambition to construct physical emptiness of the desired land of Israel, through effacing the Palestinian identity of the territory and by destroying their shared spatiality/urbanity and territoriality. It aims at the same time to force a form of ethnic cleansing and purification of the desired Land of Israel to be solely a Jewish state.

The second pattern of the Palestinian urban/territorial destruction finds expression in the active process of *construction* of the Israeli body within the Palestinian occupied reality. This is evident in the ongoing construction of Israeli networks of settlements, the Israeli-only bypass roads, industrial parks, dumpsites, and the Apartheid Wall. This pattern is also evident in the *transformation* of the Palestinian landscape, the changing of Arabic names to biblical names, the appropriation of the Palestinian cultural heritage, and traditions that are claimed, re-interpreted and represented as Israeli historical right. This form of destruction by construction aims at subjugating the Palestinian urbanity, legitimizing the Israeli enforced reality within the OPT, and the construction of territorial classification by claiming the territory to be a Jewish Israeli one (ours versus theirs).

The third pattern embodies the measures that Israel enforce to construct *control* over the OPT. The control enactment is composed from the Israeli military laws that are used to subjugate the Palestinian development and urbanization. They are also epitomized in the Israeli network of checkpoints, gates, trenches, and military bases that form the material and spatial matrix that generates and facilitates the Palestinian urbanity/territoriality destruction. The conclusion of this chapter develops the argument that the destruction of the Palestinian urbanity/territoriality by the different forms discussed above composes urbicide, on the one hand, when destruction/construction is discussed on the scale of urban settlements. When destruction targets larger spatial networks, relations and structure, territorial destruction takes place in the form of spacio-cide.

In the following sections an in-depth analysis of the above mentioned patterns is developed.

Urbicide and spacio-cide by destruction

Quick rhythm of destruction, on the scale of territory or urban areas: the massive destruction of cities and neighborhoods, and the razing of complete towns and villages

This pattern of destruction occurs within a few days, weeks, or months of a major *war* in the region, such as the 1948 war, the 1967 war and the 2002 Sharon's war on terrorism.[11] Destruction in these cases is not seen or defined as collateral damage, which is the natural consequence of the fighting. The destruction in these cases is articulated as deliberate and without any military necessity,[12] taking place after the end of the war, and not as an unavoidable result of it. The major three incidents in Palestinian history that hold this pattern of destruction are summarized below.

1948 War and the emergence of spacio-cide

The 1948 war between Arabs and Jews resulted in the creation of the state of Israel, covering over 75 percent of historical Palestine and sending 750,000 Palestinians into exile, inside and outside Palestine. Ethnic cleansing was the main framework under which the process of depopulation and re-population of the Palestinian urban fabric happened.[13] Neither collateral damage nor military necessity can describe the destruction of these towns and villages as "collateral damage," which refers to "incidental casualties and . . . property damage" that result from military action (Rogers, 1996: 15). It should be noted that most of the destruction happened after the takeover of the towns—which often happened without a fight—and after the depopulation of its inhabitants. The erasing or destruction of these localities took place by an order of the military cabinet in order to prevent the return (denial of return) of its original inhabitants. This decision also prevented the other possibility —a hostile military action in which buildings could have played some role in the logistics networks of the various armies:[14]

> During May [1948] ideas about how to consolidate and give permanence to the Palestinian exile began to crystallize, and the destruction of villages was immediately perceived as a primary means of achieving this aim . . . [Even earlier,] On 10 April, Haganah units took Abu Shusha . . . The village was destroyed that night . . . Khulda was leveled by Jewish bulldozers on 20 April . . . Abu Zureiq was completely demolished . . . Al Mansi and an Naghnaghiya, to the southeast, were also levelled. By mid-1949, the majority of [the 350 depopulated Arab villages] were either completely or partially in ruins or uninhabitable.
>
> (Morris, 1998: 189)

FIGURE 3.4 Location of destroyed villages in historic Palestine, 1948

Source: Author

A total of 46,367 buildings[15] were completely erased from the 418 settlements (urban and rural), also 123 schools and 1223 mosques, which included many historical and significant buildings of architectural heritage dating back to the eleventh century; in addition, eight churches and sixty-eight holy shrines were put into ruins. This is a dramatic indication of the fact that the cultural landscape suffered from widespread and massive destruction (see Figure 3.4) and covered all types of buildings (civic, educational and religious buildings). Furthermore, the typology of the buildings destroyed mean that we must reject the Israeli claim that destruction happened out of military necessity or for security reasons, a pretension that continues to appear after every major Israeli act of military devastation of the Palestinian urbanity (see Figure 3.5).

The destruction of these villages is seen in this context as a spacio-cide attempt, in which the locality as an individual physical entity loses its significance, as its destruction alone does not count or affect the national identity. What matters in this form of massive destruction is the erasure of the spatial relations between these villages that are converted on the scale of the territory to be nodes, and the links between them compose the territorial spatiality. The erasing of these nodes (villages) erased the territorial spatiality and in effect the territorial identity of that territory through the disappearance of the rural vernacular nature of that region.

FIGURE 3.5 Village of Indur in the Nazareth area before its destruction in 1948; an example that reflects the urban character of destroyed villages and that destruction targeted all types of building and was not only for military targets

Source: gnuckx, Flickr-Creative Common Pictures, www.flickr.com/search/?q=Palestine+1948&l=4

Of course, the destruction did not target the villages alone; what was connected to these villages was destroyed as well—the landscape, the agricultural crops, the agricultural roads. Not only was the physical material/spatial of the built environment erased but also all that it held from folklore, traditions (in clothes, cooking, local dialects). Not only were the Palestinian villages and towns under attack and devastation but also the cities, which were extensively damaged; however, the scale of destruction in cities compared to the enormous number of devastated villages eclipsed this fact in historical literature. The old town of Jaffa is a clear example. A complete neighborhood (Almansheyeh) was dynamited in April 1948; Graham (2004) argues that the Irgun saw that the control and occupation of the city could not be achieved through conventional war techniques, and that the reorganization of the city fabric through cutting a deep corridor to separate the rebellious neighborhood from the rest of the city was therefore seen as the appropriate strategy. This act of urban destruction and spatial reconfiguration is a clear case of urbicide —Pappé (2006) calls the destruction of these cities the "urbicide of Palestine." These urbicidal acts included attacking and cleansing the major urban centers in the country. They included Tiberias, Jaffa, Lud, Ramleh, Acre, Haifa, Tel-Aviv, Safad and what Pappé calls the "Phantom City of Jerusalem."

For the Palestinians this war meant being subjected to continual uprooting and being transformed into refugees in their own land and beyond it, in the attempt, following the occupation of their land and history, to banish their existence, to turn their existence from an unequivocal entity in space and time to redundant shadows exiled from space and time (Darwish, 2001).

1967 War and spacio-cidal activities

The 1967 war resulted in the takeover of the rest of mandate Palestine—causing the West Bank and Gaza Strip to fall under Israeli military occupation—as well as the expulsion of another 350,000 Palestinians[16] and the destruction of several neighborhoods, even entire towns, all over the territory. The material/spatial destruction in this period shows a clearer pattern of the strategic destruction of complete villages, towns, and parts of cities. Strategically located villages or towns were targeted with the aim of breaking the spatial connection between the destroyed areas and creating a sort of "purified" space, at the same time creating spatial territorial contiguity between the Western newly established Jewish Towns and the Jerusalem area. Other villages were destroyed to create a clean buffer zone with neighboring countries such as Syria. This form of destruction is a manifestation of spacio-cidal activities. These are some examples:

- Al Latrun villages and the towns near the Green Line (the post-1948 war armistice internationally recognized border line) were destroyed.
- The three villages of Bayt Nuba, Immwaus, and Yalu situated near the Green Line in the Latrun area, northwest Jerusalem, were completely bulldozed down after the eviction of their inhabitants. Some 6,000 people were expelled, and

1,464 buildings were totally destroyed; in addition, four mosques, five schools and many shrines were leveled to the ground.[17]

- In Qalqilya City another 1,000 buildings out of 2,000 buildings were bulldozed or blown up.
- In Al Jiftlik, 800 buildings inhabited by 6,000 people were destroyed.
- In Bayt Marsam and Bayt Awa thousands of homes were destroyed.
- In addition, hundreds of houses were destroyed in Alburj, the refugee camps of Jericho and in the Gaza Strip.[18]

In total 16,000 persons were made homeless,[19] and approximately 5,000 buildings were totally destroyed[20] (see Figure 3.6).

2000 Intifada (Sharon's war on terrorism)[21] and the urbicide of the OPT

Nadia Abu-Zahra, in her article "Nationalism for Security? Re-examining Zionism" (2005), uses some statistics collected from the Palestine Monitor (2006a). These statistics roughly reflect the scale of damage hitting the Palestinian urbanity in the OPT. From 28 September 2000 to 31 May 2005, more than 63,000 buildings were damaged: 40,220 in the West Bank and 22,807 in the Gaza Strip (Palestine Monitor, 2006a). In addition, 7,505 were completely destroyed: 2,843 in the West Bank and 4,662 in the Gaza Strip (Palestine Monitor, 2006a). They also reflect the persistent Israeli denial of Palestinian rights to urbanity and modernity as expressed by Graham (2003). A detailed study of the mechanism of this devastation will be discussed in Chapter 6, looking at the case of Nablus Old Town.

The Israeli invasion of the Palestinian territories, which started in March 2002, and the destruction of the Palestinian built environment and infrastructure was aimed at four targets:

1   Palestinian symbols of power—by targeting Ramallah city, which was functioning as a temporary capital of the Palestinians, and also the residing place of most of the Palestinian National Authority (PNA) ministries and headquarters, and by destroying PNA police and military stations in other Palestinian cities.
2   Palestinian symbols of resistance, "the myth of Palestinian resistance"—Nablus old city, Jenin refugee camp, Rafah refugee camp and Balata refugee camps are well known examples.
3   Palestinian symbols of identity—manifested in historic cities and cultural heritage sites. The old centers of Nablus and Bethlehem were heavily destroyed during these invasions.
4   Palestinian symbols of the right of return and the mark of the Palestinian Nakba represented in the refugee camps that had already been a target for several Israeli campaigns since the 1970s. The military campaign and regular Israeli military invasions of the Occupied Palestinian Territories resulted in the

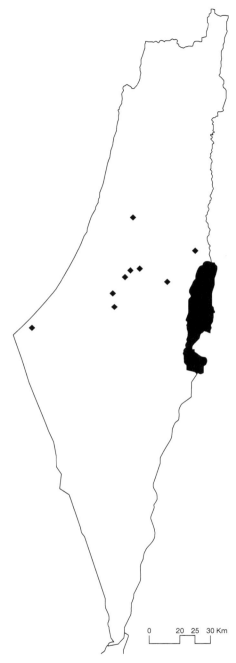

FIGURE 3.6 Location of destroyed villages and towns in the 1967 war

Source: Author

destruction of complete neighborhoods in many Palestinian cities, towns, and refugee camps. Some examples are the destruction of Nablus Old Town, Ramallah public buildings and ministries, Jenin refugee camp, and Rafah refugee camp. This type of destruction is seen as urbicidal activity, as it aims at destroying the Palestinian urbanity and the Palestinian symbols of identity (national, cultural, civic and political).

Slow rhythm: the systematic process of housing demolition[22]

The second rhythm in the first form of place destruction in the OPT is linked to the systematic housing demolition of the Palestinians. Israel adopted a parallel policy of either massive or individual housing demolition (outside the event of war). Since 1967 12,000 Palestinian homes have been demolished in the Occupied Territories, including East Jerusalem. Israel's policy of house demolition seeks to confine Palestinians to small enclaves, leaving most of the land free for Israeli settlement. Israel's policy of demolishing Palestinian homes is part of a larger policy to expel Palestinians from their traditional lands on the West Bank, render Israel's occupation permanent, and destroy any chances for a viable independent Palestinian state, according to Jeff Halper (1999). Two different kinds of house demolitions are found:[23]

1   Punitive demolitions over the years: Israel has demolished Palestinian houses as a punitive measure since the beginning of the occupation in 1967. A total of 2,506 buildings have been demolished in the scope of this policy.[24]
2   Building without permit: permits are rarely issued by the Israeli authorities.

This pattern of destruction is seen by scholars (Graham, 2003, Coward 2004, 2006) as a form of urbicide as it aims at creating Jewish-only zones, especially in the Jerusalem area, by subjugating the Palestinian development and demography in that area. It aims at the same time to liberate spatial continuity between the major Israeli settlement blocks that facilitate their development. Coward (2004) argues that the logics of urbicide can be seen in the Israeli policy of demolishing Palestinian houses (in both the West Bank and Gaza). He states that:

> Israel has implemented a dual program of destroying the houses of Palestinians (Ginbar, 1997). On the one hand it has deployed its defence forces to destroy those houses that are thought to harbour terrorists (Burke, 2001: 21; Reeves, 2000: 17). On the other hand Israel has utilized stringent planning regulations to ensure that Palestinians cannot build on land adjacent to Jewish settlements (that are themselves built on occupied territory and deemed illegal in light of UN resolutions) or in contested areas such as East Jerusalem. These planning regulations have been reinforced by an aggressive policy of demolition where houses are found to have been built without the requisite permission.
>
> (Coward, 2004: 17)

Urbicide and spacio-cide by construction

The 1948 War: territorial spacio-cide and urbicide by re/construction and transformation

An active process of constructing a new Jewish town on or adjacent to a destroyed Palestinian built area started to materialize almost in parallel with the destruction and dispassion. A new physical and spatial organization of urbanity from settlement scale to territory scale was formulated. Landscape identity transformation was a parallel process, with looting of the traditional landscape and agricultural crops pattern. The traditional Palestinian landscape was replaced with new landscape types, for example, by planting pine forests establishing natural parks near or over the ruins of some destroyed villages. In the cities that had significant cultural heritage, their heritage was reclaimed, transformed and appropriated to represent a biblical history that later became the idol of the Israeli promoted cultural heritage. This is evident, for example, in the taking over of the Arabic Jaffa city from its inhabitants and appropriating it as an Israeli artist city. Jewidizing and de-arabizing place names went parallel with the other processes at the national level. This process of territorial transformation is best described in Meron Benvenisti's book *Sacred Landscape: The Buried History of the Holy Land since 1948* (2000). Benvenisti demonstrates the way the Israelis transformed the "human geography" of Palestine directly after the 1948 Nakba (catastrophe). The book examines in a detailed manner the renaming of the land and its human sites as part of the anti-repatriation policy that Israel Zionist generals adopted after the war. Benvenisti is one of the few Israelis who dare to describe the policy that was pursued as "ethnic cleansing." According to Benvenisti, the ethnic cleansing included "Hebrewizing [sic] Arab names, the building of Jewish settlements over deserted Arab villages, and the refusal to allow a collective return." The Nakba is presented here as loss of land and houses, and the focus of the analysis is the territorial dimension of the event, marginalizing the human experience of this loss in link with the loss of normal life and cultural production. The same process of transformation continued even after the 1967 war and the occupation of the West Bank and Gaza Strip. A strong example is the transformation of the Al Latrun area into Canada Park. The built environment has always been the place where the material testimonies of a history as commonly shared and co-memorized is concentrated. "Culture" refers to the customs, practices, languages, values and world views that define social groups such as those based on ethnicity, region, or common interests. The Palestinian society in Palestine prior to 1948 consisted of three main groups: the townspeople (*baladin*), the settled farmers (*fellahin*), and the nomadic Bedouin tribes. Some 80 percent of the Palestinian population depended on agriculture, with over 800 villages scattered from the coastal plains to the Jordan River (Khalidi, 1999). Many were economically and socially independent, and difficulties in communication and environment produced strong individualistic traits within the communities: different dialects, different crops, different food, and different clothes. With the destruction of almost half of these entities and the traditional Palestinian society in 1948, much of Palestinian culture ceased to exist. As Edward Said has noted, to write of Palestinian culture is to write of dispossession and exile:

> The most obvious and saddest impression is the staggering dimensions of the Nakba. In every spot you look at, you know there were people with their own local history and geography that sustained them for centuries. Now they are refugees living in exile for over half a century. Numbers alone cannot fully describe this human experience. Life has been snuffed out of 675 towns and villages. But in every one of them, indeed in every house and in every plot of land, life was destroyed and there is a story to be told.
>
> (Abu Sitta, 2005, BADIL interview)

The construction of Israeli settlements, Israeli-only bypass roads, and the Apartheid Wall

In this section we will deal with the Israeli construction policies in the OPT. It may appear strange to place this category within the history of place destruction of Palestine. However, as Graham (2005) demonstrates, Israeli settlements, strategically placed within the Palestinian topography, have destructive urbicidal impacts on the Palestinian urbanity. Settlements in the OPT serve geopolitical purposes and are part of the Zionist vision of territorial spatial control and territorial continuity.[25] Their objectives include enforcing a Jewish Israeli identity in the Palestinian territory and undermining the existing Palestinian urban and territorial identity.

A decade after Israel occupied the remaining parts of Palestine, the Israeli "ethnocracy" reached its peak, as Yiftachel (2002) describes it. Following the 1977 rise to power of the rightist Menahem Begin and his Likud party, Israeli policies began to create irreversible facts on the ground, manifested by the massive settlement program in the OPT. Motives of Jewish survival were used again and manipulated to justify the new settlement projects. Colonialism and settlements programs were enforced and placed in the midst of the Palestinian geographical reality. Ancient Jewish time and history was manipulated and reinterpreted into a contemporary political and colonial ambition, settling Jews on what was interpreted as biblical sites, thereby shaping anew the nature of Zionist and Palestinian geographies and identities. Not satisfied with the slow initial pace of Jewish settlements in the OPT, the Israeli government commenced a new strategy in the early 1980s. The Jewish control and settlement in the OPT, according to Yiftachel (2002), have caused a major change in the representation of space as it erased in late 1970 the Green Line (the 1949 armistice line internationally recognized border) from official maps, atlases, and state publications. Yiftachel points out that the political objectives of these settlement projects were to cement control over the entire "Greater Israel." The project of "Greater Israel" has been

adopted by several government officials over many years to follow the implementation of the settlements project. Yitzhak Shamir stated in a Parliament
speech:

> This is our goal: territorial wholeness. It should not be encroached or
> fragmented. This is an a priori principle; it is beyond argument. You should
> not ask why. Why this land is ours require no explanation. Is there any other
> nation that argues about its homeland, its size and dimensions, about
> territories, territorial compromise, or anything to that effect?
>
> (Knesset protocol, 17 June 1991, translated by
> Yiftachel, 2006: 66)

According to the Badil report (2004a), the Israeli colonization spread to the
West Bank and Gaza Strip after 1967, and by August 2005 the subjective estimates
of the US Central Intelligence Agency counted twenty-nine Israeli "settlements
and civilian land use sites" in East Jerusalem, 242 in the remaining West Bank,
and 42 in the Israeli-occupied Golan Heights (CIA 2006, Figure 7.10). While these
built-up areas are relatively small, their influence extends through the entire West
Bank. At the outset of the Oslo peace process, an Israeli Civil Administration report
revealed that 1,000,000 Palestinians in the West Bank had access to 273 km², or
less than 5 percent, of the West Bank (BADIL, 2004a). At the same time, 114,600
Jewish colonists had access to 3,850 km² (BADIL, 2004a). The Jewish expansion
continued apace using military laws and instruments to confiscated land. It was
estimated that by the 1980s around 52 percent of the OPT was classified as Israeli
state land.

The Jewish settlements effectively encircle and cut off existing Palestinian towns
and villages from each other in accordance with the same policy adopted inside
Israel. Weizman and Segal (2003) argue that each of the three topographical strips
of the OPT (Jordan valley, fertile plains, and mountains) in a strange and almost
perfect correlation between latitude, political ideology, and urban form, became
an arena for another phase of the Israeli settlement project (called civilian occupation), promoted by politicians with different agendas to appeal to settlers.
Weizman and Segal further assert that the building of Israeli settlements in the
OPT is part of the Israeli military strategy of sovereignty, and it is used as a tool
of control to limit the urbanization process of the Palestinian cities and towns.
They explain that the strategic location of these settlements over the OPT hills
is well designed and planned (forming a network of Jewish entities within the
Palestinian inhabited areas) to enforce the enclavization[26] and identification
of Palestinian territories as distinct from the Israeli ones. This form of enclavization
is seen and explained by Martin Coward (2004, 2006) as another form of urbicide,
explained as establishing zones of separation that enforce the perception of
differentiation between Jews and Arabs as distinct from each other. Its purpose
would be:

To fulfill the Israeli ambition of creating homogenous Jewish state 'cleansed' from Arabs that are not seen within any future Israeli state. Israeli Urbicide comprises the transformation of agonistic heterogeneity into an antagonism. This destruction establishes zones of separation which naturalize the perception that Arabs and Jews are distinct and separate. This consolidates Israel as a homogeneous entity predicated on a claim to an origin distinct from that of the Arabs. These zones of separation thus naturalize the exclusion of Arabs who are regarded as both heterogeneous to, and thus not welcome within, the Israeli state.

(Coward, 2006)

Weizman and Segal (2003) explain how the changing landscape in the Occupied Palestinian Territories does not simply signify power relations, but functions as an instrument of domination and control (see Figure 3.7). The structuring of the settlement networks is not necessarily a result of an existing power situation, but is a tool meant to create it and preserve it. They further demonstrate that the organization of these settlements solidify the division between the Jewish and the Palestinian physical and spatial entities by creating multiple separation and provisional boundaries that relate to one other through surveillance and control. They see this process as an intensification and ramification of power that could be achieved in this form only because of the particular terrain. The settlement project creates a new geography in the heart of the Palestinian one; it creates urbicide when discussed on the level of one urban area as we will see in the case study, while it generate larger spacio-cidal impacts if discussed at the level of the whole territory. The network of the settlements with their connecting network of bypass roads and infrastructure are an active spatial restructuring policy.

An important mechanism in restricting Palestinian mobility has been the 974 km of colonist-only roads[27] (PCBS, 2005) with 500 km more planned (ARIJ, 2006). These roads connect areas claimed in 1948 to areas annexed later, even in recent times. Another intifada has raged in the occupied territories in 2000. Since then, as Abu-Zahra (2005) explains, Palestinians' lives are under siege conditions, enduring a nearly total blockade around every town and crippling economic stoppages, as well as continual Israeli tank and helicopter-gunship attacks on civilian areas. Even before this new intifada, Palestinians in the West Bank, Gaza, and East Jerusalem had continued to live with many of the administrative encumbrances of the Israeli military and civilian occupation. They had watched as Israeli settlements expanded, Israeli settlers multiplied, roads accessible only to Israelis redefined the territory, and Israelis confiscated Palestinian land and demolished Palestinian homes.

The construction of what is euphemistically called a "security barrier" or, more accurately, an Apartheid Wall began in 2002. In October 2003 the Israeli military designated 18,000 acres of Palestinian land as "closed zones" (UNOCHA 2003); this land is enclaved between the Apartheid Wall and the Green Line (the 1949 armistice line between Israel and Jordan, which served as the de facto border

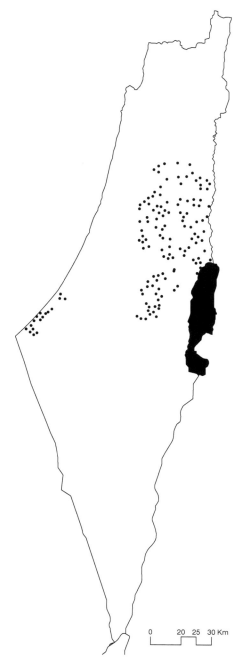

FIGURE 3.7 Location of Jewish colonies in the Occupied Palestinian Territories, 2002

Source: Author

between Israel and the West Bank after Israel militarily occupied the West Bank in 1967). Entry and exit were to be governed by a permit system based on people's color-coded identity cards, corresponding to the Israeli Population Registry of Palestinians. At the time, more than 7,000 Palestinians resided in these areas in the northern West Bank (UNOCHA, 2003). They were subject to the closures, encirclements, and barricaded roads that made their movement impossible. See Figures 3.8 and 3.9.

Urbicide and spacio-cide by control

This will be discussed in detail in Chapter 6, applied to the case of Nablus.

In November 2003, the UN Office for the Coordination of Humanitarian Affairs (OCHA) reported 757 barriers "blocking Palestinian roads and towns in the West Bank and severely restricting movement for 2.3 million Palestinians." OCHA categorized these as follows: 73 manned checkpoints, 58 ditches blocking vehicular access, 95 concrete blocks, 34 road gates, 33 wall gates for Palestinians, and 464 earth mounds blocking vehicular access (UNOCHA, 2003). Abu-Zahra (2005) touches upon the unbearable life that the Palestinians have to go through.

Synthesis

An evolving pattern can be traced in the history of place destruction/construction in Palestine. Active, widespread destruction/construction took place during and between the three main historical events of armed confrontation (either in the form of war or in the form of armed/civil uprising Intifada) between the Israelis and the Palestinians in 1948, 1967, and 2002. However, the active Israeli construction of Jewish towns and colonies, both in historic Palestine after the 1948 war and in the occupied Palestinian Territories after 1977 aimed at establishing an Israeli territorial sovereignty with a coordinated rhythm of placement/replacement.

Destruction/re-construction patterns

In the 1948 war, an aggressive destruction had befallen the Palestinian place/space, to accomplish the Zionist ambition of territorial acquisition and the territorial construction of a Jewish state in the western part of historic Palestine. This devastation was fuelled by the Zionist strategy of seizing as much territory as possible with as few Arabs as possible. In doing so territorial emptiness was achieved to fulfill the Zionist slogan "land without people for people without land" and to make it possible to reproduce and reconstruct an Israeli history and reality in the same place. In parallel, an active construction movement of newly planned Jewish towns either over the destroyed Palestinian places or in a totally new setting took place. This form of active spatial destruction, reorganization and interpretation generates clear spacio-cidal activities as can be seen in Figure 3.10.

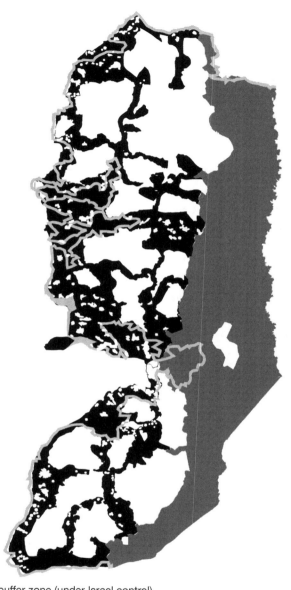

■ Eastern military buffer zone (under Israel control)

■ Area C, under Israeli military control

▨ The Separation Apartheid Wall

FIGURE 3.8 An abstract map of the dynamics of control in the occupied Palestinian territories (West Bank) that exemplifies the invisible layer of the Israeli physical network of control; urbicide by control

Source: Author

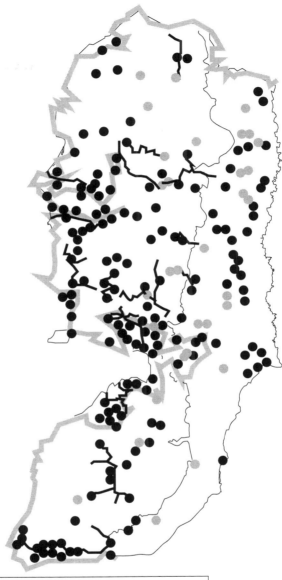

FIGURE 3.9 An abstract map of the physical elements of the Israeli network of
control in the occupied Palestinian territories (West Bank), the
settlements, the bypass roads and the Apartheid Wall; urbicide by
construction

Source: Author

Efrat (2003) points out the fact that the very notion of "Hamifdal Hazioni" (the Zionist Enterprise, or Zionist Project) enfolds the highly institutionalized, explicitly synthetic and actively constructive nature of the process of land appropriation (or re-appropriation) and nation building by Jews in the twentieth century. Efrat argues that any attempt to "normalize" Zionism by over-emphasizing aspects such as spontaneous immigration, organic settlements or market forces misses the point, which is "the artificial essence of Zionism," as Efrat calls it. He further argues that the grounding of Zionism rhetoric lies in "the notion of 'negation', 'inversion', syntheses or 'combination'; Zionism its self definition as constrained, corrective, redemptive intervention in historical time and geographic space" (Efrat, 2003: 61).

In the 1967 war, a more selective spacio-cidal strategic destruction of the Palestinian places was pursued for territorial control, targeting the border Palestinian cities as well as the villages between Israeli military controlled areas on the border with other Arab countries such as Jordan and Syria. On the other hand, further destructive acts took place in order to construct territorial continuity between the western part of the newly established State of Israel and the Jerusalem Area (the claimed capital of Israel). Other devastations were exercised for ideological reasons—such as the destruction of the Almaghareb quarter in front of the Dome of the Rock—with the purpose of claiming territorial sovereignty on the city. From 1977 onwards and for the same motives of territorial expansion and sovereignty, a progressive strategic construction of Jewish colonies, Israeli bypass roads, Israeli military bases, and Israeli industrial parks materialized all over the Occupied Palestinian Territories.

Sharon Rotbard's (2003) argument on the Israeli architectural and planning policies in the OPT supports the above argument. He asserts that every act of architecture executed by the Jews in Israel is in itself an act of Zionism, whether intentional or not. He points out that those buildings in Israel are inherently political and because their aim is usually to divide the land, create an identity or expand the nation, they are often linked to some greater political agenda. He further states that "the building of a sovereign state for the Jewish people is an industry for the fabrication of political realities" (Rotbard, 2003: 40).

In the 2002 Intifada, the enormous destruction in most of the Palestinian cities, towns and refugee camps was actively designed to destruct and to achieve territorial sovereignty and control within the very Palestinian urban place. At the same time it destroyed and undermined the essence of the Palestinian urbanity and modernity constituting urbicide:

> The Israel–Palestine war is not simply a struggle over territory between two national entities, it is driven by Israel's systematic denial of modern urban life to the Palestinians. One of the lessons of the battle of Jenin is that the bulldozer that demolishes houses is also a weapon in the wider strategy to prevent the Palestinians from creating a modern, normal, urban society.
>
> (Graham, 2003: 53)

Destruction/construction significance

Disappearance/emergence

The 1948 war resulted in the vanishing of Palestine—or *Filasteen* in Arabic—from the geopolitical map of the Middle East. The expulsions, destruction of cities, towns and villages, the loss of life and exile formed a concluding chapter that described and materialized the disappearance of what was once Palestine. A new emerging state of Israel was to surface; a new history, urbanity and identity were to be formulated. At the same time new Palestinian spaces were to be constructed and physically manifested outside what was once Palestine. Thus, Palestine became (at least for Palestinians in exile) an idea, a memory of place:

> In this century of course Palestine *was* "rebuilt," it *was* "reconstituted," it *was* "re-established" as the state of Israel in 1948.
>
> (Said, 1979a: 2)

Nassar points out a similar vision of the impacts of the 1948 war on the emptying of historic Palestine from its indigenous inhabitants:

> In 1948 the Palestinians "disappeared"—more than two thirds of the population was expelled from over 418 villages, towns and cities—most of which were subsequently ruined—making the early photographic image of Palestine as "Land without people" look like a self-fulfilling prophecy.
>
> (Nassar, 2006: 224)

Enforcement/resistance

The 1967 war concluded with the second Palestinian exodus; consequently a condition of disposal, war and loss was to be experienced once again. The West Bank and Gaza Strip became under the Israeli military occupation. Enforced military laws, military control measures and tools started to materialize and be visualized. Israeli Jewish entities are forcefully emerging and colliding with the Palestinian geographic reality, consequently reshaping and re-engineering the geopolitical, historical authenticity of what is left from Palestine. Meanwhile an emerging Palestinian Nationalist mobilization in post-1967 Palestine has started to take shape. Through it a Palestinian identity of resistance is to be formulated in the OPT and in Israeli space itself.

Salim Tamari suggests that: "As pressures arise for maintaining Jewish hegemony in the political sphere, against the increasing role of Palestinians in its economy, the Israeli state will have to acquire an infinitely more repressive character." He concludes on a reflective note: "Paradoxically, the conditions experienced by Palestinians living under occupation have generated an unprecedented movement for national independence precisely at a time when their daily activities are more embedded [sic] into the lives of their conquerors than ever before" (Tamari, 1981: 95).

Contiguity/fragmentation: exclaves/enclaves and the 2002 re-occupation

After the breakup of the second Intifada 2000, a strict Israel military cordon was implemented (as discussed earlier in the chapter). An accelerated process of enclaving the Palestinian built areas materialized. This enclaving is manifested by the existing Jewish colonies (which, after a long process of formation, are now fully developed), Jewish bypass roads, and the newly constructed Israeli military checkpoints, road blocks, road gates, and the Apartheid Wall. The Israeli colonies exclaves or islands in spatial terms draw the contours for the process of formation and consolidation of Jewish parcels of land in the heart of the Palestinian territory, while the subsequent enterprise by these exclaves is to expand and multiply as Falah (2003: 182–183) explains. These Jewish exclaves forcefully and slowly emerged within the Palestine built environment connected by a network of bypass roads (and infrastructure) that serve the Jewish inhabitants of the new colonies and that Palestinians are forbidden to use. The spatial dynamics of these new Jewish colonies produced a new geographical reality in the OPT, in which the Palestinian built-up areas are totally cut out from their natural surroundings by the Israeli military network of control. The Palestinian local communities are thus transformed into floating enclaves within the Palestinian territory itself, as seen in Figure 3.9. The spatial metaphorical reality of these Palestinian enclaves makes them look like small pockets of land lying outside the main flows and networks shaping the territory, consequently appearing as strangers in their natural setting, and naturalizing as well the presence of their conqueror. The dynamics of "enclaving" bears a strong similarity to the kind of spatial partitioning usually known under labels such as *zoning* and *redlining* when applied to discriminatory manipulation of space and its allocation for the benefit and power. All such ways of partitioning seek to reinforce and reproduce spatial, economic, and military hegemony through fragmentation and manipulation of territorial, social, and economic space according to Falah (2003: 185).

Transformations of urbanity, territoriality and identity

The long process of destruction, construction, and transformations taking place in historic Palestine after 1948 and more recently in the OPT influenced significantly the identity of this region over time. It is argued that spacio-cide and urbicide deliberately target identity in its broader term and that this identity transformation is more evident on the territorial scale. Charting the different mechanisms, forms, rhythms, and epochs of destruction and reconstruction that constitute this identity destruction over time can be seen in Figure 3.10. As we argued before, identity needs time to be un/re/constructed. Furthermore, the form of its physical and spatial dimensions are important constitutive elements of a given place identity, here territorial identity (in an abstract way). In territorial identity the physical tissue is presented in the villages, towns, and cities that are connected, together with dynamic spatial networks, namely the spatial tissue. The destruction of the physical entities (nodes) caused tremendous impacts on the territorial spatial networks, whose devastation generated the disappearance of Palestine as geopolitical entity. This was presented in this chapter in the charting of the actual destruction of buildings (presented in number for every urbicidal and spacio-cidal

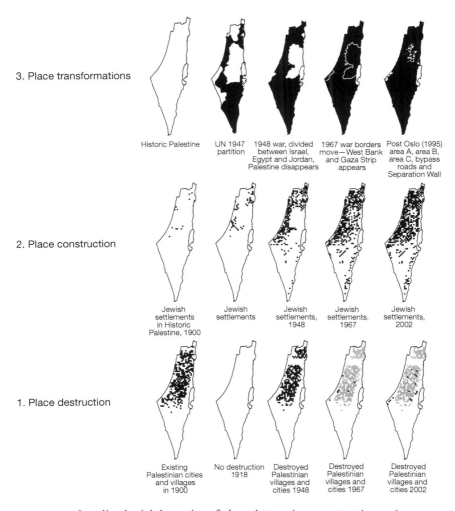

FIGURE 3.10 Israeli colonial dynamics of place destruction, construction and transformation in historic Palestine

Source: Author

activities) and larger physical entities such as neighborhoods and villages. This territorial form destruction is sustained by further transformations through construction of other physical entities such as the radical transformation of the landscape as well as the construction of a network of control over the territory. The territorial destruction and transformation took place on different levels and scales of resolution, from the destruction of individual buildings by the systematic home demolition policies to the devastation of urban areas through enclaving and exclaving, and the construction of Israeli colonies and control processes on the scale of every Palestinian city and town, and finally reshaped the physical/spatial territorial reality and identity. These processes were presented in this chapter in synthesizing the Israeli policies of urbicide, spacio-cide by construction and control in the OPT. The experience of this territorial identity transformation is presented partially in the 1948 war impacts on the Palestinian cultural identity and collective memory. Finally, the destruction of the territorial identity by spacio-cide was derived by the perceptions and meanings the Holy Land was associated with in the Zionist ideology. These territorial transformations consequently reshaped the perceptions and meanings of "Palestine" as a homeland in the contemporary Palestinian conception to "Palestine" as an item of the lost paradise and the last homeland. In this framework of values and transformations of meanings, the Palestinians perceive themselves as the victims and the new exiles of the Holy Land. As Said (1979a) states, "to write of Palestinian culture is to write about disposition and exile" (a topic that is not fully elaborated in this chapter).

Notes

1 Commonly, "geographic scale" can be referred to as a "graduated series, usually a nested hierarchy of bounded spaces of differing size, such as the local, regional, national and supranational," "each with a distinct geographic scope, that is, territorial extent" (Delaney and Leitner, 1997).

2 Sack's tendencies deals with the territorial relationships in social and spatial contexts.

3 A myth is an unproved or false collective belief that is used to justify a social institution, or a traditional or legendary story, usually concerning some being or hero or event that surrounds a given territory with special value to a certain group. This can be seen in that signification of place and identity by connecting it to religious beliefs.

4 These tendencies are defined or explained by Sack as ten reasons that he labeled potential reasons for, or causes of, territoriality, or potential consequences or effects of territoriality (Sack, 1983: 60).

5 Sack's definition of territorial emptiness is not satisfactory as it focuses on the social dimension and negates the physical one. I argue that constructing territorial emptiness in political and armed conflict is an important issue within enforcing power and control over territory. This can be achieved by physically emptying the territory through ethnic cleansing as in the Bosnian case.

6 Maxim Rodinson, a French historian, stated: "The element that made it possible to connect these aspirations of Jewish shopkeepers, peddlers, craftsmen, and intellectuals in Russia and elsewhere to the conceptual orbit of imperialism was one small detail that seemed to be of no importance: Palestine was inhabited by another people."

7 Western photographers who were concerned with the biblical landscape and the Judeo-Christian history of Palestine removed irrelevant Palestinians from photographs.

The result of such a perspective and viewing of Palestine, whether by politics or in photographs, creates a condition wherein Zionist leaders can use this concept in their propaganda about "the deserted Land." Chaim Weizman, the first Israeli president, declared in the French Zionist Federation in Paris, in 1914, that: "there is a country which happens to be Palestine, a country, a people, and on the other hand there exists the Jewish people, and it has no country. What else is necessary, then, than to fit the gem into the ring, to unite this people with this country?" (Weizmann, 2001; also quoted in Sheik Hassan, 2005).

8   In war, the enemy is generally demonized, with ethnic slurs being used to dehumanize them to the point where killing them becomes morally acceptable. Cited in Encyclobedia.com and www.reference.com/browse/wiki/Dehumanization.I

9   "Plan Dalet" or "Plan D" was the name given by the Zionist High Command to the general plan for military operations within the framework of which the Zionists launched successive offensives in April and early May 1948 in various parts of Palestine. These offensives, which entailed the destruction of the Palestinian Arab community and the expulsion and pauperization of the bulk of the Palestine Arabs, were calculated to achieve the military *fait accompli* upon which the state of Israel was to be based (Khalidi, 1961).

10 Palestinian resistance started earlier than the 1948 war. During the Mandate epoch the Palestinian resistance to the British colonial power and the rejection of the Zionist project were popular unorganized forms of resistance.

11 It is in the event of the war that Israel uses the chance to carry out massive destruction of Palestinian built environment, as history has shown

12 On 20 May 1948, the United Nations appointed a mediator, Count Folke Bernadotte of Sweden. In his first report, Count Bernadotte wrote: "Zionist pillaging on a grand scale and the destruction of villages without apparent military necessity."

13 Many researchers have mentioned it in their description. See, for example, Morris (1989), Khalidi (1992), and others.

14 After the expulsion Josef Weits and his colleagues on the transfer committee sought, in October 1948, to amplify and consolidate the demographic transformations of Palestine by: (1) preventing the Palestinians refugees from returning to their homes and villages; (2) the destruction of Palestinian Arab villages; (3) settlement of Jews in Arab villages and towns, and the distribution of Arab lands among Jewish settlements; (4) setting ways of absorbing the Palestinian refugees in Arab countries, such as Iraq, Syria, Lebanon and Jordan, and launching a propaganda campaign to discourage Palestinian return.

15 "Buildings" here means both one-story and multi-story buildings.

16 The author collected the number of destroyed buildings during all historical stages from different sources, but mainly from Khalidi (1999) and Abu-sitta (2005).

17 "We were ordered to block the entrances of the villages and prevent inhabitants returning to the village from their hideouts after they had heard Israeli broadcasts urging them to go back to their homes. The order was to shoot over their heads and tell them not to enter the village. Beit Nuba [sic] is built of fine quarry stones; some of the houses are magnificent. Every house is surrounded by an orchard, olive trees, apricots, vines and presses. They are well kept. Among the trees there are carefully tended vegetable beds . . . At noon the first bulldozer arrived and pulled down the first house at the edge of the village. Within ten minutes the house was turned into rubble, including its entire contents; the olive trees, cypresses were all uprooted" (Masalha, 2002).

18 Cited in the *Daily Star* (Beirut), 21 July 1967

19 From review and calculations obtained from different sources on the topic, mainly from Khalidi (1992), Masalha (2002), and Falah (1996).

20 In the summer of 1971, the IDF destroyed approximately 2,000 houses in the refugee camps of the Gaza Strip, including Rafah. Bulldozers plowed through dense urban areas to create wide patrol roads to facilitate the general mobility of Israeli forces

(Electronic Intifada, Human Rights, "A History of Destruction," Badil Report, http://electronicintifada.net/content/history-destruction/1665).

21 Sharon declares "war against terrorism" suicide bombings kill at least 14, injure 37, CNN.com/world, 2 April 2002.

22 Jeff Halber, "The Israeli Committee against House Demolition," www.icahd.org.

23 "Through No Fault of Their Own: Israel's Punitive House Demolitions in the al-Aqsa Intifada" B'tselem Report, November 2004.

24 More details on the settlements destructive consequences on the Palestinian urbanity will be discussed in details in Chapter 6.

25 BADIL Occasional Bulletin No. 19, June 2004 http://www.badil.org/Publications/Bulletins/Bulletin-19.htm,

26 The notions exclave is defined by The exclaves problem as it still exists in so many places throughout the world is, then, essentially this: The presence of part of one state in the territory of another creates inevitable tensions arising from the desire of the enclaving country, or host state, to include the outlier within the purview of its economic and civil administration, and the conflicting desire of the parent, or home state, to maintain normal communication with the exclaves and to administer them in the same way that the home state administers contiguous portions of the homeland' and enclave is defined as a country or part of a country mostly surrounded by the territory of another country (Catudal, 1979: 2)

27 This pattern should be seen, as it has been in evolution for almost half a century and the map presents a snapshot of a dynamic colonizing process at a fixed point of time.

4

Nablus
Historical perspective

> *The story of every city can be read through a succession of deposits: the*
> *sedimentary strata of history.*
>
> Mumford (1945: 222)

There is still a consensus that looks at the city as composed of different stages
that are captured in space. This chapter attempts to investigate the time factor that
shapes the identity of Nablus city. Identity is articulated here as a dynamic non-
fixed feature in a city's history. This identity is subject to changes, transformations and ruptures (by wars, natural disasters, and urban development) over time.
Moudon (1994) argues that the urban morphology of a given city tends to change
in response to the context of city development; an essential component of the urban
landscape is the historical process that shaped it. Writing a historical account for
a much contested site such as the case of the Palestinian context brings many
conflicted stories. Much of the modern history of Palestine as highlighted by
Doumani (1995) has been written from the top down and from the outside in. The
history of the region has been written either from the perspective of the dominant
social classes in Palestine or from that of tourists, pilgrims, diplomats, immigrants,
spies, and others located outside the indigenous society. However, a much
contested biblical history brings another account of the same site. History in this
chapter is used as a tool to define urbanity and its constituting elements of identity,
including the spatial component. The chapter also aims to highlight the richness
of the urban morphology of Nablus city and the major structuring elements of its
identity, which has been developing since the Roman times, in order to better
understand its collapse during Israeli invasions of 2002–2005.

Therefore, insofar as the contemporary history of modern Nablus is the focus
of this research, a very short historical background to Nablus's ancient site of
Shechem will be given, based on archaeological excavation campaigns since the
1950s.

Historical urban development of Nablus City

Nablus, as with any traditional "Arabic" city, had successive layers of history that shaped its existing urban fabric. Nablus is the largest Palestinian city in the Occupied Palestinian Territories. It lies 66 km to the north of Jerusalem, as shown in Figure 4.1. It is located at a junction in a pass that links the Mediterranean coastal plain in the west to the Jordan Valley in the east. It is strategically located on main trade and pilgrimage routes. It connects with Beirut in the north, Damascus in the northeast, Amman in the east, Mecca in the south, and via Jerusalem to Cairo in the southwest.

Shechem

The first settlement established in the Nablus area was the Canaanite city of Shechem, known today as Tell Balata. Schechem meant "shoulder" in reference to its location near Mount Gerizim. It is located at the eastern entrance of modern Nablus, between Mount Ebal and Mount Gerizim. Shechem was mentioned in the Egyptian execration texts and the Khu-Sebek inscription from the nineteenth century BC that describes an expedition to Canaan in which the Egyptians "reached a foreign country of which the name was Sekmem" (Wilson, 1969: 230). Literary and archaeological data alike attest to the importance of the city, and a series of excavations was carried out during the last century by the Austro-German Expedition, 1913–1934, and the Joint American Expedition, 1956, 1968–1969. The excavations revealed the occupational history of the site. Evidence of Chalcolithic period, Bronze Age, Iron Age, Hellenistic and Roman remains were uncovered. The greatest moments of the city's history were during the rule of Labaya, one of the strongest Canaanite rulers, who annexed great cities and established a strong kingdom with Shechem as its centre. Shechem was the most important Canaanite city in higher Mount of Palestine at the end of the thirteenth century BC as mentioned in the Amarna Letter in the fourteenth century. It was strategically located, controlling major north–south and east–west roads, but it lacked natural defenses and for that reason required heavy fortification. In addition to Jacob's Well (400 m to the southeast and now a Christian site) as the main water source, the city derived its water supply via a conduit from a cave in Mount Gerizim, while the fertile plain of Askar provided the city with food (Wright, 1965: 214–228).

El-Fanni (1999) stresses that the military role of the town flourished during the campaign of Alexander the Great as he made it a camp for his soldiers. Alexander also permitted the Samaritans to live in the town and to build their temple on the summit of Mount Gerizim. The Samaritan temple was destroyed several times, then destroyed and fully abandoned during the early Roman period. The last destruction has been attributed to John Hyrcanus between 127 and 107 BC.

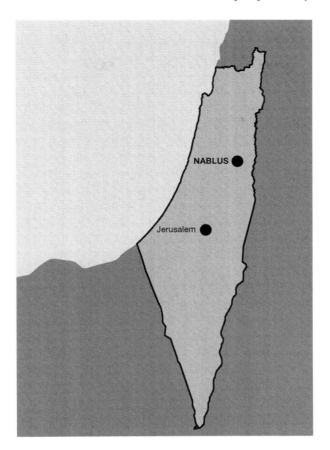

FIGURE 4.1 Nablus aerial map
Source: Author

Roman city of Neapolis

The Roman history and city structure formed part of several pieces of research on the territory and on the city itself (Abel, 1938; Al-Dabbagh and Murad, 1978; Kalboune, 1992; El-Fanni, 1999, 2007). Because of the important impacts of this epoch on modern Nablus, a brief account of the period will be given in this section.

The second phase of Nablus site development took place during Roman times. In 67 AD in honor of his father, the emperor Vespasian, the Roman general Titus (later emperor) founded the settlement of Flavia Neapolis two kilometers west of the ruined town of Shechem. In 244 AD, Neapolis was raised to the status of a colony with the title Colonna Julia Carsergia Neapolis. The city contained all the typical elements of a Roman city; some can be seen within the urban fabric of modern Nablus while others were uncovered during excavations for infrastructure installations. The complete structure of Neapolis was found on the Madaba map in the sixth century AD. It was mentioned on the first city coins issued during the reign of Domitian. The city of Nablus flourished as a major centre during the second century AD. Major public building projects were planned, including the hippodrome, the theatre, and other public buildings. The Roman temple of Zeus was erected on Mount Gerizim during the reign of Antoninus Pius. A Roman city plan is usually structured by the intersection of two main streets; the north–south axis—the *Cardo*—and the east–west axis—the *Documanos*—with a grid system dividing the main neighborhoods. In Nablus they did not follow the typical Roman city plan. As can be seen in Figure 4.2 the plan structure here was adapted to fit the special topography of the location; they therefore used one structuring principal street, the east–west axis (the *Documanos*). The sixth century Byzantine Mosaic of Madaba confirms this plan in its mosaic drawing presenting the wall with the eastern and western gates into the city, the east–west colonnaded street (the *Documanos*), and the main structures of the Roman city, such as the theatre, which is the largest found in Palestine, the hippodrome, and the huge water canals under the city. Beside these, there were other features, such as the aqueducts, the temple, and the main forum. A necropolis on the slopes of Mount Gerizim was excavated, in addition to the remains of a stairway that connects Nablus city with the Roman temple on top of Mount Gerizim.

The regular street pattern dating from Roman times is still discernible in the structure of the city, as seen in Figure 4.2. In some places excavations have revealed portions of Roman buildings; in other places these are still visible at lower levels. The main public buildings, such as the larger mosques, the bazaars and *khan*, which no doubt have been constructed over earlier Roman buildings, are still to be found along the main east–west axis of the city. According to El-Fanni (1999), based on his excavations, the city urban form developed in three phases, as seen in Figure 4.3. The first was in 76 AD in which three major neighborhoods were constructed, known by the same names up to the present day: Alqisaria to the east, which was the soldiers' residence, Alqaryun in the middle, and the Al Sumara to the west, which was the residence of the Samaritan community. The second phase took place in 130 AD, during the period of Hadrian; the city grew by the construction of another three neighborhoods: Alhabale in the northeastern part of the city, Algarb in the northwestern part of the city, and the Alyasmeneh between the two. The third and final phase was during the time of Filip the Arab in 244 AD in which the seventh neighborhood of Shwaitre was constructed to complete the known boundaries of the city.

The Romans were succeeded by the Byzantines. With the increase of Christianity in this period several public buildings were constructed, such as the Maria Theotokos (Greek for "Mother of God") on the summit of Mount Gerizim. (Its octagonal shape, walls, part of the mosaic floor, and a baptismal well have been excavated and can still be seen.) The church replaced the Roman temple; apart from the building of other churches in the city, such as Jacob well church, the plan of the city has kept its Roman structure.

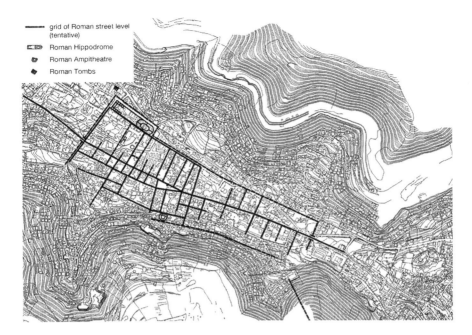

FIGURE 4.2 Nablus Roman structure map

Source: Courtesy of Nablus Municipality

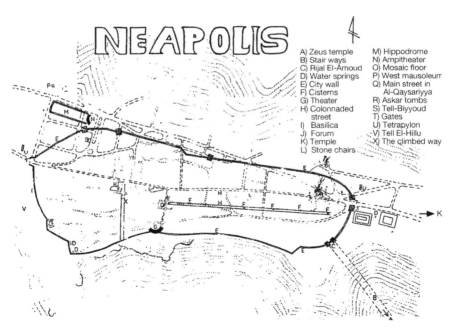

NEAPOLIS

A) Zeus temple
B) Stair ways
C) Rijal El-Amoud
D) Water springs
E) City wall
F) Cisterns
G) Theater
H) Colonnaded
   street
I) Basilica
J) Forum
K) Temple
L) Stone chairs

M) Hippodrome
N) Ampitheater
O) Mosaic floor
P) West mausoleum
Q) Main street in
   Al-Qaysariyya
R) Askar tombs
S) Tell-Biyyoud
T) Gates
U) Tetrapylon
V) Tell El-Hillu
X) The climbed way

FIGURE 4.3 Nablus Roman structure and buildings

Source: Courtesy of Nablus Municipality

Early Islamic period 636–492 AD

In the first half of the seventh century AD the Arabs conquered the region and Neapolis became Nablus. Umayyad Abbasid Fatimids and Suljuqs regained the city. The Islamic rulers did not change much of the city plan in the beginning of their rule as Nablus was taken over through a peace agreement with its inhabitants. Their major contribution to the city was the extension of the existing neighborhoods (Alhabaleh and Alyasmeneh Quarters) for they did not settle inside the city but on its borders. Several mosques were built during this period, as some inscriptions found in Alsaton mosque indicate the date of construction to be 646 AD; this is the first sign that the Arab Moslems settled in Nablus. The Arab domination from 636 AD onwards involved no immediate modification of the town plan. There was no building of mosques: instead, churches were adapted to function as mosques. Nablus had the usual factors working for its growth, namely religious and economic factors, as well as the intellectual factor. The economy flourished in this period because of the city's location on the north–south trade road in Palestine as well as on the roads to Egypt, Jordan and Syria. This was a main growth factor, which became manifest not only in the number and diversity of guilds established in its markets but also in the establishment of main trade markets such as the covered markets (Khan Eltujar), as well as the establishment of many hotels, *khans* and *wakaleh*.

As argued by Qamhieh (1992), through three ages of time many transformations and modifications were implemented in Nablus to readapt the city to the new religion and its needs, from building mosques, *madrasa*, and *hammams*, rebuilding many houses in its neighborhoods as the population grew and to meet the needs of Islamic families and communities. The Muslims built a new mosque on the site known later as Khan Al-Tujjar, around which the Islamic houses were gathered and extended to east and along the valley. The Samaritan and Christian quarters occupied the southern side of the city, and the Islamic quarters were on the northern side, according Al-Nimr (1976).

Al-Yaquby, a geographer from Jerusalem visited Nablus and described it:

> Nablus lies between two mountains, has plenty of olive groves, it is called a Small Damascus, its markets from the gate to the gate, while the other reaches to the town centre where there is the Great Mosque, it is clean and finely tiled, there is a river in it, and it is built from stone with strange Dawamis.
>
> (Al-Yaqubi cited in Qamhieh, 1992)

From Al-Yaqubi's description it can be seen that the city has kept its Roman plan, as a long city stretching from east to west, The main street (which used to be the Roman colonnaded street) connecting the eastern and western gates is still a main structuring element. The Great Mosque (the converted Byzantine church) occupied the central space in the town, which is an important characteristic of Islamic towns.

The Crusaders period 1099–1187

The Crusades campaigns to Palestine also resulted in the control of Nablus in 1099. The town was called Nablus by then (Benvenisti, 1970). Because of the central geographical location, Nablus (as Crusaders called it) was the meeting place of the king and his court to discuss the kingdom's condition. Nablus was described by travelers who passed by and who praised the city and its surroundings. Daniel the Russian reported:

> The land of Nables is very rich in various fruit trees, figs, nuts and olives. The plantations resemble dense forests surrounding the town, the territory also was fertile of wheat. The entire region is notable for its beauty and its rich produce includes oil, wine grain and fruits. The city of Jerusalem obtains its food stuff from Nables
>
> (Qamhieh, 1992 after Benvenisti, 1970)

Ayubbis

The city was later conquered by Muslim troops led by Slah Aldin Alayubi. An active reconstruction of the damaged buildings took place, and the transformation of churches to mosques was a major activity, but it did not change the existing urban fabric of the city.

The city entered new stage of its history after a major earthquake in the year 1201/597. Nearly all town buildings were badly affected apart from those in the Samaritans part. About 30,000 inhabitants were killed, and the survivors were dispersed to the surrounding villages as described by Al-Nimr (1976).

Mamluks

The major changes in the city urban fabric took place during Mamluks period. The city's original plan remained in its Roman format, but the city buildings began to have Mamluks' architecture style, known for its pointed arches, cross-vaulted houses and special decorated entrances, full of inscriptions and dates. A new architectural typology emerged in the city fabric; many buildings were erected on strategic summits for watching and warning the inhabitants of any sudden attacks. (Maqam Imad Al-Din on Mount Ebal and Maqam al-Shykh Ghanim on Mount Gerizim are two examples of these buildings.) Many school building were established inside the city.

Ottoman period 1517–1918

During Ottoman rule the city of Nablus experienced very important additions and changes. According to Qamhie (1992), at the beginning of the sixteenth century Khan Elwakaleh was built at the western parts of the city. The main addition was the opening of the second main street connecting the city from east to west, which is the main bazaar or Suq Al Qumash (cloth market), parallel to the Roman colonnaded street, which later became An-Naser street. The city quarters were fully established in this period, and the six quarters took the shape we know now, after many changes occurred and new houses were constructed. Al-Nimr (1976) describes the development on the level of neighborhood by explaining how another twelve smaller neighborhoods branched from the main six quarters without clear division (names were given to certain areas only to be identified clearly), such as: Alhanbaly quarter (Haret Alhanbaly) due to its location near Alhanbaly mosque; also the nut quarter (Haret Aljozeh) due to the existence of a big nut tree in the center of Alqysaryeh neighborhood; and Alsumara quarter according to the Samaritans living in the Alyasmeneh neighborhood. For each quarter a mosque and *hammam* (bath) were erected, and a sheikh was appointed, responsible for the inhabitants. Palaces began to appear in the urban fabric of the city. Doumani (1995) stresses the role of Prince Yousf Al-Nimer—who became the ruler of Nablus region, Jabal Nablus—in developing the city's status. He built a new palace on northeastern side of the city, which became the residence of Nablus governors for at least two centuries. Around this palace many new buildings were built, and this later became the Alhabaleh quarter.

Prince Yosuf engrossed himself in the economic revival of the city. He built a soap factory and encouraged trade movement and agriculture. At that time Nablus became glorious, and the inhabitants became wealthy. An active public building construction took place during the Ottoman rule. Water canals were constructed, such as the canal for the Alqaryun spring, and many water fountains (*Subul*) were built all over the city. Restoration and maintenance work for the main public buildings were an important achievement of Omar Aga, the grandson of Prince Yosuf, who established security in the city, which flourished with an economic and industrial revival. The trading products from Nablus—as mentioned by Al-Nimr (1976)—were cotton and wool products and iron, silver, and copper industries, besides, of course, its famous soap. Nablus became an important educational centre, and students from all over the empire came to study here. Nablus had flourished and these were its golden days.

H. B. Tristram described Nablus during this period:

> Its beauty can hardly be exaggerated . . . Clusters of white-roofed houses nestling in the bosom of a mass of trees, olive, palm, orange, apricot, and many another varying the carpet with every shade of green . . . Everything fresh, green, soft, and picturesque, with verdure, shade and water every-where. There is a softness in the colouring, a rich blue haze from the many springs and streamlets, which mellows every hard outline.
>
> (Tristram, 1866)

In 1836 a serious earthquake hit the city; many were killed and the Alhabaleh quarter suffered from serious damage according to Al-Nimr (1976). The middle of the nineteenth century witnessed active building and construction activities in which Kahn Altujar was replaced by a big trade hall in the middle of the impressive bazaar street that ran the length of the town, Suq Al-Sultan. At this point Nablus urban fabric included five mosques, two of which were originally Christian churches as reported by Mills (1864).

At the end of the nineteenth century Nablus reached its peak in terms of both the development of its urbanity and landscape and its other activities such as economy and industry. Mary Rogers described Nablus at that time:

> The great gates, which were on the point of being closed, were thrown back for us, and we rode through dark arcades and narrow streets to the house of . . . One morning we walked through the stony arched narrow tortuous streets out of the nearest gate, and rose on to the raised road or terrace, which nearly encircles the town. He [her guide] led me to the hill beyond the burial-ground, whence I could see the whole extent of Nablus, with its mosques and minarets, its irregular groups of houses with domes and terraced roofs, its dark archways and colonnades, and the gardens of lemon and oranges around.
>
> (Rogers, 1865)

The first construction work outside the city borders was done by the Turkish governor in 1875: he built the Al-Qeshleh on the eastern entrance of the city, in the narrowest point of the valley, as an arsenal and a military resident for the Turkish army (see Figure 4.4). It later became the main prison during the British mandate,

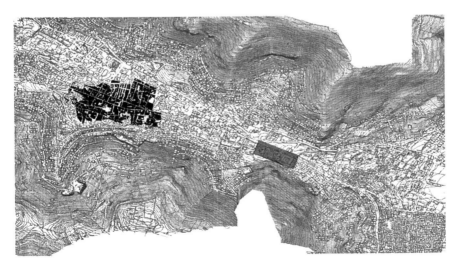

FIGURE 4.4 Location of the Turkish governor headquarters outside the old town

Source: Courtesy of Nablus Municipality

Jordanian rule, and the Israeli occupation, and the Palestinian national authority used parts of it as the ministry of foreign affairs. It was destroyed by the Israeli invasion. Also in 1875 a Latin convent and a protestant school and a chapel were erected, as were a new *khan* and a new street that led to the open centre (Scholch, 1982).

In 1883 the Turkish Al-Mutasaref (the mayor) bought part of the garden next to An-Naser mosque and converted it into the main square of the town, and the clock tower was built on the silver anniversary of sultan Abd Al-Hamid (Al-Nimr, 1976). The city wall was made up of rows of detached fortified houses (Khatib, 1986). Qamhieh (1992) argues that the economic rise of Nablus led to another expression of building activity. In 1887 the Christian monastery of Saint Josef was built on the slopes of Mount Ebal, and in 1888 the National Hospital was erected on the slopes of Mount Ebal.

Wilson visited the area in 1860 and produced several paintings of Nablus (see Doumani, 1995). Nablus was the subject of research and visits by travelers who wrote and produced pictures of Nablus (see Figure 4.5, which is a picture made in 1898 by the Photography Department of the American Colony Jerusalem).

The British Mandate

During the First World War Nablus was the center of the Ottomans' Seventh army. The city was victim to hunger and exhaustion during war times. In 1916 the Ottomans lost the war, and the French divided the Arab world with British army. Palestine came under British Mandate from 1917 to 1948. In September 1918, three days after the capture of Nablus, aviators of 1st Austrian squadron photographed Nablus from the west side. The photo shows the town nestling in a valley, with the slopes of Mount Gerizim on the left and Mount Ebal on the right). On the fringe of the densely built old core are numerous large buildings and the newly built hospital. Several minarets and a tall rectangular clock tower rise above the houses, many of which have sloped tiled roofs. There are some orchards along the borders of the town, and also within it. Beyond the town's far (eastern) end, at the narrowest point of the valley, stands a large, rectangular, flat-roofed structure: the Turkish barracks erected in 1875. When Juassen visited Nablus in 1926, he drew a map of the city with photos as shown in Figure 4.5.
Al-Nimr (1976) stresses the role of the 1927 earthquake, which affected Nablus badly. About 600 houses were demolished, fifty persons were killed, and thousands of people became homeless (see Figure 4.6).

The Municipality built camps to re-house people in the eastern part near Rijal Alamoud, which later became Al-Jabalyeh quarter. This was the first large development outside the old town. The number of inhabitants reached to 25,000 (Al-Nimr, 1976). Juassen took several images of the city at this time, as shown in Figure 4.6.

FIGURE 4.5 Nablus image in 1898 with its Ottoman urban fabric

Source: Library of Congress Prints and Photographs Division Washington, DC 20540 USA

FIGURE 4.6 Nablus earthquake of 1927

Source: Library of Congress Prints and Photographs Division Washington, DC 20540 USA

The Jordanian rule 1948

The 1948 Arab–Israeli war put the West Bank under Jordanian authority; Nablus, as part of the West Bank, was under that authority. Nablus became a center for receiving the refugees from occupied Palestine: three refugee camps were built near Nablus city, and the population doubled as a result, causing many economic difficulties. The same year 3,700 housing units were built in the town as described by Khatib (1986).

During the Jordanian mandate, as a result of the disconnection between the West Bank and the occupied parts of Palestine in 1948, Nablus expansion moved towards the East Bank (Trans Jordan), where new relations had been established. The villages of Balta, Askar, Al-Juneid, and Rafidia were added to the municipal boundaries.

The Israeli occupation 1967

In 1967, Nablus was occupied by the Israeli army. The hard years of occupation caused much damage to infrastructure of the city, and three refugee camps were added to accommodate the people who had fled to the city. The city development occurred mainly up the mountain slopes, to the east towards Jerusalem, and to the east-west axis connecting Nablus with surrounding villages later to be included in the municipality boundaries. The impact of Israeli occupation on Nablus and the Palestinian Occupied Territories has been discussed in Chapter 3 and will be further discussed in Chapter 6.

The Palestinian Authority 1994

With the beginning of the peace process, important institutions settled in Nablus, such as the Palestinian telecommunication company. Political and cultural progress was accompanied by endeavors to solve many long standing problems of the steady growing population, refugee camps, spatial limitations, and traffic infrastructure. During this period new streets were built on the slopes, opening up areas for housing development. Most important was the improvement of the social infrastructure— new schools, nursery schools, cultural centers and hospitals were built. Two new schools were built in the historic center, providing an important incentive to develop the historic center.

Nablus Old Town: a city of collage

It is argued and has been evident throughout the analysis that the urban culture of Nablus Old Town, like many other old cities, is made up of a mix of historical, cultural, and architectural layers, from Roman, Byzantine, and Islamic periods. This overlapping of historic layers indicates a long urban development process— formation, growth, development, changes, and transformations as well as many interactions throughout time and place. Consequently each layer may add to the urban form a number of architectural and urban elements, creating a relatively a homogenous and integrated whole. Political events as well as economic, social and cultural changes throughout history have affected this historic development process and contributed much to its morphological characteristics. The continuity of cultural and social life throughout the city's history, which can be seen in the wealth of religious and cultural events and venues, is strongly reflected in its urban physical and spatial patterns.

The existing layer of Nablus Old town is a collage from the different historical layers discussed in this chapter. Many physical elements and spatial patterns are still evident from these different historical layers. For example, the Roman hippodrome, the amphitheatre, the street's grid fragments, the reused roman stones, the springs, and the water tunnels are still part of the urban dynamics of the twenty-first century city. The dominant structure in the Old Town is an Ottoman one, though there are many remnants from other Islamic, and crusader periods that interact with the authoritative Ottoman patterns and buildings. Many houses and buildings date back to the Mamluks, while many buildings that have been created in the Byzantine and Crusaders epochs are still present in the urban fabric, though their function and use has been transformed or adapted with the changing needs of daily life or the transforming social and cultural fabrics. Al Kabeer Mosque is a strong example of this process of transformation and adaptation. The building was originally constructed as Roman temple, then a Byzantine church, then a Moslem mosque, then a Crusader church and finally a Mosque again. The collage and composition of the Old Town's building material are a live document of this type of historical transformation, change and adaptation through time.

The extensions of Nablus Old Town clearly materializes the colonial and then modern tissue that composes the existing modern Nablus city.

The city also represents the development of the co-existence of its three religious groups whose divinity was established in the Old Town's several neighborhoods (the Samaritans, the Christian and the Moslem quarters) who used since their establishment to live together as Palestinian Nabulsi rather than as Muslims, Christian or Jews. This form of co-existence is a representative and a significant element of the city identity. Its social solidarity and network regardless of religious beliefs explicitly materializes the non-material heritage that qualifies the development of the city's values, customs and traditions.

5

Nablus

A city of heritage

Urban morphology

Urban morphology is the study of the city as human habitat. Urban morphologists analyze a city's evolution from its formative years to its subsequent transformations, identifying and dissecting its various components. For this school of thought the city is the accumulation and the integration of many individual and small group actions, themselves governed by cultural traditions and shaped by social and economic forces over time. (Moudon, 1997) Urban morphologists focus on the tangible results of social and economic forces: they study the outcomes of ideas and intentions as they take shape on the ground and mould our cities. Buildings, gardens, streets, parks, and monuments are among the main elements of morphological analysis. The social construction of place can be analyzed in three ways: as the meaning attributed to specific physical places, as a community of social interactions, and as a discourse about place (Harvey, 1993), each of which contributes to producing power relations. Moudon (1997) argues that these elements also exist in a state of tight and dynamic interrelationship: built structures shaping and being shaped by the open spaces around them, public streets serving and being used by private land owners along them. The dynamic state of the city and the pervasive relationship between its elements have led many urban morphologists to prefer the term "urban morphogenesis" to describe their field of study.

The urban morphological conceptual framework as a methodological approach studies the urban form not only by investigating the material components of urbanity but by analyzing the spatial, natural setting and the physical elements of a city. The spatial pattern is defined by Butina and Bently (1991) as "the specific land utilization and pattern of activates that particular parts of the city generate."

In general the urban morphology approach emphasizes the social and economic dimensions of form because it portrays elements of urban form in a dynamic fashion, as the city changes through time. It also highlights the interplay between elements of form at different scales or resolutions; for instance, a building fits on a lot, which fits on a block, which fits into a network of streets, which fit into districts, and so on—a phenomenon called nesting. Finally, it helps to demonstrate differences and similarities in the cultural dimension of form because urban form elements are explained as they relate to the people making them and to the time at which they are made. In short, the approach integrates the micro and macro scales of the urban landscape with its time dimension and stresses both the cultural and historical dimensions of city building.

The morphogenetic approach is integrative with, but not inclusive of, other approaches: in its focus on the objective, material city, it does not account for individual or collective perceptions of the environment (the subjective city, as per Conzen, 1978).

Muratori sees that the key to historical urban morphology is the building as a priori synthesis. The design method of the school of Muratori is based on the dialectic relationship between complementary and reversible moments in historic typological research and the stages of design development (Petruccioli, 1998).

In Italy it was Gianfranco Caniggia (1933–1987) who took over the mission and continued Muratorian tradition (Moudon, 1997). Through his work and publications he concentrated on building types as being the elemental root of urban form. According to him, every building is a product of modifications to previously existing buildings, in a never-ending process of derivations.

The urban morphogenetic approach flourished in the UK and Italy. The French approach was part of the dissolution of the Beaux-Arts that had different characteristics. Just like the other schools, it rose out of a reaction against modernism and its rejection of history; it is the school of architecture in Versailles, which was founded by Jean Castex, Philippe Panerai, and sociologist Jean-Charles de Paule (Moudon, 1997). Two important general characteristics differentiate the approach of the French school of Versailles: one relates to the dialectic of urban form and social action; and the second is related to the dialectic between modern and non-modern, but with a distinction from the Italian school in that the social component here comes first.

The three multi-disciplinary fields or schools have three main principles upon which the new urban morphologists have developed as the bases for morphological analysis. First, there is agreement that the city or town can be "read" and analyzed via the medium of its physical characteristics: streets, plots and buildings that, in turn, form the topographical arrangement of the built urban environment (town plan). Second, because these physical characteristics undergo continuous transformation and replacement, only historically can we understand this urban form without separating it from the processes of change to which it is subjected. And third, urban form can be understood at different levels of resolution: building/ lot, the street/block, the city and the region (these characteristics are of the major concern of this study and are part of the adopted methodology). Moudon (1997) synthesizes the common characteristics between the schools of thoughts on urban morphology in reading the city time, form, and resolution. Moudon claims that these elements constitute the three fundamental components of urban morphological research that are present, she asserts, in all studies, whether by geographers or architects, and whether they focus on a medieval, baroque, or contemporary city.

The contemporary developments in this line of research is materialized in the Dutch school, in which N. J. Habraken articulates environment as the background against which architects build the "extraordinary." The built environment for him is a self-organizing entity. Habraken (2000) stresses a profound recent shift in the structure of the everyday environment. One effect of these transformations, he argues, has been the loss of implicit common understanding that previously enabled architects to formally enhance and innovate: "Our subject, then, is not architecture, but built environment. It is innately familiar. Anew, we observe what always has been with us—not to discover, much less to invent, but to recognize" (Habraken, 1998: 1).

Habraken argues that in order to understand something as complex as our built environment we must seek what is common in its many manifestations and constant in its transformations. By learning to see environment in terms of change, we also learn to understand the ways in which we organize ourselves as agents acting upon it. Such a spatial order is created by means of types of all kind (houses, streets, courts, squares, shops, workshops, gardens, monuments, etc.) and morphological relations between those types. It provides a method to decompose the city into different layers of information, enabling simultaneous (re)grouping of layers and elements in order to make comparisons to identify the conceptual foundation of the city as a built work, an artifact, with its own specific logic of morphological organization. The Order of Form for him is observed in how the built environment operates on different "levels." This hierarchy may differ somewhat from time to time or place to place, but it always has the same characteristics. While the control of space for him bring to light territorial hierarchies that are different from those found in physical form, the formal and the territorial hierarchies mutually influence and interpret one another; in the context of meaning and social understanding they are revealed in patterns, types, systems, and other regularities that can be seen in the environment in endless variety.

Similarly, Andréa Loeckx, a Belgian scholar in urban morphology who builds up Muraturi's conception of urban form, claims that analysis and design are complementary operations. They both generate better understanding of the built environment and enhance the urban design process. He argues that similarities of analysis and design lie in the similarity of their respective object, the similarity between reality and projected reality. This peculiar relationship between the existing position and the design project was characterized above as an analogy. Thus the similarity of analysis and design can rightly be called an analogy: analysis and design project are analogical operations:

> Since analysis and design have similar objects, these must be discussed in the same language, using the same terms. This means that terms like "type,"

"urban structure,""privacy regulation," "private/public," "scale level," etc. are not only analytical entities, brought about by the analytical breakdown of our environment. They are also, to the same extent, the very words we should use in conceiving new environments. Metaphorically comprehensible writing needs the same language we use for reading.

(Loeckx *et al.*, 1996: 22)

Place as experience

Townscape was developed in Britain from the 1950s as a reaction to the "any-where" quality of the modernist environments then being introduced (Butina and Bently, 1991).

According to Gordon Cullen (1971), *precincts, enclosures, focal points and the kinesthetic experience* of the built environment emerge as the main components of identity.

Advocating respect for identity, Cullen calls for the reshaping of our sensitivity "to the local gods" of geography, climate, and culture. The kinesthetic emphasis reflects the stress Cullen places on vision as the main means by which people perceive the environment (1971).

He explains that environments are experienced as "a serial vision" that defines the urban landscape as a series of related spaces, so as the user moves through the environment he perceives constantly changing relationships between existing views and emerging views, "hereness" and "thereness." Cullen (1959) developed this approach within the field of urban design in order to understand how the place is perceived by people—i.e. how various components of the place are contributing together to provide it with a unique character. Gordon Cullen suggests three ways/dimensions for understanding a place:

1   *Serial vision*—sequential vision concerning existing and emerging view within an urban place.
2   *Place*—concerning position, an experience stemming from exposure and enclosure.
3   *Content*—this and that, concerning the variety and richness of the activities. Using this framework, we are identifying townscape elements providing a strong townscape character to the place, owing to its spatial configuration and—most of all—uniqueness of activities.

Cullen's approach is to investigate the qualities of existing urban environments, and analyze them to derive common themes that might be replicated in contemporary design. He developed the concept "sense of place." In his work Cullen addressed several notions that might contribute to this sense of place, such as the notions of possession, "hereness" and "thereness," the interplay between the known and the unknown, linking and joining, and the various modes of relationships between buildings, objects, activities and spaces. He was interested in the human scale of towns and cities and therefore analyzed the urban experience from the perspective of the people on the street. From this he sought to establish the experience's fundamental components. To capture what he termed the "serial vision" of the city, he used a technique of sequential drawings which offered an unfolding succession of views of related spaces. Writing of Cullen and the townscape movement, Joseph Rykwert says:

> Insistent on the continuity of the urban fabric . . . [the] teaching had a picturesque slant and presented the city as a selection of episodes; the lack of response to social or economic reality condemned it—for all the valuable things it had to say—to a local role.

(2002: 149)

Another important component of the townscape approach is the city skyline, which refers to profile of buildings. It constitutes a group of building height profiles forming the topography of the city. It also offers incredible panoramic views of the city and exists coherently with the environment. The scene of the city and its surroundings reflects the relationship between its natural and built forms. Different cities have their own city skylines and city structure, representing the city's image and public realm. Most cities create their unique city skylines through some statutory and design guidelines.

Nablus morphological characteristics

The city of Nablus is situated at the highest and narrowest point of an east–west valley, at the watershed. To the east a plain opens into the valley of the Jordan; to the west the land slopes gently down to the Mediterranean. This ideal topographic site, linked to an ample supply of fresh water, was the prerequisite for its long and turbulent history as a settlement. The existing structure of the historic center of Nablus city is a characteristic feature of the latest Arabic and Islamic culture. This is clearly manifested in the structure and form of the network of the streets and alleys, and in its domes, vaulted houses and *souqs*. The existing architectural layer reflect the Mamluks and Ottoman architecture, even though the pattern of the Roman city can still be read in some parts despite the impetuous social and political changes through the ages. The main street of the city forks a short distance after the east entrance of the historic city in front of the Great Mosque (Jami' Al-Kabeer). Its two branches and the connecting paths between contain the main bazaars. In front of the other big Mosque (Jami' An-Naser) there is an open square with a clock tower, both dating from the late nineteenth century. Nine similar mosques, some other churches, and bathhouses (*hammams*) are very characteristic of Nablus; many old soap factories are other important elements. Side streets and blind alleys lead to entrances and further into courtyard houses lying intricately next to or above one another. Large and complex palaces with many courtyards and deteriorated upper parts are also to be found, today often divided into small units and reused as a modest living space. Modern implantations are mainly schools, some apartment houses, and the intrusion of the surrounding roads serving the needs of modern traffic. The most important feature that has been preserved in the old core of Nablus is its configuration, which is best described by its open spaces, streets and paths; this configuration includes most of the traditional functional associations, such as mosques and bazaars, along the central axis of the city. These features give the old town great value both historically and architecturally; they are without doubt the oldest and most lasting elements of a city.

To get an in-depth analysis of the existing identity of Nablus Old Town, different elements of the urban form (physical layout, urban tissue [material and spatial tissues] and land use patterns), the arrangements and links between different elements on different scales and levels of resolution—as well as understanding the experience the townscape generates—are to be investigated in the coming sections.

Physical layout

The plan of Nablus displays the accumulative character of transformation, adaptation, and appropriation of its historical urbanity to the emerging forms, functions, and building types without losing its original pattern. The formation of the plan reflects the impacts of topography in shaping the urban form. The Roman grid pattern can be traced in the city in the linear covered *souqs* area in contrast to the mazy alleys structure in the old city. Thus as seen in Figure 5.1, the street structure is composed of two major veins that start from the Great Mosque; other secondary narrower streets ramble from them, defining the courtyard houses and providing access to the residential areas. The city urban form is complex in terms of its spatial structure, relations, and hierarchy. The figure plan of the city—which presents the coherence and relationship between voids and spaces—reflects the evolution of the city fabric that extends in hierarchical format from the macro city form to the underlying structure of the individual buildings' complexes and clusters. As seen in Figure 5.1 these buildings and clusters have irregular compact agglomerations that consequently create organic patterns of connection between buildings and open spaces. These spatial hierarchies enabled independent and segregated urban clusters within the urban fabric, which in turn composed a larger ratio of compact building masses with small courtyards, which consequently have created the compact form of the city. The building mass is composed of compact buildings within a complex and seemingly disordered overall structure. This is also probably due to the need for protection and the sense of security. With this arrangement, urban space—that is, space defined by an enclosure of buildings— is widely spread in the form of courtyards inside houses.

FIGURE 5.1 Figure plan: street structure in Nablus Old Town

Source: Courtesy of Nablus Municipality

Urban tissue

Urban tissue, as earlier highlighted, reflects the material built and spatial tissues from which the urban form is made. It refers to the interweaving of built and open spaces that are normally based on certain typological and morphological patterns that make the urban form. The traditional city pattern in Arabic cities with their courtyard houses is the major typology that dominates the town plan. They are interwoven with public buildings, installations that are interconnected with the clear spatial public, semi-public, and private spaces hierarchy.

Built tissue

The built tissue displays the building types that exist inside Nablus Old Town. Buildings typology can be classified into two main categories: residential (housing) and public buildings. Six major building types exist in Nablus Old Town: residential buildings and public buildings that include five major typologies—military, religious, industrial, commercial, and leisure buildings.

Residential buildings are of two types: houses and rulers' big palaces. The house—or *Dar/Beit* as locals call it—is the dwelling place. As the Old Town of Nablus has a mountainous character, the land determines house form and house orientation. The topography of Nablus had great impacts on plans, arrangements, and buildings' orientation, with heights limited to three stories in many parts of the city. It is understood that several other factors have influenced the urban fabric formation, and characteristics such as the different historical and cultural layers are reflected and anticipated in its architecture and cultural identity. Assi (2000) argues that the courtyard type was the traditional type that had been used in Palestine till the end of the nineteenth century. This type is based on a central plan, as shown in Figure 5.2, with inward spatial layouts for rooms; different rooms for different function are organized around the courtyard. The courtyard and its layout allow the adaptation of weather conditions and provide a less harsh atmosphere in this inner space and for the rooms around it. The courtyard house typology is the essential urban fabric that is noticeable in all the urban tissue of Nablus Old Town (apart from the central hall house that emerged in later periods and the clustered shape house). It has been the most popular typology from old times up to the early 1920s, according to Assi (2000). The concept of a house planned around a courtyard or open space appeared in the Middle East with the earliest cities there (Hakim, 1986). Courtyard houses in Nablus as in other Arabic cities are clustered together into a walled complex around a courtyard. The cluster form starts with a nuclear room; then new rooms can be added over time to serve the growth of the extended family. Normally the expansion of houses is horizontal unless the inner yard spaces are covered, in which case a vertical extension takes place.

Palaces in Nablus Old Town are very important landmarks in the townscape. Historically they had a double function as residential and as governmental

FIGURE 5.2 Courtyard house of Abdel Hadi Palace

Source: Author

buildings (Qamhieh, 1992). Figure 5.3 show that there are five main big palaces in Nablus Old Town. They are situated in the old neighborhoods representing the ruling family in one historical epoch. They are Al Toqan palace in Alqaryun quarter, A'shur palace in Algharb quarter, Al Nimer Palace in Alhabaleh qarter, Abedl Hadi Palace in Alqaryun, and Al Nabulsi palace in Habs Eldam.

Military buildings represent the barracks and military schools that are specific among the governmental edifices due to their specific purpose. The barracks are represented by huge blocks of buildings. In Nablus the building of Al-Muqata'a in the eastern extension of the Old Town can be seen as a major military type of building that was built in the end of nineteenth century. This complex has been used since its construction by the Ottomans as their headquarters of military offices and as a prison. The same use has been traced in this building during the British Mandate and during the Israeli occupation of the city. After the Oslo Peace agreement the building was used by the Palestinian Ministry of Interior and the Ministry of Exterior main offices in addition to the main prison building.

Religious institutions and buildings are those buildings that are used to practice religion, for example, mosques, synagogues, and churches. They can also be buildings and institutions of both administrative and educational purpose, such as Madrasa and court houses Al'adleyeh'. In fact, many religious buildings can be indicated in the city during the early Islamic period and are shown in Figure 5.4.

Mosques are one of the most important religious factors in the Islamic religion. As shown in Figure 5.4 there are eleven mosques inside the Old Town; many of these mosques have been converted from ancient churches or temples. Qamhieh (1992) describes two types of mosque: the big Friday mosque (*Jame'*) that is usually located in the commercial core; and smaller neighborhood mosques that are to be found in every neighborhood (*Masjed*) for the daily five prayers. Besides mosques there are eight shrines; two *Zawayaeh* (pl. *Zawiyah*) in the Old Town. The shrine is a place where the Islamic group proceeds with their liturgies. And there are six *Mqam*, that is, the tomb of a famous religious figure. Many religious activities and rituals take place in these types of buildings on special religious occasions.

The *Madrasah* type of building can be found either attached to a mosque or incorporated within a mosque building. The *madrasa*, as described by Hakim (1986) is a school for the training of spiritual and legal leaders, and became one of the most typical institutions of the Muslim world of the twelfth century. In Nablus Old Town there is only one *madrasah*—on the second floor of Albeek Mosque.

Churches and synagogues have existed in Nablus Old Town for centuries. Nablus is known for its history of tolerating the three religious faiths of Islam, Christianity, and Jewish. The three religious groups lived together for centuries, and each has its own religious buildings. There are two churches in the Old Town dating back to the eighteenth and nineteenth centuries. These churches are still used by the Christian population that inhabits the Rafedia neighborhood in the western new extensions of the city.

The Samaritans used to have a synagogue within the Old Town. At the beginning of the twentieth century when they moved from the Old Town to the

FIGURE 5.3 Location of palaces in Nablus Old Town

Source: Author

FIGURE 5.4 Location of religious buildings map

Source: Author

Legend:
1 Mosque
2 Church
3 Maqam
4 Synagogue

FIGURE 5.5 Mosque image on the western entrance of the Old Town

Source: Author

western new extension of the city, they sold their synagogue to their Muslim neighbor, as mentioned by Al-Nimr (1976), and established a new synagogue at the summit of Mount Jerzim that they claim to be the Holy Mountain of "Altur" mentioned in the Bible and Q'uran.

Industrial buildings in Nablus Old Town are exemplified in the traditional soap industry that is one of the ancient industries in the city. Major families had their own soap factories, which produced handmade soap over many years. (The soap factory is called *Al-Masbaneh* or *Sabaneh*). Nablus is famous for its traditional olive soap industry, which dates back many centuries. The soap is produced in stunning old buildings with exquisite architectural detail, the crumbling façade betraying its historical grandeur. The traditional art of olive soap making is an essential part of Nablus's identity and cultural heritage. Olive oil was the most important product of the hinterland of Nablus, and soap made from olive oil was the most important manufactured commodity of the city. The olive oil and soap industries had a great impact on social lives. The olive-based villages in the core hill areas of Jabal Nablus were fully integrated into the networks of urban merchants, and the soap industry underwent a remarkable expansion (Doumani, 1995).

About thirty-four soap factories are found in the Old Town. Every important and wealthy family owned its own soap factory, which was built near their houses or palaces (see Figure 5.6a, b, c). Qamhieh (1992) stresses the socio-economic role these buildings demonstrate as they are symbols of social status and of power and wealth to their owners. Examples are Toqan Soap factory, Nablusi, Abdel Hadi soap factories and many others. A special street in the western part of the city called Almasbeen Alqaryun Quarter is linked to the large number of soap factories along this street. During the twentieth century traditional soap industry was a very important element in the economic flourishing of Nablus. The introduction of new technologies to the soap industry badly affected this traditional industry and led to its decay. Consequently a rapid transformation and appropriation of several soap factories buildings took place, while others have been abandoned or have been left in ruins.

Commercial buildings—referring to the bazaar (*suq* or *kasbah*)—are considered one of the most significant socio-spatial systems of traditional Arabic cities. The location and the socio-economic role of bazaars compose a very important structuring element in the city urban fabric from a spatial perspective. The Friday mosque, which is the main religious and political center of the city, and the bazaar are always found together, and the Friday mosque is sometimes located next to or part of the bazaar. The bazaar was not only the commercial center of cities but also the center of social, cultural, political, and religious activities. Mansour Falamaki (1992) has described the Iranian bazaar as the center of social representation in a city—like the piazza for European cities during the Middle Ages and Hiroba in Japanese cities. In Nablus Old Town, as shown in Figure 5.7 and Figure 5.8, the spatial core, which is called Suq or Khan Altujar, is expanded from west to east and the main route connects this core to the rest of the commercial

meter

0   50   100   200

FIGURE 5.6A Location of soap factories

Source: Author

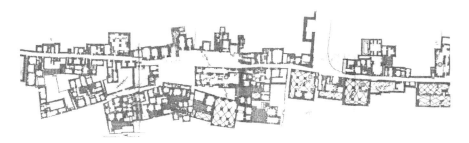

FIGURE 5.6B Ground floor plan of Masaben Street, a concentration of traditional soap factories in the Alqaryun neighborhood

Source: Qamhieh, 1992

FIGURE 5.6C Image from traditional soap production

Source: Nablus soap G. Eric and Edith Matson Photograph Collection at the Library of Congress

system. On its eastern edge the big Friday mosque 'Aljame' Alkabeer is located. Other mosques can be found along or near the main commercial routes. Other public buildings are also connected to the bazaar system—for example, Hammam Alshifa', Khan Hineyeh and Abdel Hadi Soap Factory. Nablus Old Town bazaars have been very famous for centuries. In 1864 Mills described the town's commercial bazaars:

> These are the Eastern shops or market-places, and they are comparatively numerous in Nablus. They are grouped according to the merchandise they contain, and situated principally in the main street. One is for vegetables of all kinds; another for dried fruits—raisins, olives, figs, etc; and last, but not least, comes the group of well stores of tobacco. The principal bazaar is arched, and is very large and fine in Nablus. It is the finest, by far, in Palestine, and equals any, so far as I observed, in the largest towns of the Turkish Empire. This is the clothing emporium, and is well furnished with the bright silk production of Damascus and Aleppo—the Abs of Baghdad—calicos and prints from Manchester, in varieties too numerous to be named—as well as the production of the town itself.
>
> (Mills, 1864: 88)

The two main commercial streets that are known as Khan Altujar covered *souq* and An Naser street are the main *kasbah* that structure the whole town around them.

Leisure buildings can be seen in the six neighborhoods of the Old Town; such buildings represent the socio-cultural activities of the city. They are presented in both the *hammams* and the hotels.

The hammam (Turkish bath) is the public steam bath house of Roman and Byzantine origin. Usually the hammamat (the plural of hammam) were used during the morning by men and in the afternoon by women. They had to serve different purposes: hygienic, social, recreational, and indirectly religious, argues Qamheih (1992). Ismail (1982) highlights other functions for the hammam as a centre for recreation and relaxation and as a place where massage is available after taking a bath. He further argues that the hammam also served as a social institution by strengthening the social interaction, bonds, and relations among the quarter people. See Figure 5.9, which shows the interior of a hammam in Nablus. Moreover the hammam was used for special social occasions such as weddings and educational celebrations—for example, school graduation and the celebration of compilation of memorizing the Qur'an.

Figure 5.10 shows the eight *hammams* in the Old Town. Only two *hammams* are still operating there: Hammam Alshifa' (Aljaded) and Hammam Alsumarah). The other *hammams* have either changed their function—Hammam Alkhallil is now used for storage, for example—or they have fallen into ruins—Hammam Alresh is such a case.

FIGURE 5.7 Map of *souqs* and *khans* and commercial *souqs*

Source: Author

FIGURES 5.8A AND 5.8B
Pictures from main
streets

Source: Author

meter

0   50   100   200

FIGURE 5.9 Location of *hammams* in Nablus Old Town

Source: Author

FIGURE 5.10 Picture of a *hammam*

Source: Author

Hotels (khans) and the caravanserai are the two building types that were used to host strangers in the Old Town. There are only a small number of hotels (*khan*) in the Old Town (see Figure 5.11) because strangers were not allowed to stay overnight unless they were tradesmen or guests, according to Qamhieh (1992). The most important hotel was Khan Altujar in Suq Alsultan. Its name means "the merchant's hotel," and it is at the center of the cloth bazaar, Souq Alqimash. There are four hotels (*khan*) in the Old Town. Only two still function as lodging places: Hindyeh and Alsaha. The others, such as Khan Altujar, have changed their function and become shops. The *caravanserais, Al Wakalat* (the plural of *al Wakalah*) were the merchants' hotels. Their location near the main bazaars and the town gates gave them a strategic location to be the appropriate place for traveling merchants to use. Unsal describe the main *caravansarai*:

> In these caravanserais the merchants found proper accommodation where they could attend to the safety of their goods and wares, to repair their vehicles, and find the needs of their animals. In times of wars these buildings were used for storing food and ammunitions.
>
> (Unsal, 1959: 15)

FIGURE 5.11 Location of major *khans* in Nablus Old Town

Source: Author

The only *caravanserai* within Nablus Old Town is Alwakaklah Alfarrokheyah, named after the Mamluks prince Farrokh, who built it in 1620, according to Al-Nimr (1976). It is also called Al Wakalah AlGharbeyeh (the western *caravanserai*) as it lies near the western gate of the town. Its gateway leads into an open courtyard, with an arched arcade around. The ground floor was used for lodging camels and horses, and for hay storage.

The public buildings discussed above are important structuring elements of the city's spatial dynamics; at the same time they can be regarded as significant landmarks in the townscape. Many activities (social, religious, cultural, and economic) take place around these buildings, which adds to their importance to the town's identity. Nablus Old Town is an important destination for shopping in its main bazaars and a place to pray Friday prayers in its major *Jame*'s (An Naser and Alkabeer). It is also a place of many cultural activities during Ramadan and the Holy feasts. Alsuq Nazel is a very important Ramadan market that has taken place in the Old Town's main square (Bab Alsaha) for decades.

Spatial tissue

The spatial tissue is the second constituting element of the urban tissue that provides the three-dimensional aspect of the urban form. The spatial tissue is based on the network of open spaces and streets. A street in the Old Town is a long space between two walls. These walls have no openings facing the street and they are built from the local yellowish Jama'een stone. The possibility of knowing what is behind the walls is minimal for a stranger in the city. The façade architecture is introvert, with detailed decorative elements in the main entrance façade and without aesthetic function on the other sides, giving importance to the inner courtyard as the major private space.

The layouts of old cities in Palestine still bear witness in many places to their Hellenistic and Roman past as in the case of Nablus where the Roman grid system can be still witnessed in the existing street layout. In the Middle Ages, certain streets were paved to avoid mud and puddles and some were illuminated at night. In certain sectors in old Nablus, such as Souq Albasal, the pathways beneath the porticos remained, while the roadway became reduced to a simple pathway for pedestrians because of two rows of stalls. Streets within Nablus Old Town can be divided into different groups according to their importance, location, density, and use. They vary from the simple passages between different buildings of the town that can best be called alleys to the main spines or thoroughfares that are called *casabas*. The major thoroughfares in old Nablus lead from the east gate of the city wall towards the west, branching from the main thoroughfares in a series of alleys or boroughs (*harat*) and a number of irregular dead-end alleys or "cul-de-sac" lanes that are a circulation providing access to groups of dwellings inside the clustered houses of *hush*. There is a predominant balance between the geometry of streets and spaces and their forms. The spatial hierarchy of street and open areas clearly distinguishes public, private, and semi-private spaces. The primary circulation system defines the edges of the residential quarters while the secondary system provides access into residential quarters.

The hierarchal division of street order in the Old Town is connected to the following factors: the type of activities, size in terms of width, and location in connection to the built tissue. The streets are divided to main streets, secondary streets, minor streets, and dead-end streets, as shown in Figures 5.12a, b, c, and d.

The main streets in Nablus Old Town form the backbone of the street network; their importance lies in their accommodation of important public buildings such as soap factories, churches and mosques (for example, An- Naser, Al-Hanbaly, and Al-Kabeer). They also contain within their borders the main markets or bazaars, such as Suq al-Sultan and Khan Altujar. They follow the natural topography line of the valley, and consist of two east–west spines that dominate the urban fabric. The first street stretches through the area from the Great Mosque (Jami' Al-Kabeer) in the east to Al-Khader Mosque in the west (it is now called An-Naser Street used to be the Roman colonnaded street), and the second street stretches from the Great Mosque east to Blacksmith Market or Suq Alhadadeen West. The size and shape of the street networks are very different, and the hierarchy of the street networks and their relevant independent agglomeration of buildings and open spaces dominate the urban fabric of Old Nablus. They are generally wide enough. Their maximum width reaches thirteen meters to accommodate pedestrian traffic and vehicular volume at certain hours. The only exceptions are certain markets that are tiled and covered, such as Khan Altujar. The important streets are organized into markets—*souqs*—such as the vegetable market, cloth market, and jewelry market. Normally they are covered by cross-vaulted or barrel-vaulted roofs— Souq Alqumash (the cloth market) is an example. Facing the streets are shops occupied in the daytime; they have a façade of two meters and are opened out by two shutters, an upper one serving as a lean-to and the lower, generally smaller, for a shop display or to hold goods. These shops are normally between three and four meters deep. The back part of the shop is often an extended workshop opening to back street. It should be noted that neither merchants nor craftsmen live in their shops, which close at night.

The secondary streets connect the main streets; at the same time they compose the main routes within and between the adjacent quarters. They tend to be the connection between the main housing complexes *Hush*—private and semi-private spaces—and the main public spaces. Usually they exist in busy commercial areas, with less pedestrian density compared to the main streets; furthermore their width is small so they cannot accommodate vehicular traffic. Minor streets provide access or linkage to areas within quarters, more likely residential areas that are not connected to secondary streets Figures 5.12b, c, and d give examples. The dead-end streets or as they are called "cul-de-sacs," are private properties, owned and shared by their users, mainly the residents. They do not have any particular pattern of linkage to main or secondary streets, and they could be connected to any of the other types of streets mentioned above.

FIGURE 5.12A Location of the main two *Qasbas* (main streets)

Source: Author

5.12B, 5.12C, AND 5.12D Pictures of secondary streets

Source: Author

Open spaces, gardens, and nodes represent the other element of the spatial tissue in Nablus Old Town. "Traditional Arabic cities" generally did not have a place of public assembly corresponding to the church square or the space in front of the town hall in European cities of the period. The place for religious gathering was the Great Mosque, which has always had a vast courtyard surrounded by a portico (Elisséeff, 1980). In traditional Arabic cities there would be several little squares bordered by houses—*saha*—such as Saha Alqaryun and Saha Al-Manarah, and, above all, squares at crossroads—*Muraba'ah* or *Musalabeh*—that represent the known form of a node, such as Musalabeh Ahmed and Musalabeh Souq Albasal, as Qamhieh (1992) describes them. Figure 5.13 demonstrates two types of open spaces in Nablus Old Town fabric—namely, public open spaces (squares) and private gardens (*basteen*) and yards. There are also two types of open public squares: city squares, which function at the city level, such as An-Naser square, also called Saha Al-Manarah; and neighborhood squares, which function at the neighborhood level and are smaller in size, for example, Sahet Alteneh in Alqaryun quarter.

Squares in "Islamic cities" were known only in late medieval times; they were used for military parades, plying sports, commercial activities, public executions, political gatherings, and extensions for the Friday mosque. The main open public space in old Nablus is Al-Manarh Square, which was built next to An-Naser Mosque in the late nineteenth century; later, the clock tower and a fountain (which was brought from Hammam Al Qadi) were built in the square (Al-Nimr, 1976).

Private gardens exist in many houses and palaces. Until the beginning of the twentieth century, the Old Town of Nablus was surrounded by private gardens of fruit trees and vegetation plains, with plentiful water resources (Qamheih, 1992). The Old Town did not have public green spaces inside its wall until 1883, when Sahet Al-Manarah was established with a few of the trees left from the replaced garden. Private gardens are found in big houses and palaces. Usually, they are located in the inner courtyards or a backyard garden. See Figure 5.14.

The most evident feature of architecture in "Islamic cities" is the focus on *interior space as opposed to the outside or façade*. The most typical expression of this focus on inner space is in houses. Rectangular dwelling units typically are organized around an inner courtyard. The façade of the house offers high windowless walls interrupted only by a single low door. The courtyard allows for outdoor activities with protection from wind and sun. The courtyard also serves as an air well into which the cool, night air can sink. And the plain, thick-walled street façade of the house with few or no windows is designed to withstand severe elements, such as hot winds and sand.

Most private houses in Nablus Old Town are invariably inward-looking courtyard houses, as we discussed earlier. A bent corridor (for privacy) leads from the gated entry from the public lane into a courtyards paved with tiles, often planted with shade trees and with a pool at the centre. Surrounding the courtyard are the principal rooms of the house. Different sides of the courtyard may provide separate accommodation for sections of the extended family.

FIGURE 5.13A and 5.13B Pictures of (a) Alqaryun square and (b) Almanara square

Source: Author

■ Private gardens

▨ Private courtyards

FIGURE 5.14 Map of open spaces system

Source: Author and Qamhieh, 1992

Land use patterns

The land use pattern is the third constructing element of the urban form. In Nablus Old Town the land use pattern can be described as mixed use without a clear distinction, more particularly in the central commercial zone, where the same building can be used both for commercial activities in the ground floor and for other purposes in the other floors—residential areas, offices, medical clinics, and so on. There are other functions that can be found in individual or large complexes, such as soap factories, *hammams*, and other public buildings. The main *kasbah* (streets) contain the concentrated mixed use of different types of commercial, administrative, educational, handcraft, and residential activities. This can be seen also along the secondary streets, but in less density, and gradually it is minimized until we enter the pure residential areas in the main quarters of the city. In conclusion, we can see in Nablus Old Town the following land use is revealed:

1   The plan varies with mixed functions and activities that can be related to: the historical layers of the city (Roman archaeological site, the hippodrome); other activities that are connected mainly with the inhabitants' cultural and religious customs (shrines, *zawaya*); others connected with the economy such as soap factories; and others connected with land ownership and land parceling.
2   It appears that the land use pattern, as in other Arabic traditional cities, is much connected to the central Great Mosque and other mosques in the different residential quarters.
3   Stores and shops vary in the types of goods they sell according to their location on the main *casaba* or on secondary streets; for example, the main stores that sell main products such as wheat and the vegetable market are on the main *casaba* while smaller shops selling secondary products such as groceries and herbs are more likely to be found along secondary and minor streets.
4   Streets widths also vary according to commercial activities as dense pedestrian circulation is foreseen along the main *casaba* and secondary streets, with maximum width that can reach twelve to thirteen meters, while on minor streets pedestrian movement is less with street width can reach to three meters only.
5   Open public spaces are also connected to different land use patterns in the city, where most small open spaces and main squares are concentrated in the city centre, where dense commercial activities take place. Small open spaces can be found in front of or near many mosques in the urban tissue and are used as extra space for the increased number of prayers during special religious occasions such as the Holy Month of Ramadan, the main feasts and Friday prayer.
6   There are other land uses inside the urban fabric of the city: agricultural land at the level of the quarter or at the level of the city, for example, the big gardens annexed to palaces and big houses such as Abdel Hadi palace in the Alqaryun quarter.

Built/spatial interconnections on different levels and scales of resolution

The built fabric composes a major element of the urban tissue as it denotes the cluster of houses and agglomerations that compose the several neighborhoods. The built fabric can be analyzed at different scales of resolution: building, block, plot, quarter, neighborhood, city, and region. The parceling structure defines compact land subdivisions of "islands of dwelling groups" surrounded by narrow streets. The subdivision of the traditional parceling system creates self-contained neighborhoods—*harat*—which are an accumulation of numerous dwelling environments reflecting their own character. The subdivision system accommodates many parcels for a mixture of uses and sizes interwoven together. It seems to be a more durable element than their relevant built form.

Plots

The subdivision system is most evident around the main arteries, for usually the ground floor consists of commercial shops while the upper floors are dominated by schools, as is the case of the main covered *khan* (Souq al Qumash), or by residences, as is the case of the buildings on the main commercial streets, or by residences only in residential quarters. Plot configuration shows significant variations while the geometry of lots is almost regular. Along the main *casaba* (An Naser Street), plots form rather short narrow strips. They tend to be oblongs, and are laid at right angles to the street line and parallel to each other. Plots can occupy the full frontage and so form rows or serial lines of diverse buildings along the side of the street. Each side of the *casaba* consists of a single plot series reaching a depth of about three meters, with their frontages not exceeding two and a half meters to allow the accommodation of a maximum number of shops on a minimum of available total street front.

Block (hush *system*)

A residential quarter is formed by the composition of neighborhood block units that are known as *hush*, which are organized along quarter streets. The *hush* is a closed, autonomous, physical, and social unit. A common descent for the families living in the quarter is fundamental for the ordering of it. The quarter is confined by other quarters, all situated back to back with each other. The boundaries are also marked by large gates at the entrance of each quarter. The neighborhood unit of the Old Town closes itself from the public street and turns its "blind" façades towards it—a typical characteristic of traditional Arab cities. The social hierarchy used to be expressed internally, since the social rank is shown through the proximity to the public street. The inner house always had a higher social rank than the house situated closer to the entrance of the blind alley. The composition of primary pattern units surrounding a cul-de-sac forms a neighborhood unit, which constitutes the territory for a community unit. The neighborhood unit is a socially

FIGURE 5.15A Location of *hush* of major large families. The circle shades are for major *hush* in Nablus, while the numbers refer to other *hush* and their locations

Source: Author

FIGURE 5.15B Example of the *hush* unit plan and picture of Alatuut

Source: Qamhieh, 1992

and physically closed pattern unit. The blind alley is a narrow semi-private lane, which opens up to the quarter street through a gateway. The solidarity within a community unit is strong, since it is based on kinship among the families. The community has a hierarchic social structure, with a family in a leading position living in the house at the inner end of the neighborhood unit. Figure 5.15a and Figure 5.15b demonstrate the composition of the *hush* in the neighborhood blocks.

Quarters

The historic city of Nablus is composed largely of dense residential quarters or *harat* (plural *hara*) that are subdivided to neighborhoods, each of which is a self-supporting urban unit with its own cohesive socio-ethnic and cultural character. Residential quarters surround the local mosque (*Masjid*) where the five daily prayers are held. Each quarter has a high degree of independence, as it has its own *hammam*, bakery, mosque, and shops. The residents usually share a common origin and social, economic and professional status. For example, the various quarters of the city were connected with a street network as a major element that segregated and integrated each quarter with the rest of the city parts. The Old Town is divided into six quarters (*hara*, as mentioned), each containing several neighborhoods. Each quarter is an entity in itself with special characteristics that give it its own image and identity, and make it easy to recognize while moving inside the Old Town. Further, they can be an external reference when visually spotted from outside the Old Town. Alyasmeeneh quarter, for example, is known for its asymmetric sloped dark alleys, while Alqaryun is very famous for its large number of soap factories, and Alhabaleh quarter for its late nineteenth-century buildings.

Centrality and significance of Nablus City at the regional and national levels

Religious route

The city has a long history in connection to three religious beliefs. It has a major significance for Judaism, and it is also important to Christianity and Islam. Besides Abraham's ties to the area, the city contains religious sites such as Joseph's Tomb, Jacob's well and also the location of the destroyed Samaritan temple. Nearby there is a Greek Orthodox monastery that is associated with that of the Biblical figure Jacob. Mount Gerizim in Nablus is holy to the Samaritan community, who remember it as the site of their ancient temple. The two historic churches inside the Old Town also reflect the town's importance for Christians as the town accommodated Christianity for many years. The several mosques inside the Old Town assert its significant role in the Muslims' religious life as well. Many historical sites in the Nablus area are connected to the three religious beliefs—for example, Maqam Mujeer Eldeen on Ebal Mountain and Al Khadrah Mosque inside the Old Town, a place where prophet Yakuub mourned his son.

Cultural heritage centre

Nablus, an ancient Canaanite town, has remains dating back to *c.*2000 BC, about the time when the city was held by Egypt. The Samaritans made it their capital and built a temple on nearby Gerizim to rival that of Jerusalem. Nablus still has a small community of Samaritans who are considered the smallest religious group in the world. Nablus Old Town has been an important mark of the Palestinian cultural heritage among other important sites, such as Jerusalem and Bethlehem. Its importance is derived from being an inhabited site since at least since the fourth century BC. The many historical and archaeological sites in Nablus and around it are witnesses of this historical and cultural significance. The villages of Jabal Nablus—and Nablus itself, in fact—were Palestine's main economic and manufacturing "capital." The majority of Palestine's inhabitants lived in the hilly region, and its history, consequently, is representative of what transpired for most Palestinians (Doumani, 1995).

This picturesque history of Nablus endowed it with many archaeological sites, including Jacob's well, Joseph's tomb, the Roman amphitheatre and hippo-drome, and many beautiful mosques, some of which were built on the remains of Byzantine churches, remains from the Mamluks period, and the dominant existing structure from Ottoman times. UNESCO and other international organizations connected to cultural heritage assured the significance of Nablus as a cultural heritage site. UNESCO stated that the historic Old Town of Nablus was of "Outstanding universal value according to Article 12 of the World Heritage Convention" (UNOCHA, 2004: 2).

One of the results was that Nablus Old Town was listed as important heritage site in *Inventory of Cultural and Natural Heritage Sites of Potential Outstanding Universal Value in Palestine*, published in June 2005. Fowler (2011) analyzes the *Inventory*, which identifies and documents twenty sites in what is in effect a provisional tentative list for World Heritage nomination. It includes Bethle-hem and Tell -Sultan (archaeological Jericho), and Hebron Old Town, Mount Gerizim and the Samaritans, Qumran, the Dead Sea, Nablus Old Town and ancient Samaria in a landscape associated with John the Baptist. Nablus together with Jerusalem, Bethlehem and Hebron compose the major urban historic cores in the Palestinian historical landscape, in addition to many rural vernacular villages and hundreds of archaeological sites.

Educational centre

Nablus city is the home to An-Najah University (which obtained university status in 1977). This university serves all northern Occupied Palestinian Territories cities, such as Jenin, Tulkarem, and Qalelia. Many high schools and colleges, such as Alrawda College, are present in the city as well. The city has produced numerous writers, poets, and academicians—for example, Ibrahim Toqan and Fadwa Toqan.

Economic centre

Nablus and its surrounding environs have been the economic centre of Palestine from the eighteenth century onwards. Nablus contained what Doumani calls the "social life" of the four major commodities of the Jabal Nablus region: textiles, cotton, olive oil, and soap. This type of economic and commercial dynamic created a strong relationship with the cultural context of localized merchant peasant trade, regional trade networks, the political economy of commercialized and monetized agricultural production, and state and manufacturing relations.

> The production of soap was capital intensive and allowed partaking in the related strategies of accumulation: money-lending, landownership, urban real estate, and regional trade. In this process of transformation, an evolving middling peasantry reproduced urban institutions in the countryside and brought it into the orbit of urban, Islamic, legal institution.
>
> (Doumani, 1995: 45)

Nablus is considered to be the market centre for the northern region in the OPT, where wheat and olives are grown and sheep and goats are grazed. Nablus is an agricultural and commercial trade centre dealing in traditional industries such as production of soap, olive oil, and handicrafts. Other industries include furniture production, tile production, stone quarrying, textile manufacturing and leather tanning. The city is also a regional trading centre for live produce. It is the location of the Palestine Stock Exchange and of leading information and communication technology organizations such as Palestine Telecommunication Company and AMRA Information Technology.

Centre of the Palestinian resistance

During the British Mandate (1918–1948) Nablus became the core of Palestinian nationalism, and it was the center of resistance against the British. Nablus city was considered one of several centers of rebellion in the first intifada (1987–1993) and was one of the first locations in the Occupied Palestinian Territories to witness the initial impact of the second intifada that broke out after 28 September 2000. The city is known in the region as what Doumani (2004) calls the city's epithet, the "Mountain of Fire": "an appellation deriving from a local legend that Napoleon, upon approaching Nablus, met his defeat when the inhabitants set forests and olive groves ablaze, burning the French soldiers' (Doumani, 2004: 13).

Doumani describes this historical legend connected with Nablus area because it speaks of one of the traditions for which the Nablus region is famous: as a centre of resistance to outside control. The seminal moments in popular memory for the modern period, aside from the encounter with the French troops during Napoleon's ill-fated adventure in Palestine, are its leadership of the 1834 rebellion against the invading Egyptian troops of Muhammad Ali Pasha, its role as the beating heart of the Great Revolt against the British (1936–39), and, finally, its centrality in the two intifada against the Israeli occupation, according to Doumani (2004). Nablus has been a major economic, political, and cultural centre for Palestinians. Several leading families in Palestinian history stem from Nablus, including the Toqan family and the Abel Hadi Family. It has played an important role in Palestinian political history as well, especially as a centre for Palestinian nationalism outside the family rivalries of Jerusalem. Nablus Old Town is the centre of the Palestinian resistance in the OPT, together with Balata refugee camp, located at the eastern entrance to Nablus city, and Jenin Refugee camp, and they are very well know for the history of resistance to the Israeli occupation.

Hence, Nablus city plays a very important role at the regional and national level as it is an urban center for cultural, religious, educational, and economic life, and the centre of the Palestinian national resistance to the Israeli occupation.

Townscape components: understanding the city as an experience

> *[The townscape is] . . . the art of giving visual coherence and organization to the jumble of buildings, streets and spaces that make up the urban environment.*
> (Cullen, 1971)

The previously mentioned urban morphological elements and the rich, complex townscape shape the structure of Nablus's ancient core. The townscape of a place can be understood by the experience that place gives. The relationship between light and dark, the sequential views, the symmetry and asymmetry of the passageways, the skyline, the street line and many other factors shape and formulate the experience of specific places and spaces. In this section the major elements that strongly affect the identity and image of the Old Town will be highlighted.

The serial (sequential) vision of the city

The hierarchy of street layouts and the variety in scale and configuration of open spaces have created an image of *surprise* and *mystery* achieved through the variety, intimacy, and intricacy of the urban spaces, from squares to streets to arcades and to courtyards.

In general the street patterns and coverage system is a special characteristic of Nablus Old Town that generates a special experience of the spatial and built tissue. The maze of narrow lanes and dead-end alleys that are vaulted in places to afford shelter from the sun and the rain in winter, give the old town a picturesque and charming character. It is noted that periodically a minaret or an ornamental doorway provides a landmark to help orient the town visitors. This amazing street pattern resulted from building positions and spatial structure, which is influenced by building line, height, masses, texture, and color. The openings form and make

FIGURE 5.16A and 5.16B Panoramic views

Source: Courtesy of Abed Qusini

patterns, with the special usage of decorative elements within the buildings themselves and within other structure giving the city its spectacular identity and image. The succession of interacted visual sequences through the alleys and streets form the integration of architectural vocabulary, porches, gateways, and the variety of functions in the old neighborhoods, and the glimpse of minaret towers helps in enhancing the value of the urban space and creates a varied urban experience, while following the changing atmosphere between different urban land use zones, which reflects a sense of rhythm and progression. The urban tissue of the Old Town is in sharp contrast to the scale of the open area and the density of the surrounding buildings. Hence, this contrast moves the visual sequence from the dramatic dark passages, cacophonous with commercial activity, to a vast, open, serene, precinct space path in light and dark. The openings and the enclosures in the urban tissue along the streets and alleys, established by the remarkable public buildings, have all contributed to the visual sequences and differentiation of the townscape. Added to the advantageous attribute of the landscape itself is street furniture; these monuments are nodes and landmarks that participate in evoking the characteristics of the townscape patterns.

City skyline

The town portrait "is the result of a cumulative process, and very legible. The land marks that stand out in this picture are symbols of collective life; they advertise civic priorities, and make palpable the hierarchy of public institutions" (Kostof, 1991). Hence the dominant accent of Nablus's skyline as seen in Figures 5.16a and 5.16b is formulated by the featured clusters, domes, and pitched roofs of the houses, and the interplay of horizontal and vertical elements of sacred places, their domes and the mass of minarets that are piled high in the sky. However, their visual prominences are enhanced by sky-aspiring properties. The shapes of the skyline matter to the residents and to visitors as it is the familiar fond icon of the town's form, a vision to cherish, and it is the guide that leads the residents to their homes. It is also their urban advertisement to the world, the front that is presented to visitors, and disseminated shorthand for a broader audience still.

Nablus identity: synthesis

From the previous analysis along with the discussion in Chapter 4, it can be seen that the Old Town of Nablus city has a significant historical, cultural, social, economic, religious, and architectural importance. This significance is embedded in its rich history that is evident in the collage of several historical layers found in the urban form (physical layout, land use, urban tissue, and townscape). The most significant characteristics principle is the way in which its historical layers are composed. On the one hand, the assimilation of different layers within a consistent and living urban continuum created a relatively coherent and complex urban entity. However, each historical period produced its own morphogenesis. Each production would generate a rupture to the balance of the already existing urban form. The urban form then would create dynamism to go back to the coherence and balance it used to have before the production process. This coherence dynamic is maintained through out the process of incorporating, adapting, and altering previous morphogenesis to the changing needs and growth of the community.

The existing urban tissue of the Old Town is a consistent juxtaposition of the physical urban tissue and the spatial arrangements between them. The inter-connection of buildings of various typologies adjacent to each other with a high degree of responsive and contextualization is the major characteristic of the existing urban tissue. The tissue is highly ordered and regulated in a hierarchical order, consequently generating a coherent townscape. Within the dense urban tissue groups of different building typologies and complexes are evident. These complexes are well integrated in the traditional urban form. They are composed from major public buildings that materialize the landmarks in the town's tissue. Their history, architecture, scale, arrangements, and function contributed to the remarkable identity and image of Nablus Old Town. Nablus is therefore famous for its soap factories, *hammams*, *kahns*, old mosques, bazaars, and palaces. The dominant courtyard house and *hush* complex adds to the quality and significance of the Old Town identity. The courtyard house typology is similar to traditional houses in Damascus old city, which is why many people and scholars call it Beit Shami in reference to Damascus. The process of production and commerce has always been located adjacent to residential clusters without any physical segregation, resulting in a highly mixed use pattern. The assimilation of the different historical layers that produced different building typologies generated remarkable "internal capacity" to accommodate changes and adapt to transform-ations in their essential elements without disruption of their structure and links. The spatial layout and patterns have also affected the urban appearance of the Old Town. The streets network contributed to the formal and visual composition in the Old Town. The spatial patterns are composed of the street network with different hierarchies from the main and secondary to the dead-end alleys. Open spaces added to the organic composition of the spatial patterns that shaped the town with its special character and provided a special spatial experience while moving from the central public space to the smaller neighborhood squares. Nodes materialized in the major entrances to the town along with the intersection of the major streets generating remarked spatial dynamics. The Old Town is also extremely valuable for its bustling commercial centre and the concentration of crafts activities. The social fabric, relations, and activities add to Nablus Old Town's unique identity. The cultural dynamics and activities are also part of Nablus's known identity as a place of traditions and rich culture. The Old Town identity can be highlighted by analyzing and understanding the different factors that contributed to this identity emerging and shaping. This historical reading is combined with the urban form in which the material physical elements are represented in building typologies, the spatial patterns and arrangements, and the social, cultural, economic, and political dynamics. All together they comprise what is called place or city identity.

The perceived identity and meaning of Nablus Old Town

Lynch's (1960) model of charting users' mental maps that people use to help them find their way through cities is composed of five fundamental, reasonably invariant elements: paths, edges, districts, nodes, and landmarks.

For him, "Identity, structure and meaning combine in different ways to create the image of the city or its parts" (Lynch, 1960: 7). Recognizable identity and structure are essential to meaning and, therefore, image. Lynch's conception of identity implies distinctiveness, individuality, and oneness of a place. It is clear from this approach that environmental images are "the result of a two-way process between the observer and the environment" (Lynch 1960: 8). According to Lynch, the elements of city image combine to highlight identity and strengthen urban character; that is, the perceived interactions of landmarks, paths, nodes, and edges within a district combine to create identity. The structure of a city is thus portrayed as the key to the users' orientation and recognition:

> People use many different clues to establish (environmental) structure of the recognition of characteristic form[1] or activity[3] in areas or centers, sequential linkages[2], directional relations[1, 2], time[3] and distance[1], landmarks[1, 2, 3], path or edge continuities[1], gradients[1], panoramas[2], and many others.
>
> (Lynch, 1981: 135)

In contrast to the Conzenian historical–geographical approach, environmental psychology examines the relationship between environments and human behavior, with "environment" broadly interpreted to include the "natural world," society, the built environment, and the informational environment. The environmental–psychological approach is used to interpret public perceptions of urban form. It also emphasizes the understanding of urban form, but does so from a different perspective—namely, from people's subjective recognition. The concept of place identity is a theoretical necessity for understanding the impact of the urban environment on the individual. Place identity for this stream of theory refers to clusters of perceptions in the form of images, meanings, memories, facts, ideas, beliefs, values, and behavior tendencies relevant to the individual's existence in the physical world. These clusters are related to the development of self-identity, which is largely a product of socialization. Coping in an urban setting requires socialization in the physical world at any number of periods during the life cycle. The urban environment comprises diverse physical settings, and place identity associated with different settings provides norms and values that regulate behavior patterns in given milieus. Thus, the individual behaves and interacts in certain ways in settings that involve crowding, privacy, and territoriality. Place identity is both enduring and changing. Enduring family/household influences often determine what happens when the child becomes an adult, while the changing character of place identity, mainly due to technology and demographic patterns, may explain changes in self-identity (Proshansky and Fabian, 1986).

Place identity is thus perceived and articulated in what Proshansky (1978) called an affective-evaluative component. This finds expression within individuals' preferences for, or sense of emotional belonging to, particular environments. Place identity is a predominantly cognitive structure to be discovered in the heads of individuals. To be sure, it is also a highly contextualized form of identification, deriving from individuals' engagements with their material contexts of action and interaction (Proshansky *et al.*, 1983). Even recent social psychological revisions of the concept, such as that proposed by Bonauito *et al.* (1996), have retained a view of place identity as a mental entity, the nature and intensity of which varies from individual to individual. The measured elements are connected with issues of preferences, perception, value, importance, likeliness, attachments, and others. For the purpose of this research certain issues were investigated that link with the research questions and objectives.

Many important researchers have developed this field of research and approach, among them, Rachel Kaplan, Stephen Kaplan, Robert L. Ryan, Edward Soja, and Henri Proshansky.

The diverse ways in which different groups see the same place are important for public policy, as their common imagery can furnish the raw material for the symbols and collective memories of group communications (Lynch, 1960: 25).

As such, mental images uncover the "consensual view" of a city in terms of meaning and major identity and orientation features; they also serve as a statistic-ally reliable measure for urban legibility and as a basic ingredient in urban design. Lynch defines both legibility and imageability as:

> that quality in a physical object which gives it a high probability of evoking a strong image in any given observer. It is that shape, color, or management, which facilitates the making of vividly identified, powerfully structured, highly useful mental images of the environment.
>
> (Lynch, 1960: 9)

On the other hand Lynch defines "public images" as the common mental pictures carried by large numbers of a city's inhabitants—areas of agreement of what might be expected to appear in the interaction of a single physical reality, a common culture, and a basic physiological nature. External representations of mental images include graphic depictions and verbal descriptions, such as: sketches and cognitive maps, and verbal descriptions of temporal characteristics of the built environment; visual identification of typical architectural characteristics on drawings; statements of attitudes or values towards an environment; and combined verbal descriptions of experience, feelings, and attitudes towards an environment. These definitions of the term "image" break down its complexity, while the theoretical use of the term considers the concept as a larger, more comprehensive mental representation of a person's subjective knowledge of reality. The following sections attempt to reveal the features and symbols that have withstood the passage of time in the collective memory of Nablus user groups. They attempt to find out how the historic city is remembered and valued by different user groups. Further, they aim to investigate the different urban meanings and sensations among user groups to figure out how to acquire better knowledge of the city. They further explore the qualitative and quantitative changes to memory retention and environmental image development to evaluate the city image in war and post-war. As such, the ultimate goal is to use the collective memory that will help in formulating a set of guidelines and urban design scenarios for post-disaster urban reconstruction projects.

The identity researched here is itself "dynamic," as it already includes elements of "making" and "unmaking" because of the destruction of 2002. The conflict and military occupation are expected to alter user groups' mental maps of the city before its destruction. These mental maps are not the "pure" image of the city prior destruction as they include also the traumatic experience of destruction and reconstruction.

The synthesis of the mental maps of all user groups (inhabitants, visitors and vendors) is shown in Figure 5.17. The most important elements in structuring the city identity are nodes represented by squares such as Bab esaha, followed by Alkabeer mosque as the main node on the eastern entrance. The most important path is Khan Etujar, followed by An-Naser street.

Paths with more architectural homogeneity and historical significance were the most legible attributes—Khan Etujar and Albasal market, for example. In general, the main east–west paths dominate the overall image of the town as opposed to other directly connecting systems.

The most important attributes of linear district legibility are strong functional themes such as high status, and the contrast in physical, spatial, and functional characteristics. The most important attributes of landmark legibility are of historical, architectural, and functional significance, as well as visual prominence.

Associated meaning with Nablus Old Town

Because of the complicated political situation and degradation reflected by the two national intifada, people tend to tie the historic centre with national resistance as an "undefeatable" place. Thus, the main landmarks gain more importance in people's mental image of the city, and that in return reinforces the city's identity as a symbol of national and cultural identity. Relph defines this place identity: "The identity of a place is comprised of three inter-related components, each irreducible to the other—physical features or appearances, observable activities, functions and meanings of symbols" (Relph, 1976a: 61).

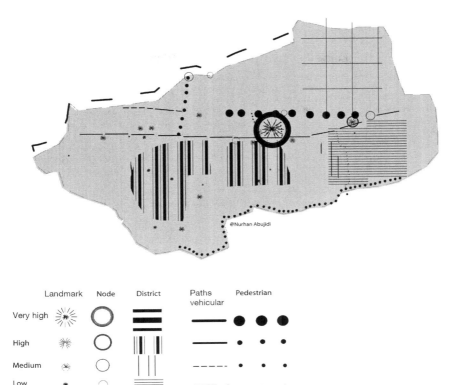

FIGURE 5.17 Users' mental map of Nablus Old Town

Source: Author

People's perception of the city and its importance is projected in many expressions of attachment, belonging, and sincerity. Some 80 percent of those interviewed described Nablus Old Town as "my city, my home," "the place that makes me relax and relieves stress," "the inheritance of our grandfathers." The city connects to the glorious past of the Nabulsi community as the main commanders of the surrounding villages and cities during the nineteenth and early twentieth centuries. Devine describes this action: "The environment can provide a set of symbols that both individuals and groups of people can identify with as well as representing an expression of identities" (Devine *et al.*, 1997: 38).

Moreover, it was noticed from the interviews that Nablus Old Town provided people with feelings of self-esteem, for commercial and economical reasons. For a long period of time Nablus was represented as the economical capital of Palestine, as a centre for trading and industry. The wealthy traders of Nablus and wealthy families originate mainly from the old city; their big fabulous palaces, such as Tuqan palace and Abdel Hadi palace, and the big families' houses, such as Hashem and Alnimer, are still witnesses to the recent past economic glory of the city. Since the sixteenth century, Nablus has been famous for its soap industry. Nablus's historic urban fabric contains more than thirty old soap factories from different historic epochs; therefore people's mental image and perception of the city's identity was strongly tied to these recognizable elements of antiquity. Jacobi defines such elements: "When traditional meanings comprise integral components of experience, development or identity, their affective and symbolic salience for group's members increases" (Jacobi and Stokolos, 1983: 46).

We can conclude that Nablus Old Town in general has played an important role in maintaining the different user groups' identities and their capacity in symbolizing social memories. This has been more and more noticed in the Palestinian context, as historic places represent the Palestinian right to exist in the country and their sovereignty during the long period of Israeli military occupation of their country. Evidence from interviews suggests that Nablus inhabitants have perceived the Old Town largely in ways that enhance their distinctiveness, self-esteem, self-efficacy, and cohesion, which stresses the continuity of the past with the present. Moreover, the city was seen and valued by user groups as representative of their identity first as the Nabulsi community among other Palestinians and also as Palestinians with a distinctive national identity. For example 78 percent referred to this issue in the interviews in this way: "Nablus is my identity, my roots, my culture, and my sign of existence." Correspondents expressed other feelings and values that have strong connections to national resistance to military occupation. For example there is a link between Nablus's historic center and the Palestinian national resistance to the British Mandate (1917–1948) and later to the Israeli occupation (1967–current). This has been associated with feelings of nationalism, bravery, hopes of freedom, heroism, self-sacrifices, courage, and idealism. The "historic value" and "pride" in the built heritage rank highly among residents; there is a powerful link between historic places and memory. On a personal level, people can become deeply attached to places in a way that is critical to their well-being. Whether such places are conserved, transformed, or destroyed, these places are still crucial elements for the maintenance of people's memories and sense of identity. At a group level, certain places are significant because they trigger social memory. Hayden (1995) calls such places "storehouses of memory."

Political and ideological conflicts reinforce the values, meanings, and importance of historic places in people's mental image as resources of self-esteem and confidence. Cultural heritage became a source and symbol of identity that has a special significance for people and places in periods of transition when configurations and meanings are subject to interpretation and change (political and ideological conflict in this particular case). Moreover, it increases people's awareness of the importance and values of cultural heritage.

6

Urbicide in Nablus
2002–2005

The specificity of the complex Palestinian condition and the Nablus urbicide case in 2002 (in comparison to other urbicide cases) is materialized in its distinctive combination of the three forms of urbicide that have been discussed earlier— namely, urbicide by destruction, by construction, and by control. It is argued that the extreme urbicide by destruction in Nablus Old Town followed the atrocious wanton destruction of the urban as a political body and a place of identity. The other specificity of the Nablus urbicide case is presented in the high technology weapons that were used inside the Old Town and caused its destruction. The specific concern of this case is the relationship between spatiality and the constitution of identities in extreme colonial conditions.

The urbicide episode in Nablus can be approached from several interconnected perspectives by investigating the generating mechanisms of destruction, then the actual urbicidal destruction and its consequences and impacts on the material/spatial, socio-economic/cultural and human aspects of urbanity (not all aspects will be analyzed to the same level of detail). Thus, exploring what has been destroyed, how it was destroyed, and what has been produced as a consequence of destruction will take place from two perspectives. The objective dimension of this assessment relies upon charting the physical destruction of the urban tissue (nature, pattern, and mechanisms of destruction).[1]

This chapter stresses the earlier developed assumption that urbicide is not only the physical/spatial destruction of urbanity that embodies urbicide by destruction (direct urbicide). Other forms of urbicide exist in the Palestinian Occupied Territories that are, in effect, the antithesis of destruction and can be, seemingly paradoxically, termed urbicide *by construction and control*. This is embodied in the construction and forceful juxtaposition of the Israeli "colonial urbanity" and reality within the Palestinian urbanity and territoriality through the active Israeli process and policy of settlements projects and their network of bypass roads. This is also evident in the construction of the Israeli military matrix (network) of control from checkpoints, military bases, and the Apartheid Wall. This chapter argues that this form of urbicide by construction and control operates in a twofold manner. First, it generates urbicidal acts within Palestinian space by enclaving the Palestinian territories into small islands, subjugating its natural development and urbanization. Second, it goes on to coordinate actions that cause extreme physical destruction by colonial transformation and the strangulation of Palestinian space.

Historical readings and a review of the Palestinian experiences of urbicide indicate that this phenomenon follows a certain logic of development. This chapter proposes three stages in the urbicide process, beginning with the prerequisite of *politics*, which paves the way for *action*, which then creates the *effect* of urbicide.

The *politics* prerequisites stage can be defined as the preliminary framework that eventually allows the action of urbicide to materialize. This framework consists of a state of ignorance and denial of the "other," manifested in the dehumanization and demonization of the urbanity/spatiality of the "other." This is combined with mechanisms by which this "other" is controlled, a typical complex in colonial subjugation.

The stage of *action* is embodied in the military operations that target and destroy various aspects of urbanity.

The subsequent phase of manifest *effect* is the resulting new physical/spatial condition of the city, which becomes a place, space, and state of exception—a state that alters the human perception and experience of self and place.

Politics: urbicide by construction and control

Surveillance and control in the Occupied Palestinian Territories

David Lyon defines "surveillance" as "the focused, systematic and routine attention to personal details for purposes of influence, management, protection or direction" (Lyon, 2007: 14). This definition stresses the technical and human management objectives of surveillance but does not address other non-technical, spatial, time, and socio-economic aspects that this chapter deems essential in order to understand surveillance in a colonial context. The spatial surveillance that this chapter details below marks a major shift in the Israeli surveillance system and its network of installation. This development started to materialize after the Oslo Agreement of 1992 and gained visibility after the onset of the Al-Aqsa Intifada in 2000. This shift can be observed in surveillance architecture and techniques, spatial and time dimensions, and population management. The newly developed surveillance network incorporates such high-technology elements as cameras, small airplanes (drones), checkpoints, inspections using laser technology, and the Apartheid (or Separation) Wall. This surveillance consequently succeeded in managing the Palestinian subject's spatial inclusion or exclusion from Israeli laws and responsibility. It also manages—and sometimes stops—the spatial flows and activities of the Palestinian subject, impacting significantly on aspects of their daily life. The other shift is observed in the Palestinian subject's experience of the Israeli exercise of power, which is designed to give the impression that power is in Palestinian hands post-Oslo when, in fact, Israel still holds the power. Consequently, this exercise of power and the Palestinians' resistance create several forms and layers of the states or spaces of exception that offer unique spatial experiences. Such spaces of exception, detailed below, go beyond Agamben's definition of exception. Agamben presents the state of exception in diametric opposition to the normal state of affairs (along the lines of inside/outside, sovereign/*homo sacer*, normal/abnormal, private/public, and so on). The state of exception, for him, is one in which a sovereign exercises absolute power over the victim, who cannot resist and who has no rights since all laws are suspended and all notions are confused. These conditions are undoubtedly present in the Palestinian state of exception, yet the Palestinian states/spaces of exception are much broader. They entail all aspects of life.

The Israeli control and surveillance network comprises one part of the larger Israeli occupation machine, which also includes several other cogs: the Jewish settlements project, the destruction of Palestinian villages, the military laws, land confiscation, and so on (see Figure 6.1). The surveillance network is a very important element in that it enables Israel to exercise full control over the territory and resources, and at the same time it manages Palestinians' activity flows in space and time. It is structured around six interconnected systems of surveillance: the Apartheid Wall; territorial subdivision and zoning; checkpoints; Israeli-only bypass roads; military bases; and the special set of military laws that support all other systems. (Jewish settlements are presented in this analysis as being deployed partially for surveillance and control purposes, among other functions.) The surveillance network produces fragmented Palestinian spatial conditions and multi-layered experiences of exception.

Since its military occupation of the Palestinian territories after the 1967 war, Israel has actively implemented surveillance networks and techniques to construct control over the OPT. The control is enforced by Israeli military laws that subjugate Palestinian development and urbanization, and by the network of checkpoints, gates, trenches, and military bases that form the material and spatial matrix that is devastating Palestinian urbanity/territoriality. The case of Nablus city illustrates the different scales that the Israeli surveillance and control network touches, and the many techniques and mechanisms that are used.

Spatial surveillance and control in Nablus

In Nablus, as elsewhere in the OPT, there is surveillance over space. The Israeli authorities have established a surveillance system throughout the occupied territories that penetrates every Palestinian city, village, and camp. This network functions on different scales, from the territorial to the urban, and even to the level of neighborhoods and individual houses during times of military invasion. Since

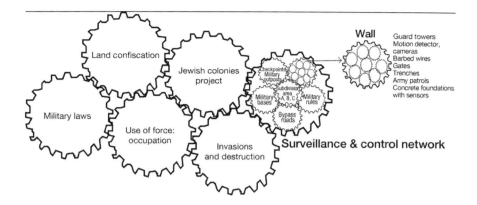

FIGURE 6.1 The Israeli military occupation machine "cogwheels"

Source: Author

the early 1980s, Israel has developed a strategy of control over key Palestinian spatial and physical structures. A network of strategic "points" was established around the main Palestinian urban areas, manifest in settlements, checkpoints, army bases, and industrial parks. These points are connected by the "lines" of the massive system of highways and bypass roads; the Apartheid Wall is seen as a border line. One might hypothesize that this wall embodies a permanent state of exception manifested as an exceptional barrier. The eastern edge of the West Bank, declared by the Israeli authorities to be a combat zone and a "closed military area," can be seen as an edging surface of the territories. The layout of this network of points, lines, and surfaces comprises what Jeff Halper (1999) has defined as the "matrix of control." The physical network reflects the visible material layer of the matrix. The other two layers are invisible. These are projected, first, in the military laws imposed on the Palestinian territories since 1967 and, second, in the use of force—the occupation itself: checkpoints, Israeli dumps, Israeli industrial parks, Israeli holy places, Israeli military bases, and Israeli-only bypass roads (see Figures 3.8 and 3.9 in Chapter 3).

The control points of the previously discussed permanent physical network in Nablus operate on several levels. They are intended to control and enclave the main Palestinian centers, and to limit Palestinian urban growth. The process is recognized, first, by a tight circle of six main settlements with their master-plans and buffer zones established to enclave the area. These have imposed crucial surveillance and monitoring mechanisms on the Palestinian territories since the 1980s.

The second level is an "iron ring" of 117 full-time and partially manned check-points (at the two main city entrances, these are transformed into something more like permanent border crossings), roadblocks, metal gates, earth mounds, earth walls, and trenches that surround the city and its main entrances as shown in Figure 6.2 (UNOCHA, 2005a).

Some points of the physical network change and damage the Palestinian natural landscape and agricultural land by installing factories and industrial parks within Jewish settlements. Of the seven main Israeli industrial parks in occupied Palestine, Burqan, located to the northwest of Nablus, is the largest.[2]

The lines of the physical network are the Apartheid Wall and the bypass roads. They are constructed to facilitate access to and travel between settlements without passing through or connecting with the Palestinian-built inhabited areas. Consequently, the bypass roads often block the development of Palestinian communities in the OPT, creating borders and barriers between communities and routes that were once connected and contiguous. The bypass roads also form clear axes for Israeli control throughout the OPT. These roads are classified as forbidden: Palestinian travel is restricted or entirely prohibited on forty-one roads and sections of roads within the West Bank, including many of the main traffic arteries (B'tselem, 2005). Nablus is surrounded by three main bypass roads: road 60, road 57, and the road connecting E'bal military base with the Shave Shomron settlement.

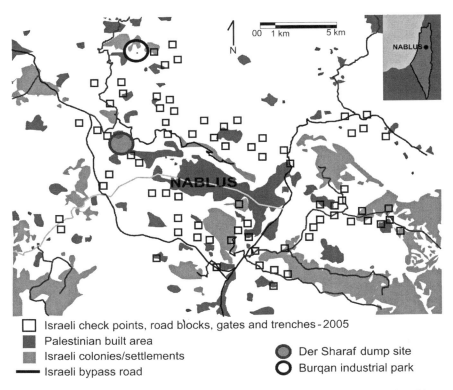

Legend:
- Israeli check points, road blocks, gates and trenches - 2005
- Palestinian built area
- Israeli colonies/settlements
- Israeli bypass road
- Der Sharaf dump site
- Burqan industrial park

FIGURE 6.2 Location of the Israeli physical network of control points around Nablus

Source: Author

The Israeli Apartheid Wall, another line of the physical network, gouges through the Palestinian territories from the west. Its track constitutes another border that confiscates Palestinian land, reproduces and enforces Israeli control, and limits Palestinian urban growth. The wall carves and solidifies the division concept and parallels the other elements of Israeli control, especially the bypass roads and settlements. It can be interpreted as the starkest embodiment, on a material plane, of the logic of a permanent state of exception.

The occupying power reconfigures the urban/neighborhood level during military invasions and special operations. The temporary physical network of control is implemented on the city, sub-district, or neighborhood scale; it is intensified during "temporary"[3] Israeli military incursions into Palestinian cities (in this case Nablus). This network is more often assigned to secure control within target areas; it is made up of military outposts, sniper positions, gates, dividing lines, temporary checkpoints within city borders, and temporary buffer zones.

Snipers and military outposts became common during Israeli invasions into Nablus; Figure 6.3 shows the location of the twenty-eight positions that have been registered inside the Old Town alone.[4] Snipers and forced routes (holes blown through the internal walls of houses to allow access from one building to the next) played important roles as surprise elements in the battle of April 2002; these two techniques were not usually employed during the first intifada. These strategies enabled the Israeli army to control the battlefield with its heavy machinery, and were an important developmental shift in the Israeli military's strategy inside Palestinian urban areas. The nexus between the territorial/urban permanent and temporary physical networks of control—discussed earlier—generates a total Israeli military administration of the Palestinian physical and spatial structure. During military invasions special measures are added to the Israeli surveillance and military control network. Between 2002 and 2005, frequent military Israeli invasions occurred in the Old Town of Nablus and the nearby Balata refugee camp. In all instances, the Israeli army used its existing physical network of control to infiltrate and control urban space and dominate the city. During these events new, temporary physical networks of control were superimposed on the existing networks, consisting of sniper and military outposts, iron gates, temporary roadblocks, trenches, and a dividing system. This system divided Nablus New Town into east and west with a physical demarcation line, called "Tora Bora" by the residents, as shown in Figure 6.4. This comprises a mound of dirt constructed by the Israeli army near the destroyed governorate building (Muqata'a) and the city prison.

Legal and juridical aspects of control in the OPT

The juridical/legal dimension adds another facet to Israeli military and spatial control over the OPT and Nablus. Many laws have been created since the Israeli occupation in 1967 to enforce the occupation machine. Even before 1967, the British "emergency laws" of 1945 were used against both the Jews and the Arabs.

FIGURE 6.3 Location of Israeli military outposts and snipers inside the Old Town during the 2002 military invasion

Source: Author

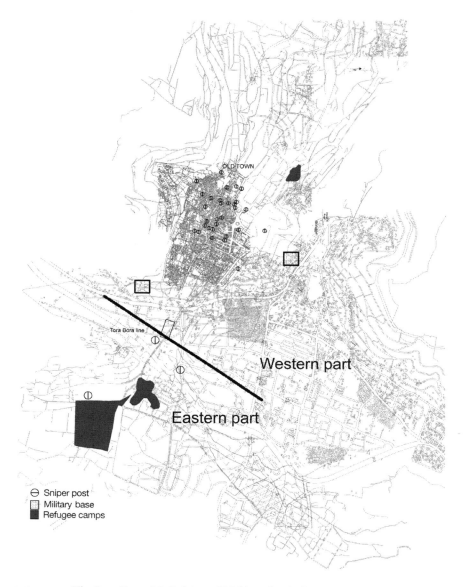

FIGURE 6.4 The Israeli spatial division of Nablus city during the June 2002 invasion

Source: Author

Of these, Law 124 gives the military governor the right, on grounds of "security," to suspend citizens' rights, including freedom of movement: the army needs only to declare a zone forbidden "for security reasons" and Arabs no longer have the right to enter it without the authorization of the military governor. The state of Israel has since used these laws against the Arab population. To justify their retention, the "state of emergency" has not been formally lifted since 1948. Many other laws have been enacted as well, such as planning laws for Palestinian cities and villages, military laws, curfew laws, invasion laws, ownership and construction laws, and other laws that will be discussed in other sections of this chapter.

The innumerable restrictive military laws imposed on the occupied territories give Israel total control and administration of these areas and their inhabitants. They also generate paradoxes in everyday life experience. Siege and mobility laws, for example, have made life unbearable in the OPT since 2000 and the installation of the new checkpoints system. The network of surveillance and control, supported by the elastic and numerous military laws, is designed to control the territories spatially and, at same time, to act as a tool to manage the social and economic flows within the OPT.

Several waves of internal migration have occurred at the level of Nablus city and at the regional level—from Nablus to Ramallah and Bethlehem. These waves generated new patterns of socio-economic and spatial flows and mobility within the occupied territories. Thus, a concentration of certain activities (social, economic, religious, cultural, and administrative) can be observed in the OPT. For example, Nablus is no longer the economic center. Rather, Ramallah has become the open city that supports most regional activities, and is now the Palestinian business, administrative, and cultural center.

Action: military operations and urbicide by destruction

The process created by the politics and mechanism of construction and control enabled the Israeli army to reoccupy and have full authority over Palestinian cities. Between 2002 and 2005, frequent military Israeli invasions occurred in the Old Town of Nablus and the nearby Balata refugee camp. In all these invasions, the Israeli army used its existing physical network of control to infiltrate and control urban space and dominate the city.

The urban fabric of the Old Town core of Nablus (traditional Arabic city morphology) has encouraged the Palestinian resistance to take refuge in its maze-like alleys since the first intifada of 1987. The density and morphology of the Old Town has hampered Israel's capability to control this space and move within it. This, in turn, has led to the mythical construction of Nablus as the "impenetrable city," the "Castle of Resistance," and the "Mountain of Fire"[5] in the Palestinian discourse according to Doumani (2004).

These factors influenced how both the Israeli military and the Palestinian resistance prepared for the event of Israeli military re-occupation in April 2002.

On the Palestinian side, the legendary immunity of Nablus reinforced the perception that the Israeli army would not risk entering the Old Town or try to hold it in any military operation on the ground (Abujidi and Verschure, 2006).

Recalling its previous experience in the Old Town, the Israeli army saw the morphology and structure of Nablus itself as the major line of defense preventing it from controlling the city. Consequently, reorganizing this space and destroying the city became the only possible effective strategy to establish military control over Nablus. This is evident in the Israeli army commander Aviv Kokhavi's view of how the Old Town should be reorganized, despite the fact that it is a densely populated area:

> Kokhavi [chief of military units] was adamant that the only way to "control the flow of terrorists out of the city" is to exercise some basic acts of urban planning, in effect to reorganize the complexities he so admired into a simplified urban layout that will serve his operational needs, and to dig deep trenches all around the city "and [build] a road running across its length from east to west, channeling all access in and out of the city into two check points" one at each side of the city.
>
> (Weizman, 2004a: 6)

The massive damage that occurred in Nablus during these events was explained by the Israeli army and official Israeli media as collateral damage necessary to eradicate the Palestinian resistance. The international and the Israeli human rights organizations gave a contradictory reasoning for destruction. For example, the International Council on Monuments and Sites (ICOMOS) report (2002), the Amnesty International report (2002), and the report of the Israeli organizations for human rights (B'tselem, 2002)[6] identify that the destruction of Nablus Old Town was far from being collateral damage or damage for security reasons; rather it was a wanton deliberate destruction of the Palestinian cultural identity.

Invasion patterns and mechanisms

Four patterns of invasion used during these four years of systematic Israeli military operations are revealed from our fieldwork and research:

1 *Long-term invasion.* This type of invasion normally lasts for several weeks or months. It is typically implemented by imposing a tight siege and curfew on the Old Town core and on large sectors of the city of Nablus. For example, in April 2002, during an invasion that lasted for two weeks, both the old city and the greater Nablus area were under tight siege and a strict curfew. The June 2002 invasion, which lasted for 160 days, was also enforced by means of a continuous curfew imposed on large sectors of the city besides the Old Town. Such long-term invasions take on some of the characteristics of a

prolonged invasion in the more classical sense of spatial domination and control.

2   *Short-term invasion.* This type of invasion lasts from a few days to up to two weeks. It is accompanied by a curfew policy affecting different sections of the urban area besides the Old Town. For example, the December 2003– January 2004 invasion lasted for ten days and imposed a strict curfew on the Old Town, although the attack focused only on the Al-Qaryun quarter.

3   *Overnight incursion.* This type of operation lasts for one night, starting at midnight and concluding at dawn. This model of incursion has become the norm in the nighttime existence of the Old Town of Nablus. Since 2004, overnight incursions have followed a regular pattern: no night can pass without the presence of the IDF in the narrow alleys of the Old Town, a kind of permanent incursion feature of this space.

4   *Daylight incursion lasting several hours.* This mode of incursion lasts for a few hours during the day. A few Israeli jeeps enter the Old Town, either in order to detain some "suspect" from the Palestinian resistance or to create a state of terror among the town's visitors and vendors.[7]

In 2004 the city of Nablus was subjected to two long-term, ten short-term, and countless overnight and daylight incursions. During 2003 alone, Nablus was under curfew for a total of 4,232 hours.[8] In this chapter investigation of the three major invasions and military operation in Nablus will be discussed, with a focus on the April 2002 major operation, the "Operation Defensive Shield":

•   April 2002: A homogenous uniform curfew and siege were enforced on the whole Nablus area (including the Nablus Old Town).
•   June 2002: Different forms of curfew and siege were imposed on different sectors of the Nablus area. This time the city was divided into three different sections: Nablus Old Town, refugee camps and the Greater Nablus Area (New Nablus). This facilitated the military control, by tightening the curfew on specific targeted areas beside the old town.
•   2004 and 2005: Only the Nablus Old Town was targeted, reoccupied and placed under curfew.

2002 military invasion "Operation Defensive Shield"

After a series of suicide bombings in Israeli cities, the military decision to launch "Operation Defensive Shield" and undertake a re-occupation of the Palestinian cities was launched. On the eve of 3 April 2002, the Israeli military troops invaded Nablus city from different accesses and directions. The Israeli army used the main military bases and Israeli settlements surrounding the city as their headquarters from which the military operation took place. During its main attacks, the Israeli army was well equipped with detailed maps and aerial photographs of the Old Town:

Once the IDF surrounded the old city there were five days of fighting concentrating on two parts of the old city: the Kasbah and Al-Yasmeneh. The Israeli soldiers had good street maps and aerial photos of the town; they seemed to know where to go and what houses to enter and search.

(cited in Abu Shmais, 2004)

Forced routes: penetrating through the urban fabric

The Palestinian fighters closed all the entrances of Nablus old city ahead of the Israeli military invasion to the city—hearing the news from previously invaded Palestinian cities such as Ramallah, Bethlehem, and Jenin, they knew it was the turn of Nablus, which was the last to be invaded. The entrances were blocked with sandbags, trash cans were filled with sand, and homemade mines were planted (Hass, 2002). Once the Israeli troops surrounded the old city, they started to penetrate within the urban fabric using the forced route technique as shown in Figure 6.5. One of the tactics[9] the Israeli army used was to drill in and explode holes into the thick walls, moving from one house to another. The soldiers marked these holes with entrances and exits to guide them through (a tactic used before in Balata refugee camp in March the same year and used later in the military invasion of Jenin in 2002). This tactic was used during the invasion of April 2002. Penetration took place from different directions; one route was from the western entrances—from Al Fatimyeh School. This route was not completed; it appears that it was going to take a long time to reach inside the old town using this route, so instead bulldozers were used to clear out the blocked western entrance of Alhadadeen market. Soldiers also entered the city from the southern neighbor- hoods, going through two routes: along Alaqabeh Stairs and through the Alyasmeeneh quarter. From the north they swarmed along Suq Albasal market. It is noticeable that the forced routes technique as documented on the ground and reconstructed from interviews was used mainly in the southern parts of the city, and near the main northern entrance of Alhusien main square outside the old city borders. The northern and eastern entrances were opened by bulldozers:

"They came through the roof, ran down the stairs here and went straight to the children's room—that's right there," says Aisha as I follow her down the narrow staircase leading from the roof terrace to her apartment on the first floor of the family home in the old city of Nablus. "I begged them not to scare the children, but they just laughed in my face and started overturning the furniture, emptying the drawers, making so much noise—the children were crying, they were so frightened. But the soldiers didn't care." We continue to the next room, the living room, where she points to a wall with a built-in bookcase: "And this is where they left. They blew up the wall and continued to our neighbor's house."

(Sune, 2002)

FIGURE 6.5 Forced routes location and direction

Source: Author

Forced routes explosions were a major factor in causing extended damage to several hundred buildings. While the Israeli military narratives claim that these techniques were necessary to avoid Palestinian traps in the city's alleys, a mapping of the routes and the density of the opening inside houses reveal conclusions that contradict such a storyline.

Two openings are typically necessary to go through a building. However, it was found that many buildings had many more openings than necessary to enable the act of merely going through. From filed work we found that 56.7 percent of the 97 surveyed buildings were subject to forced routes bombings of which:

- 19.6 percent had one opening (the other entry occurring through a door or the roof);

- 16.5 percent had two openings;
- 13.4 percent had three openings;
- 4.1 percent had four openings;
- 2.1 percent had five openings;
- 1.0 percent had eight openings.

One would expect the paths of forced routes to follow linear patterns. However, the documented routes were haphazard. Moreover, the direction of these openings as documented in the field reflect that they were chaotic; for example, in one house in which five openings were documented, three of them were used to enter the same house from different directions, and this was found to be the case in many other houses. This may suggest that the soldiers from the engineering unit did not know their location.[10] This seems unlikely knowing the extensive aerial photography, city maps, and GPS technology employed by the Israeli military that would have enabled them to determine their exact locations accurately and quickly. The irrationality of the routes coupled with the large number of unnecessary openings to the structures maximized the damage to significant historic houses, keeping in mind that Nablus lies in a sensitive earthquake zone, and the damage poses long-term and severe structural problems to elements of the Old City. Forced routes played an important role in the psychological war the Israeli forces launched during their invasion.[11] Figures 6.6 and 6.7 give examples of forced routes.

Tools of destruction

During the several main Israeli army invasions, the scale of military personnel and machinery used was massive. Furthermore, the advanced military technology caused tremendous damage to the city's urban tissue. Surveys revealed that the following weaponry was used to inflict serious damage on the urban tissue of Nablus (see also Figure 6.8 and Figures 6.9a, b, and c):

- Explosives and bombs struck 42 percent of the buildings surveyed; 12 percent were totally demolished and 48 percent heavily damaged.
- Apache helicopters attacked and damaged 17 percent of the buildings surveyed; 29 percent were totally destroyed, and 52 percent suffered heavy damage.
- Bulldozers affected 9 percent of the surveyed buildings; 33 percent were totally demolished (sometimes with the inhabitants inside, as in the case of the Alshu'by family, nine members of whom were crushed alive), and 33 percent were heavily damaged.
- F-16 jet fighters struck 6 percent of the surveyed buildings.[12]
- Other types of damage were caused by multiple weapons being used at the same time. For example, houses along the Alaqabeh Stairs suffered severe damage from tank shells and Apache missiles along with F-16 missiles (12 cases were recorded).

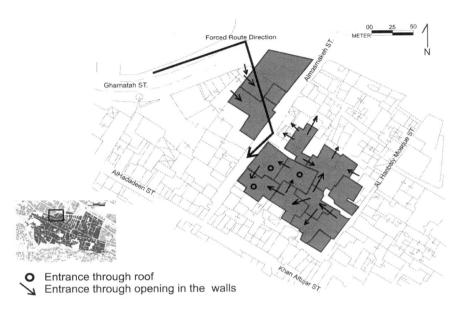

Forced Route Direction

Almasmakeh ST.

00 25 50
METER

N

Gharnatah ST.

AL Hanbaly Mosque ST.

AlHadadeen ST.

Khan Altujar ST.

O Entrance through roof
↘ Entrance through opening in the walls

FIGURE 6.6 Forced route in the Algharab neighborhood

Source: Author

FIGURE 6.7 Images of forced routes location in houses' walls and roofs

Source: Author

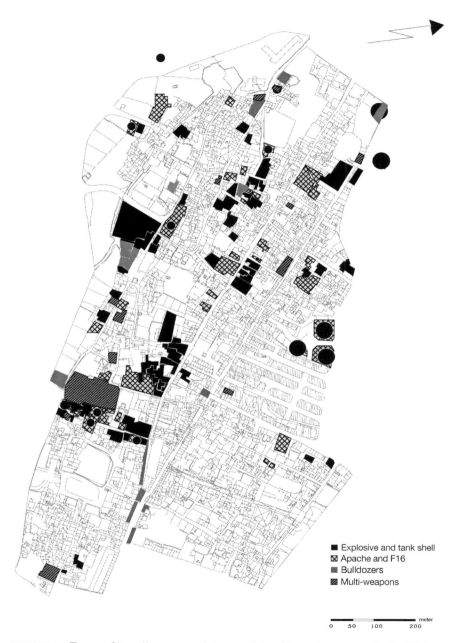

Explosive and tank shell
Apache and F16
Bulldozers
Multi-weapons

meter
0   50   100   200

FIGURE 6.8 Types of Israeli weapons that caused significant destruction in the Old
Town

Source: Author

FIGURE 6.9A, B and C

Images of different Israeli weapons used in the military invasions to Nablus Old Town

Source: Image (a) is from common wikimedia.org (http://upload. wikimedia.org/ wikipedia/commons/ a/a8/Flickr_-_Israel_ Defense_Forces_- _Standing_Guard_ in_Nablus.jpg). Images (b) and (c) courtesy of Abed Qusini

It should be noted that because of the scale of the city, when bulldozers and different types of heavy tanks entered the narrow alleys of the Old Town, they caused severe damage to its infrastructure: 80 percent of the infrastructure was severely damaged during the April 2002 invasion. According to *Alaym Daily News* on 11 April 2002: "Tanks traveling through narrow streets ruthlessly sliced off the outer walls of houses; much destruction of property by tanks was wanton and unnecessary."

Effects: consequence of urbicide on city identity

The effect of the control mechanisms and action of destruction can be seen in the resulting new physical material condition of the city and, on a psychological level, on the residents' perception and experience of this extreme "state of exception" and its repeated reproduction.

Impacts on the material physical reality of the city

Destruction: location and level of destruction

Out of the large number of frequent Israeli army invasions in the Old Town, Operation Defensive Shield in April 2002 is considered the heaviest single operation. It caused damage to 47.5 percent of the housing blocks that structure the Old Town's urban fabric (1,355 out of 2,850) (see Figures 6.10 and 6.11):

*   30000 m^2 (214 multi-family housing blocks), constituting 7.5 percent of the total, were completely demolished.
*   60000 m^2 (428 multi-family housing blocks), constituting 15 percent of the total, were severely damaged.
*   100000 m^2 (713 multi-family housing blocks), constituting 25 percent of the total, suffered light damage.

During other invasions, a shift in the mechanism and location of destruction is evident. Highly focused, limited-scale demolitions targeting specific sections of the city were identified and registered in the fieldwork. As shown in Figure 6.12, the December 2003–January 2004 invasion concentrated mostly on the Al Qaryun quarter of the old city, in and around the seventeenth-century Abdel Hadi Palace, a historic landmark. In total, forty-two buildings were severely damaged, in addition to three that were totally demolished. During the June 2004 invasion, destruction was focused along the main commercial Kasbah of the Old Town, and fifty-two buildings were destroyed. During the January 2005 invasion, the destruction was located in An-Najah Street, adjacent to the western borders of the Old Town, and resulted in the destruction of 162 buildings.

The size and scale of destruction are not always determined by the type of invasion. For example, the scale of destruction resulting from the overnight

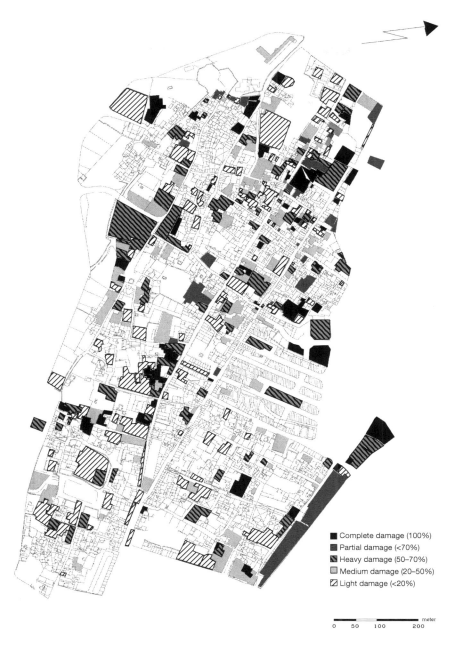

Complete damage (100%)
Partial damage (<70%)
Heavy damage (50–70%)
Medium damage (20–50%)
Light damage (<20%)

meter
0   50   100   200

FIGURE 6.10 Levels of destruction in Nablus Old Town in the 2002 invasion

Source: Author

meter
0   50   100   200

FIGURE 6.11 Location of destroyed buildings in Nablus Old Town in the 2002
invasion

Source: Author

FIGURE 6.12 Location of destroyed buildings in Nablus Old Town during the several invasions between 2002 and 2005

Damage in April–June 2002 (860 buildings)

Damage in December 2003 (42 buildings)

Damage in June 2004 (52 buildings)

Damage in August 2004 (8 buildings)

Damage in January 2005 (186 buildings)

Source: Author

incursion of January 2005 was larger than that of the short-term invasion of January 2004, which lasted ten days. Moreover, a repeated rhythm in invading and destroying the same buildings during the several invasions was registered, as shown in Figure 6.13, with each invasion accompanied by destruction, looting, and vandalism.[13] In Nablus, 21.6 percent of the surveyed buildings reported one invasion; 27.8 percent reported two invasions; 21.6 percent reported three invasions; 13.4 percent four invasions; 3.1 percent five invasions; 3.1 percent six invasions; and 3.1 percent reported eight invasions.

Many of the repeatedly invaded houses were restored after the first invasion or are presently being reconstructed. Repeated invasions have, in turn, increased the extent of damage, something that has been very little documented. Furthermore, this pattern increased the budget needed to secure and restore what has been repeatedly destroyed. Thus, the quality of restoration and reconstruction has been significantly affected, as reconstruction projects become rescue projects, thus adding another destructive factor to the city identity and its cultural significance. Here one sees what a "permanent state of exception" can mean translated into repeated invasions and destruction.

Typology and significance of destroyed buildings

- *Residential buildings* were the most heavily damaged among those surveyed; they made up 70 percent of the surveyed sample and were mainly concentrated along the southern perimeter of the Old Town. Seventy multi-family dwellings and *hush* were damaged, among them some very important and well-known *hush* of prominent families. For example, Hush Al-Jitan, an early nineteenth-century building, was badly damaged by Apache rockets; Hush Alsalu's and Hush An-Naser, eighteenth-century complex buildings, were destroyed by tank rockets. Three historic palaces also suffered from different degrees of damage, including the Abdel Hade Palace, which was heavily shelled and damaged by tanks, Apache rockets, and dynamite during invasions in both 2002 and 2003 (see also Figure 6.14, Figure 6.15 and Figure 6.16).
- *Religious buildings* constitute 8 percent of the surveyed sample. Five of the nine historic mosques suffered extensive damage.[14] Two churches dating back to the sixteenth century suffered moderate damage, while the only Samaritan[15] synagogue in the Old Town was completely destroyed.
- *Traditional industrial buildings*[16] made up 7 percent of the surveyed sample. Four of the thirty operational soap factories were destroyed: two dating back to the seventeenth and eighteenth centuries, covering an area of 1000 m², were completely demolished by F-16 jet fighters, and another two were totally burned down.
- *Commercial buildings* constituted 3 percent of the destroyed buildings. They represent shops in the traditional covered *souqs* (markets) along the two main commercial streets and the streets leading to the entrances of the city.

FIGURE 6.13 Repeated rhythm of invasion during 2002–2005

Source: Author

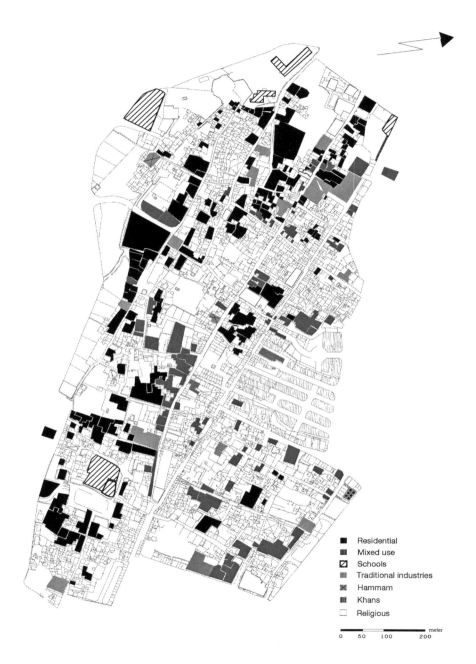

Residential
Mixed use
Schools
Traditional industries
Hammam
Khans
Religious

meter
0   50   100   200

FIGURE 6.14 Typology of destroyed buildings in the 2002 invasion

Source: Author

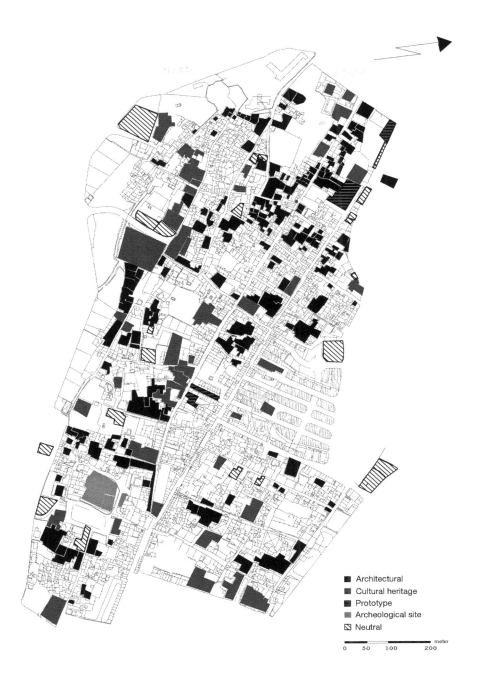

Architectural
Cultural heritage
Prototype
Archeological site
Neutral

meter
0   50   100   200

FIGURE 6.15 Significance of destroyed buildings in the 2002 invasion

Source: Author

FIGURE 6.16A Seventeenth-century Abdelhadi Palace destroyed during the 2002 Israeli invasion

Source: Courtesy of Abed Qusini

FIGURE 6.16B
Seventeenth-century Hammam Alshifa, destroyed during the 2002 Israeli invasion

Source: Courtesy of Abed Qusini

FIGURE 6.16C Nineteenth-century Alfatimye school, destroyed during the 2002
Israeli invasion

Source: Courtesy of Abed Qusini

FIGURE 6.16D Nineteenth-century traditional soap factory destroyed during the 2002
Israeli invasion

Source: Courtesy of Abed Qusini

Thirteen shops were badly damaged in Souq Alhadadeen, an important market for traditional blacksmiths near the western entrance to the city.

- *Educational buildings* represented 3 percent of total damaged structures. Three schools[17] inside and around the Old Town were documented with damage ranging from minimal (the Jamal Abdel Naser School) to heavy (the nineteenth-century Alfatemyeh School).
- *Mixed-use buildings* constituted 8 percent of the damaged buildings. These structures were residential and commercial, and were located mainly along the commercial streets of the Old Town.
- *Recreational buildings* constituted 1 percent of the damaged buildings surveyed. Among these were *hammam* (Turkish baths), such as Hammam Alshifa, a seventeenth-century complex that was severely damaged by Apache missiles.

Infrastructural damage: unavailability of basic services

According to a survey done by the Institute of Community and Public Health Birzeit University (Halileh, 2002), Nablus suffered serious damage to its entire infrastructure (see Figure 6.17). For example, the report indicated that the electrical current cuts during the re-invasion and curfew had a negative impact not only on family life but on commercial enterprises as well, with reports of substantial loss of food items that required refrigeration. In their survey, 47 percent of respondents (154 household) reported living without electricity for most or all of the period of re-invasion; 39 percent of households reported piped water shortages most or all of the time, a rate similar to that of Ramallah, again due to shelling, bombing, shooting and vandalism affecting the different levels of the water system; 39 percent reported water shortages for part of the time. During such a period, people usually rely on water wells. Of the total who had phones, 4 percent had their telephone lines cut all of the time, 7 percent most of the time, 15 percent some of the time, and the rest did not face problems with phones. On the other hand, the majority of households (84 percent) reported no problems with sewage disposal, with the rest reporting blown-up sewage pipes mostly and cesspools not being emptied, mostly reporting the problem of un-emptied garbage containers, as municipal services came to a halt during the period. Several families reported not being able to get the garbage out of the house, with garbage piling up inside their homes. On the whole, given that the areas that were mostly affected by the destruction were hardest hit in terms of loss of electricity, water and phones combined, family lives must have been very difficult indeed, especially among families with young children and elderly and disabled members.

Impacts on cultural buildings and traditions

Antiquities enshrine the collective memory of humankind as much as they preserve the cornerstones of cultural identities of the people to whose history they bear witness, and whose property they must remain. Many important buildings that

FIGURE 6.17A and B
Severe damage to
infrastructure inside
Nablus Old Town during
the 2002 invasion

Source: Courtesy of Abed
Qusini

represent Nablus's icons of identity have been destroyed by the Israeli military machine. For example, Alkhadra mosque, a twelfth century crusader church, was severely damaged by tank shells, and 85 percent of the building has been affected. Other examples are the Kan'an and Tuqan soap factories (built in the sixteenth and seventeenth centuries) and Hammam Alshifa', a seventeenth-century bathhouse that was severely damaged by Apache rockets. In the face-to-face interviews during the 2004 survey, 85 percent of the surveyed respondents stressed that Nablus Old Town was destroyed within a systematic operation targeting the Palestinian cultural identity as an important part of the Palestinian national identity. They claimed that the historical image of the city has been extremely affected by the tremendous amount of damage and by the different gaps erected within the city's urban tissue:

> Israel's destruction of many homes and public buildings in the madinas in Nablus and al Khalil (Hebron) appears systematic, suggesting a possible intent to efface those urban manifestations of Palestinian cultural heritage.
> (London Middle East
> Institute, 2002)

Several Nabulsi cultural customs have been affected by the frequent invasions and destruction of the Old Town. For example, 60 percent of the interviewed sample pointed out that their social network has been strongly affected by the continuous siege of the city. Their declining economic situation has made it impossible for them to meet the demands of some of their social activities. For example, important social festivities have been cancelled in many Nabulsi homes,[18] and social networks have been significantly touched by the insecurity presented by the frequent overnight invasions and long curfew periods. Ordinary visits by family, neighbors, and friends are disappearing from the Old Town's social tissue. Other cultural and economic patterns are also changing and diminishing in the Old Town. Ramadan shopping traditions have been missed in the last five years; "Alsuq nazel," the daily Ramadan traditional bazaar that has been organized by the municipality in the main square for hundreds of years has been cancelled for the above-mentioned reasons. Hence the Palestinian cultural identity has lost an important essence of itself manifested not only in the destruction of the cultural artifact and the built environment: this deprivation has extended to the loss of important cultural and social customs and traditions, and all that they hold.

Impacts on the spatial visual reality of the city

The widespread destruction had a significant impact on the urban tissue (the built and open spaces) in many ways:

1   There is a predominant balance between the geometry of the streets and spaces and their forms inside the Old Town. The agglomeration of buildings that is

a strong characteristic of the Old Town has been strongly affected by the many demolished buildings, consequently creating gaps within the built areas and disturbing the patterns of building fabric and open spaces that used to be composed and connected to each other. As a result, the town's figure plan now suffers from the incoherent relationship of urban solids to voids, open space and building mass. The interrelationships between urban solid and voids are perceivable through the continuity of physical structure that composes the urban tissue; this has been strongly affected by the damage, especially in the southern and western neighborhoods (see Figure 6.18), and is also evident in the façades.

2   Complete dense buildings complexes disappeared from the urban tissue, these complexes sometimes defining the old town's border line. An example is AlShu'by *hush* on Ras Al'en Street. The destruction of this complex ruined the continuity of the building border line that defined the Old Town from the southern entrance. Sometimes these blocks defined a node or street edge— the soap factories, for example, as shown in Figure 6.19.

3   Each quarter is an entity in itself with special characteristics that give it its own image and identity. This special identity makes it easy to recognize each neighborhood while moving inside the old town. For example, Alysmeneh quarter is known for its asymmetric sloped dark alleys, while Alqaryun is very famous for its large number of soap factories, while Alhabaleh quarter is known for its late nineteenth century buildings. The damage and destruction of many buildings have indeed influenced this neighborhood identity. For example, the destruction of an important building block of the two soap factories in Alghrab and the destruction of many houses in Alysmeneh has affected the layout of its dark street alleys.

4   The division system in the urban tissue varies in size and area due to variation in land use. The clustering system of *hushs* and building groups strengthen spatial flow inside the old town, which facilitates mobility from one roof to another creating a parallel spatial system. The primary circulation system defines the edges of residential quarters (the smaller units of neighborhoods) while the secondary system provides access into the residential quarters and individual *hush*. The spatial reconfiguration imposed on the Old Town by the massive destruction of many key buildings cracked and disintegrated these neighborhood-defining edges of the primary circulation routes, which can be seen as their primary defensive frontline. This is evident in the destruction of the two soap factories, which loosened the Algharb quarter as one ensemble and its definition as one strong compact unit. The quarter is now divided into two units by the newly created enormous space; in addition, the quarter's border line separating it from the Alysmeneh quarter no long exists. This new space not only exposed the Alqharb quarter to the main street of Gharnatah; it has also exposed the Alysmeneh quarter to the outer Old Town border. Thus the destruction of the two soap factories broke down a major characteristic

meter
0   50   100   200

FIGURE 6.18 New spatial reality (new spaces) inside Nablus Old Town during the
            2002 invasion

Source: Author

FIGURE 6.19 Image of two destroyed soap factories and the new created spaces

Source: Author

of the town's neighborhoods of being inaccessible to strangers who do not know very well how to maneuver within the town's narrow dark alleys (see Figures 6.19 and 6.20).

5   It further broke the social network created and facilitated via the clustering and agglomeration of buildings that in times of crises such as invasions and curfew helped in creating alternative spatial order for socio-spatial network and solidarity activities.

6   On the level of the façade the new emerging open spaces from destroyed buildings are strongly evident along the main façades of the main Kasbah and commercial streets such as An-Nasser Street. The town's skyline and street line has been strongly affected by the new emerging gaps. The succession of interacted visual sequences through the alleys and streets forms the integration of architectural vocabulary—the porches, the gateways, the variety of functions in the old neighborhoods—and the glimpse of minarets towers helps to enhance the value of the urban space and creates a varied urban experience, while following the changing atmosphere between different urban land use zones, which reflects a sense of rhythm and progression. This sense of rhythm and progression has been cut out by the creation of new spaces along the main streets facades that used to compose a continuous border line (see Figure 6.21).

FIGURE 6.20 A detail of the destruction of the two soap factories and the new spatial fragmentation of the neighborhood

Source: Author

Impacts on the socio-economic condition of the city at different levels

The Governorate of Nablus has been exceedingly affected by the Israeli tight siege because many significant economic establishments and factories exist in Nablus. According to the estimates of donor groups, the private sector suffered the most, with repairs estimated at a total of US$ 100 million, of which US$ 50 million was for commercial premises (damage to buildings and equipment and spoilage/loss of inventory). Significant damage also occurred to roads (US$ 70 million), private housing (US$ 63 million) and ancient cultural sites (US$ 52 million), as well as to electricity and water networks, schools and clinics (Donor Support Group, 2002).

From the centre to the margin

Nablus was the main hub linking the northern governorates of Jenin, Tulkarm, and Qalqilya with the central governorates of Ramallah and Jerusalem. Until 2001,

North facade of soap factories before destruction

North facade of soap factories before destruction

FIGURE 6.21 Impacts of urbicide on Nablus Old Town on the sense of rhythm and progression

Source: Author

one public transportation centre in Nablus provided services to and from all northern governorates, as well as Ramallah to the south.

Upon the implementation of heightened closure policies in 2001, it became difficult for travelers from the north to reach Nablus. After January 2002, according to an OCHA report (UNOCHA, 2005a), it was more difficult to leave Nablus for Ramallah. Taxi drivers from the north and villages to the west of Nablus started going directly to Ramallah by using tertiary roads to circumvent Nablus. The bulk of the movement restrictions—aggravated by the presence of fourteen Israeli settlements and twenty-six outposts around Nablus city—remain and in some cases are tightening. A system of permits and restricted roads continues to limit the movement of people and goods. The West Bank Barrier has made access to Israeli markets for Nablus goods more difficult.

In addition, "flying checkpoints" often appear at unexpected times or places, forcing travelers to wait between a few minutes and several hours, sometimes making it impossible to reach the intended final destination on the same day. Required travel times have tripled—and that excludes delays at checkpoints and impassable road sections that must be traversed by foot.

To cope with the strict closure of Nablus city, some services and businesses have relocated to smaller towns and rural communities in order to improve access for those outside the city. New shops and services have opened in rural communities, providing goods for local productive activity, such as seeds and fertilizers, and services such as veterinarian services, fuel and freight transportation, which reflect the greater reliance on local agricultural activities.

Facing problems in transporting supplies and finished goods in and out of the city, businesses have opened storage warehouses outside the city that are freer to facilitate movement. A B'tselem Report presents the impossibility of normal life activities due to the strict Israeli military practices to hinder mobility, surveillance, and control:

> This is a systematic destruction of all semblance of normal life through a complicated and extensive web of enforcement from passes, identity numbers, permits, routine interrogations, road blocks that require leaving home in the night to get to work, to surveillance and political assassinations.
>
> (B'tselem, 2002)

As a result of the strict siege the permanent checkpoint and closure policy, and frequent Israeli military invasions, a shift in shopping patterns has been noticed in Nablus Old Town and in Nablus commercial centre in general. Fewer people from outside the Old Town or Nablus come to buy their goods from the city, especially if they can find an alternative place outside the city. Furthermore, shoppers do not penetrate deep in the city to pursue their goods; they try to be near the old city borders to find the chance to run away in the case of a sudden Israeli military invasion. Shopping and commercial activities are therefore more concentrated around the main entrances of the Old Town with fewer activities in the main commercial *casaba* such as Khan Altujar moreover commercial activities are rare in An-Naser Street, which used to be a major commercial street before the Israeli military invasions. The Old Town's economic activities depend on shoppers from outside Nablus city (people from other Palestinians cities and villages in Nablus governorate). The strict siege and military invasion minimized accessibility to the Old Town, which now depends on the local community for its commercial and economic activities. Another fact is the absence of many seasonal markets that used to fill the Old Town with agricultural products—for example, the figs market, the olives market, and the grapes market. The insecurity and the frequent invasions make it difficult for many villagers to come and sell their products in the Old Town in the way they used to.

Migration

As a result of the frequent invasions and destruction many vacant buildings are registered inside the Old Town: around 5.2 percent of the documented buildings (twenty-two buildings) were vacant at the time of the fieldwork (see Figure 6.22). Varied reasons were identified for their vacant state: either they had not been restored after the invasion, or they had serious structural problems and required major reconstruction work entailing a large outlay of resources.

Many of the people interviewed declared that the insecurity presented by the daily and overnight invasions was a major reason behind the evacuation of the Old Town. Families with young boys prefer to move outside the Old Town because they are afraid their children will be arrested or get killed, although it is more expensive to rent outside the Old Town. Moving outside the Old Town has meant for many living apart from the rest of their family members and neighbors, as well as being far from the commercial centre. Many families who moved out later decided to go back to their houses inside the Old Town; being outside the Old Town and one's neighborhood was a difficult experience, as many returnees reported.

On the level of Nablus city in general, many employees in the Palestinian ministries that are located in Ramallah moved from Nablus city and settled down in Ramallah city to avoid the long waiting hours at checkpoints. Many small merchants moved their business to Ramallah city as well. This caused a migration pattern from Nablus Old Town to Nablus suburbs to be registered and another migration pattern from Nablus city to Ramallah city as the emerging main administrative and commercial centre after the second intifada.

Impacts on the human experience of the city

> *What we do—this is not "living." We cannot play, pray, work, study, marry, and they say we are the terrorists. This is the terror—24 hour, 7 day a week, everywhere. Nobody even knows this is a weapon. But it is killing us all, in our bodies and our minds—slowly amd quietly. There are no explosions and no*

FIGURE 6.22 Location of vacant buildings inside Nablus Old Town due to repeated invasions and destruction

Source: Author

blood—this is why the world doesn't see it. And when we scream [hand gestures for suicide bomb], nobody understands why.

("Curfew in Palestine," cited in Abujidi and Verschure, 2006)

The process and action that pave the way for creating the phenomenon of "urbicide" changes, distorts, and inverts the inhabitants' experience of their city. These events change what has come to be considered "normal" since the beginning of the Israeli occupation. Since the 1948 and 1967 wars, Palestinians within and outside the Palestinian Territories live in a permanent state of exile from what was once "Palestine."

This experience of estrangement is further reinforced by the state of emergency imposed since the establishment of the State of Israel. This state of emergency (originating from the British laws of 1945)[19] regulates and subjugates the Palestinian people's notion of normal life, an experience that hinders their differentiation between normal and emergency, civil and military, and public and private space.

During times of invasion, the exception of occupation in the Palestinian Territories since 1967 has become "normal" in comparison to the newly imposed exception established by Israeli army incursions, curfews, and the resulting destruction.

This new extreme and exaggerated exception is evident in the collective experience of detention and death, and of long periods of curfew, house raids, shelling, and building demolition. This extreme is realized in the presence of an existence of bare survival, living on the edge, where human rights and dignity no longer exist, and profound "existential humiliation" is a recurrent experience:

> When all is said and all is done, sovereign power is the control of bare life: the authority over the citizen's life and death, a concept expressed in the state of exception . . . Hence the sovereign power not only upholds the law, but also, and above all else, maintains the right to suspend the law and declare the state of exception.
>
> (De Cauter, 2004: 156, citing Agamben, 1998)

The eradication of normalcy

In both the "normal" state of exception of the 1967 Israeli occupation of the Palestinian Territories and the "extreme" state of exception during Israeli military incursions and prolonged invasions, the Palestinian body is regulated. It is systematically rendered vulnerable by the presence of a surveillance and domination that penetrates all aspects of daily life, controlling where one can travel, where and how one can work, whether one can import or export produce, medical supplies, and cooking fuel—and even whether one is safe in one's own home.[20]

Ahmed, a 20-year-old student at An-Najah University, describes the long days of curfew and regular invasion:

What is normal? Long days locked alone or with some strangers, or neighbors forced into your house. Left with very limited space, no basic services, little food, insecure, and anxious, waiting for something to happen, uncertain what it can look like, the unknown; the unexpected. Looking for few hours of relief, like a prisoner's temporary release every day for a walk in the backyard of the prison . . . We have forgotten normal.

(Interview with author, 4 August 2004)

Some 20,000 people—namely, the inhabitants of the Old Town—remained under almost continuous curfew during the June 2002 invasion, with inhabitants confined indoors for over 160 days and nights, apart from very occasional days when the restrictions were lifted for a few hours. When the curfew was lifted for a few hours, what at first seemed a relief became a source of stress, as everyday activity had to be squeezed into four short hours. The dilemma for each Palestinian, every time the curfew was lifted, was deciding what priorities to set during these four hours: going to work, going to school, paying the doctor a visit, visiting relatives, getting engaged or married, going to funerals of loved ones, taking the children for an outing, shopping for groceries, or doing a million other things that normal people can do.

A'reen Abdullah from Nablus was in such a hurry as she left her house when the curfew was lifted for the second time that she forgot to take her identity card. On her way home and a mere 100 meters from her house, she was stopped by an Israeli military patrol that demanded to see her ID. According to A'reen:

"One of the soldiers came very near to me and then suddenly took my baby out of my arms. Abdullah is only seven months old, and the soldier held him in one hand and raised him up in the air—I was terrified he would drop him. The soldiers told me they would keep the baby while I went home to get my ID, but I refused. I felt I had lost my baby forever and began to scream and weep. So did Abdullah. The soldier kept asking me if I was scared from him and I told him yes. They insisted I went home and got my ID but I told them I would never take one step away from my baby." Eventually Abdullah, the seven-month-old baby, was returned safely to his mother.

(B'tselem, 2002)

The collective experience of detention and the killing of loved ones highly affected people's collective memory of the 2002 Israeli military invasion and destruction of the city. The total number of casualties in Nablus amount to 512 deaths[21] (66 children—see DCI/PS, 2001), 3,095 injured, and thousands of detainees since the year 2000 (up to 2005).

The Israeli military invasion of 2002 became a turning point for the city and its inhabitants' personal experiences, consequently becoming a historical event and reference of the city in its inhabitants' collective memory. It is typical to hear the inhabitants say "before the big invasion" we used to do so and so (referring to "Operation Defensive Shield").

Nablus the inverted city: domestic space as military domain
(inverse geometry)

The notion of privacy disappears during times of invasion, as public and private are reconfigured by military order. A private house can be the target of a search operation, can be used for interrogation, or can be transformed arbitrarily into a "temporary" military outpost—challenging notions of ownership and privacy on the grounds of "security." The Israel army has a unique power to immediately transform any portion of urban or rural space by declaring it a "military area."

Giorgio Agamben describes this issue in his definition of the state of exception:

> It is obvious that we frequently can no longer differentiate between what is private and what public, and that both sides of the classical opposition appear to be losing their reality. The state of exception consists, not least, in the neutralization of this distinction.
>
> (Agamben, 2004: 612)

Many public buildings, such as schools and mosques, are transformed into temporary shelters for the city's displaced inhabitants. Another issue is the curfew laws that confine people to the interior of their houses, regulating the use of public space outside. The laws also restrain the use of private houses, making looking from a window or sitting on a balcony a risk in itself. Thus most intimate private space is invaded and redefined here:

> Go inside, he ordered in hysterical broken English. Inside! I am already inside! It took me a few seconds to understand that this young soldier was redefining inside to mean anything that is not visible, to him at least. My being "outside" within the "inside" was bothering him. Not only is he imposing a curfew on me, he is also redefining what is outside and what is inside within my own private sphere.
>
> (Khoury, 2004)

During invasions and military operations, the inhabitants of the city can undergo traumatic experiences by witnessing the events of shelling, house demolition, and confinement. For example, the experience of positioning military posts and snipers in family homes was extremely painful for all family members. Feelings of humiliation and anger, loss of dignity, privacy, and ownership—all come in a moment and leave their traces in the memory:

> It was more than I could bear to think of them using our bathrooms, or opening my drawers and searching and messing our clothes or personal items . . . Total strangers, they have access to all the rooms . . . they help themselves to all of our belongings; they see themselves in our mirrors and use our sheets and towels. In a way, it was almost being violated: our private

lives and intimate secrets had been forcibly opened to strangers, and we were utterly helpless to do anything about it ... feeling hopeless and helpless hurts. It hurts mentally and physically.

(Abu Shmais, 2004)

In these times of emergency, the city is forced to surrender its urban tools and imitate the life of a refugee camp, transformed into an enclave beyond any juridical sphere. Spatial normalcy and legal structuring are, in effect, "suspended" within the temporal frame created by an invasion.

Palestinian private space has been intruded on and targeted, not only to destroy people's sense of place and privacy, as Falah and Flint (2004) have argued, but also as part of the larger Israeli Palestinian struggle over land and water. Sovereignty over space is an important element in achieving geopolitical aims intrinsic to the longer-term policy imperative within the geopolitical colonial imaginary that guides the Israeli nation-state.

A powerful example illustrating the eradication of the meaning and sense of private versus public space was also noted in the forced route openings. They played an important role in the psychological war the Israeli army launched during their invasion. The *psychological* effect of these routes was to eradicate the sense of security within the Nablus community and for the Palestinian resistance fighters in the city. The routes also alarmed the conservative Nablus community by breaking down families' privacy, exposing to the neighbors or to the streets an invasion of their sphere of dignity. In an interview, Um Lutfy from Alyasmeneh quarter put it bluntly:

We are not any more mastureen [persons with privacy and pride], soldiers can appear in any moment from the door, from the neighbour's wall or from the ceiling. We have to use our head cover all the time.

(interview with author, 25 August 2004)

Threat is constant where spatiality is totally invaded and constantly open to unexpected violation.

Impacts on the perceptions and meanings of the city: colonized geographies

When the Israeli invasion took place, people recalled the events of 1948 in an attempt to comprehend and imagine what the situation might turn into as it evolved. Um Omar, a refugee from the 1967 war, a mother of five children, and a resident of the Old Town in Nablus, recalls the Israeli incursion into the city:

We were prepared that the Israelis would drive us out to the borders as they did in 1948, and 1967. I still remember the stories my mother used to tell me about their sufferings and humiliation, and decided I'd rather die here in my house with my five children than leave. We learned our lesson; we will not leave our country. We will not be refugees again.

(Um Omar, interview with the author, 28 August 2004)

Even the local population's collective memory of their own city becomes distorted and sometimes erased. Upon returning to Nablus after only a year's absence, it was difficult to remember how some areas had looked prior to the destruction. It was a frustrating experience to be unable to reconstruct an old image of the city prior to its destruction.

During the survey and in the mental image reconstruction exercise conducted, many children from the Al Qaryun quarter were asked to draw mental sketches of the Old Town in Nablus before the invasion. The result was shocking. Not only could they not remember what the damaged areas had looked like, they were unable to express anything other than damage, shootings, explosions, and ruins[22] (see Figure 6.23). Thus destruction became the new milieu of memory for future Nabulsi generations.

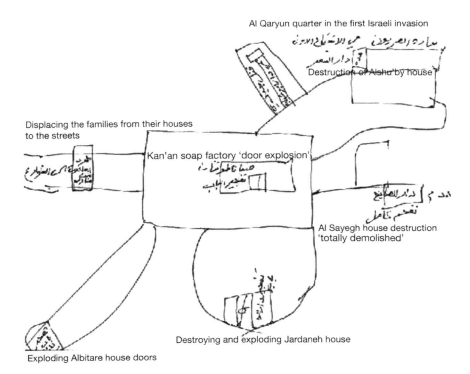

FIGURE 6.23 Al Qaryun children's mental map of Nablus Old Town after the 2002 invasion

Source: Author

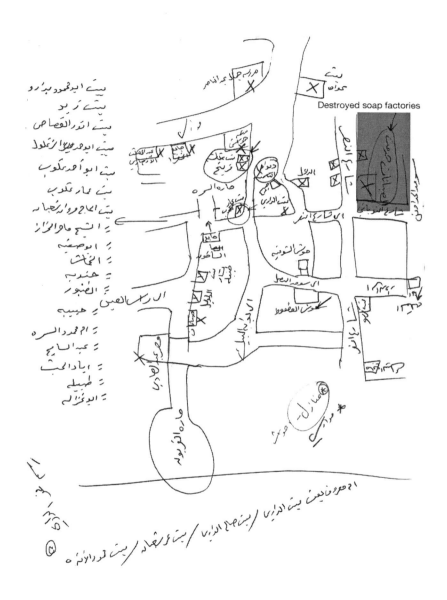

FIGURE 6.24 Example of mental maps drawn by Nablus Old Town inhabitants

Source: Interview with the author

Moreover, the narratives of many interviewees, especially the children, describe the pre-invasion Old Town as though it were a dream, a lost world from the past, an imagined metaphorical paradise. The Old Town in Nablus leaves the realm of reality and enters the discourse of legends:

> Nablus zaman [in the past]. Do you know the heaven? It was a heaven, full of people, parties, zaman it was better, it was like a palace, we could play, be free, family and friends' visits were very often. Now everything is changing . . . Ruins, soldiers, we are scared, in the first invasion we saw the bulldozers destroying our neighbor's house and crushing them under its wheels . . . We love the old town, we want to stay here.
>
> (Al Qaryun children, interview with the
> author, 4 September 2004)

Sarah Mehrag describes the links between places and memory in what she defines as *identicide*:

> The localization of memory on the material is what negotiates its survival, and by removing the material we begin to erase memory. Without landscape to trigger memory, there is no link with the past, and it recedes beyond our collective memory.
>
> (Mehrag, 2001: 91)

New mental map, perceptions and new elements of the city identity

The cognitive map of the Old Town was tested and sketched by the Old Town user groups as we saw in Chapter 4. It was not possible for the respondents to sketch their mental map of the Old Town after destruction at the same moment as they sketched it before destruction, so we depended mainly on the correspondents' descriptions of the Old Town after destruction and how the correspondents saw these changes. Around 35 percent of the correspondents unconsciously located the destroyed buildings on their sketch of the Old Town before destruction, as shown in Figure 6.24. This is a strong sign of how *destruction becomes the new milieu of people's memory.*

Notes

1 Data presented in this chapter is obtained mainly from two pieces of fieldwork in the old city of Nablus in 2003 and 2004, when 180 buildings were surveyed with structured inventory forms plus the compilation of the surveys done by the Nablus municipality. A total of 152 interviews were conducted with the old city user groups, inhabitants, vendors, and visitors, and 103 mental map sketches were made. Reconstructing and relocating the forced routes depended on the inhabitants' stories in some places where accessibility was not possible; thus the accuracy is not absolute.

2 It encompasses 80 factories and generates 810,000 m^3 of wastewater per year (Ganor, 2005).

3 What was announced as temporary is turning out to be the rule, projected in the regular invasions into Palestinian cities, especially in the Nablus area.

4 The Israeli army normally occupies strategic buildings, forcing the inhabitants either to evacuate to neighboring buildings or to stay in one room of the house (or one apartment, in the case of multi-family buildings) along with the soldiers.

5 This last appellation derives from a local legend that Napoleon, upon approaching Nablus, met his defeat when the inhabitants set forests and olive groves ablaze, burning the French soldiers. The legend reverberates to one of the traditions for which the Nablus region is famous: as a center of resistance to outside control. This tradition was manifested in the defeat of invading Egyptian troops in 1834; in its role as the beating heart of the Great Revolt against the British (1936–1939); and, finally, in its centrality in the two intifada uprisings against the Israeli occupation (Doumani, 2004).

6 See also other reports by other institutes at www.btselem.org/download/200207_defensive_shield_eng.pdf.

7 This was repeatedly reported in the interviews; people complained of such invasions hindering the commercial activities and normal life inside the Old Town, in turn discouraging people from shopping there. During our survey, we witnessed ten such invasions. The soldiers in their jeeps began throwing around the goods in front of shops; more often, they began shooting for no apparent reason.

8 Numbers are calculated from the weekly invasion reports at the website of the Palestinian Academic Society for the Study of International Affairs, Jerusalem, www.passia.org.

9 Moving through buildings to avoid the booby traps set by the Palestinian resistances declared by Israeli army officials.

10 For example, in the Alaqabeh Stairs quarter, inhabitants mentioned that the soldiers kept coming in to their house and going out to the street, the stairs, and the neighboring houses (several times) from different directions as going in a loop.

11 From the distributed statements of warnings to the residents that they would be vulnerable to attacks if they hosted any member of the resistance or facilitated their movement, to the continuous night shelling, to the vandalism inflicted on inhabitants' possessions and furniture. See reports about IDF human rights violation at www.btselem.org or www.amnestyinternational.org.

12 F-16 fighters were an important tool during these invasions; they provided air cover to the Israeli Army ground units, making it impossible for Palestinian fighters to move from one place to another over the roofs.

13 As reported by the interviewed families, as well as by human rights organizations such as B'tselem and Amnesty International.

14 For example, the Israeli Army destroyed the eastern wall of the Salah Mosque, previously a Byzantine church, and the Al Khadra Mosque, which dates back to the twelfth century and was previously a Crusader church.

15 The Samaritans can be considered the only Palestinian Jews in the post-1948 era who are, in effect, indigenous.

16 That is, traditional soap factories that are part of the heritage of the city of Nablus and its long cultural tradition.

17 Although the total number of schools within and around the Old Town area has reached five, only three were documented in the survey.

18 Sha'buneyh, the gathering of Sh'abn month (the Arabic month that is two months before Ramadan), where the head of the family invites all the women in his family to spend few days in his house; sometimes this invitation is limited to one central dinner. The same can be reported of the two major feasts in the Nabulsi Muslim community—celebrations are now limited to family visits that sometimes do not take place when they coincide with the Israeli military invasion to the city and the strict curfew.

19 In the "emergency laws" passed in 1945 by the British against the Jews and Arabs, Law 124 gives the military governor the right, this time on the pretext of "security," to suspend

all citizens' rights, including freedom of movement. The army only has to declare a zone forbidden "for security reasons" and an Arab no longer has the right to go onto his land without the authorization of the military governor. The State of Israel was to apply these laws against the Arab population. To justify the keeping of these laws of terror, the "state of emergency" has not been formally lifted since 1948.

20 This is a systematic destruction of all semblance of normal life through a complicated and extensive web of enforcement that includes passes, identity numbers, permits, routine interrogations, and road blocks that mean that people have to leave home in the middle of the night to get to work; it also means surveillance and political assassinations.

21 Prior to 2005 Nablus had experienced a high number of Palestinian deaths and injuries. In the period between 29 September 2000 and 31 October 2005, 522 Palestinians were killed in Nablus—27.8 percent of all West Bank Palestinians killed according, to OCHA (UNOCHA, 2005b: 2).

22 The adult interviewees' mental maps of the city before the invasion accorded strongly with the real pre-invasion urban fabric, although references to the damaged buildings were still much in evidence in the discourse.

Part III
Revision

7

Urbicide, states of exception and beyond

The Israeli military invasion and reoccupation of the Palestinian Territories was announced as a measure taken by the Israeli cabinet after a series of suicide bombing in several Israeli cities in March 2002. However, the reoccupation of the Palestinian territories was on the table long before the 2002 invasions.

The IDF began planning for the contingency of carrying out extensive military operations throughout the West Bank and Gaza Strip long before the deployment of Operation Defensive Shield in late March 2002. As early as 1998, during a period when hopes abounded for peace with both the Syrians and the Palestinians, the IDF's general staff faced the challenge of preparing for the failure of negotiations and the possibility of violence (Mofaz, 2002).

The Israeli military invasion and re-occupation (March 2002) of the Palestinian territories and the destruction of the Palestinian-built environment and infrastructure followed different rhythms and military strategies aimed at four targets:

1 Palestinian symbols of power (e.g., Ramallah city).
2 Palestinian symbols of resistance—"the myth of Palestinian resistance" (Nablus Old Town, Jenin refugee camp, Rafah refugee camp, and Balata refugee camp are well-known examples).
3 Palestinian symbols of identity manifested in historic cities and cultural heritage sites. The old centers of Nablus, Hebron, and Bethlehem were destroyed during these invasions
4 Palestinian symbols of the right of return and the mark of the Palestinian Nakba represented in the refugee camps, which had been the targets of several Israeli campaigns since the 1970s.

In the previous chapter we discussed in detail the urbicide case of Nablus, which was the target of multiple types of urbicide—by control, destruction and construction. It was clear that Nablus also played a very important role as the symbol of Palestinian resistance and Palestinian identity represented in its heritage sites.

Within the military invasions context and overall military strategy, Nablus was the last city to be attacked. All Palestinian cities were under attack apart from Hebron and Jericho. A gunnery force and air force made their way into the West Bank cities of Jenin, Bethlehem, Nablus, Qalqilya, and Ramallah, with the most intense fighting taking place in Jenin and Nablus. In Ramallah the destruction of the major Palestinian Authority headquarters, besides isolating Arafat in the Muqata'a, were planned to bring about the surrender of Arafat and the dissolution of the Palestinian Authority, which would lose its capacity to govern by the destruction of its major database by the destruction of its infrastructure. Most importantly it was meant weaken the Palestinian National Authority's image and power.

The destruction extended to the looting and vandalizing of many of those symbols of power:

> It was not an order from above . . . but that is the way it was understood in the field. Infantry soldiers who accompanied the unit to collect the spoils understood that they were allowed—even expected—to destroy property in these ministries . . . The result was hundreds of thousands of dollars of damage. Soldiers shattered computer screens and destroyed keyboards. In some places, they damaged banks and even broke the ATMs. There were cases of theft, too. The damage was enormous. It was extensive and unnecessary. It defied all logic.
>
> (Senior IDF Officer, *Ha'aretz*, 30 April 2002)

The so-called Operation Defensive Shield had a tremendous impact on the Palestinian cities and refugee camps in which at least 620,000 Palestinians were prevented from accessing health services, including over 330,000 children who were confined to their homes. Additionally, 500,000 children living in villages surrounding major health centers were unable to access health services during this period, according to an OCHA Report (UNOCHA, 2002).

The discussion focuses on the Jenin refugee camp for the important strategic military shift in the way the camps were destroyed.

Jenin 2002

The camp is the home to some 14,000 Palestinians, the overwhelming majority of them civilians, their place of origin mostly the Haifa area. The Jenin refugee camp is highly placed in the Palestinian collective memory as the symbol of resistance and the right of return. It is also known as the "capital of suicide bombers." The Israelis' expressed aim was to capture or kill Palestinian militants responsible for suicide bombings and other attacks that have killed more than seventy Israeli and other civilians since March 2002 (Human Rights Watch, 2002).

It is worth highlighting the Israeli perception of and position on the Palestinian refugee camps to be able to understand the environment that preceded the 2002 invasion of the Jenin refugee camp.

Refugee camps in the Israeli military doctrines

The operation in Jenin was widely seen as a success. This new direction and ideology that was adopted by the IDF drastically changed the understanding of how the army perceived Palestinians and their landscape (Graham, 2002b; Weizman, 2007).

The Israeli elite's perception of Palestinian refugee camps has a long history and at the same time influences the military doctrines developed for its destruction. During the 1960s the camp symbolized the center of Palestinian resistance, marking an increased frequency of Israeli aerial strikes targeting camps in Jordan and Lebanon. During the war in 1967, the large refugee camps in the Jericho area were to a large degree vacated, and the unofficial camps of Ajajra and Jiftlik along with several West Bank villages were cleared and razed to the ground by the Israeli army. Soon after the 1967 war, the Jordan Valley border refugee camp of Karameh became the center of the battle between the ascending resistance movement and the Israeli army. In 1972 Nabatieh refugee camp in Southern Lebanon was completely destroyed as a result of Israeli aerial strikes, and was never rebuilt. In 1982 as part of operation "Peace for Galilee" aimed at destroying the Palestine Liberation Organization (PLO) "infrastructure" in Lebanon, massive destruction would be inflicted within Lebanon with particular focus on Palestinian refugee camps. During that summer Ein el Hilweh, the largest camp in Lebanon and located in Saida, was destroyed by intensive bombing that was followed by the bulldozing of more than half of its urban fabric.

The patterns of Israeli-inflicted destruction within the camps typically varied in relation to the objectives of its military operations. During the 2002 Jenin camp operation in the northern West Bank, large parts of the camp were destroyed. The military focused on opening paths through its urban fabric as well as through the interior of buildings' fabrics, and it cleared a 10,000 square meter space in the middle of the camp. Such military interventions allowed the military to take temporary control of the camp space in order to cleanse it of its resistance fighters. On the other hand military destruction in Gaza during 1971 was part of a longer-term planning objective. Led by Ariel Sharon, at that point head of the Israeli army southern command, it has been described as design undertaken by destruction:

> where military bulldozers were ordered to carve wide roads through the fabric of three of Gaza's largest refugee camps—Jabalya, Rafah and Shati.

The new routes divided these camps into smaller neighborhoods, each of which could be accessed or isolated by infantry units. Sharon also ordered the clearing of all buildings and groves in an area he defined as a "security perimeter" around the camps, effectively isolating the built-up area from its surroundings and making it impossible for anyone to enter or leave the camps without being noticed. These ... actions caused the destruction or the damaging of about 6,000 homes in a seven month period.

(Weizman, 2007: 70)

That fall, the Israeli representative to the UN "justified" the on-going Israeli measures by comparing them to similar developments in Lebanon and Jordan where "terror-organizations had been operating actively," and where Jordan had also implemented "extreme security measures" (Sheikh Hassan, forthcoming).

Israeli politicians used a variety of justifications ranging from protecting "Arabs from killing Arabs," quelling the resistance, achieving humanitarian aims, resettlement, relocation, emigration/depopulation, to absolving Israel's moral responsibility from 1948 by erasing the spatial symbols of the Nakba.

The mere scale of destruction in Gaza in 1971 was drastic, and represents one of the many pieces of the brutal history of destruction within the Gaza strip that is still in the making. Under Israeli occupation, houses and shelters were demolished for punitive, planning, and security reasons, both inside and outside camps. This is often seen as related to other measures, such as physically delinking people from land, constructing Israeli settlements, and controlling and punishing through spatial measures.

Battle for Jenin

About 1,000 Israeli soldiers from the 5th infantry brigades invaded Jenin refugee camp from three directions on 2 April 2002. The area was declared a closed military area, access was forbidden, and a round-the-clock curfew was imposed.

For the Palestinians, the battle for the Jenin refugee camp has become a legend. Before the last of the militants surrendered, the camp saw the bloodiest fighting of Israel's offensive on West Bank towns. The brutal close-quarters combat claimed the lives of 23 Israeli soldiers and an estimated 70 Palestinians, civilians as well as fighters. In the Hart al-Hawashin neighborhood, the heart of the Jenin, the Israeli army plowed through occupied homes to broaden the alleys of the camp and make them accessible to tanks and vehicles. A new spatial reality emerged in the camp with a totally bulldozed center as shown in Figure 7.1.

D-9 bulldozer

Ofer Buchris, the commander of the 51st Battalion, developed a method that allowed relatively rapid advance without unduly exposing troops. A bulldozer was

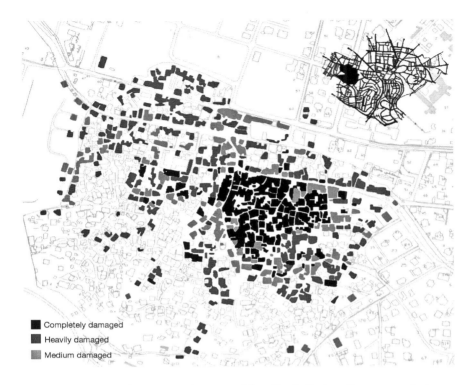

FIGURE 7.1 Levels of damage and new spatial reality in Jenin refugee camp during the 2002 invasion

Source: Author

used to ram the corner of a house, opening a hole. This ensured the house would not collapse on any inhabitants. It also gave both civilians and combatants a chance to escape. A heavily armored Achzarit Armored Personnel Carrier then backed up to the hole and discharged troops. This method allowed Buchris's unit to advance a bit faster than the rest of the attacking troops.

The systematic bulldozing of Palestinian homes began four days after Israeli forces blasted their way into the camp on the night of 3 April, strafing houses from helicopter gunships, and pounding them with tank shells. Four days later, the army razed six houses in the Damaj neighborhood on the camp's eastern parts (see Figures 7.2a and 7.2b). After thirteen soldiers were killed, Israel appeared to abandon foot patrols. Instead, the army began knocking houses down indiscriminately, creating a vast plaza of rubble in the center of the camp, a crossroads for the Israeli tanks. In a 160 by 250 meter area 140 multi-family housing blocks were completely destroyed, 1,500 were damaged, 4,000 people out of the resident population of 14,000 were made homeless (various UNRWA reports; Graham, 2002b).

FIGURE 7.2A

Image from the destruction that befell Jenin refugee camp residential center in the 2002 invasions

Source: Courtesy of Abed Qusini

FIGURE 7.2B

(below) The Israeli tanks on the borders of Jenin Refugee camp in the 2000 invasion

Source: Courtesy of Abed Qusinii

Human Rights Watch's research demonstrates that, during their incursion into the Jenin refugee camp, Israeli forces committed serious violations of international humanitarian law, some amounting prima facie to war crimes.

Shifts and parallels

> *The operation began on March 29th and ended on April 15th, and marked a change in Israel's methodology of destruction, as an estimated 4,000 people became homeless The Israeli army systematically invaded six of the largest cities in the OPT as well as all surrounding towns villages and refugee camps.*
>
> (United Nations Secretary General, 2002; Human Rights Watch, 2002; Ahmed, 2011)

Electricity cables, water pipes, sewage lines, and telephone wires were rendered unusable through soldier vandalism and army tactics. A large part of the damage in Jenin was caused by the intentional widening of the streets, allowing tanks and other military equipment access. This destruction caused irreparable damage to many buildings and caused many others to become uninhabitable and unsafe (Human Rights Watch, 2002)

In a similar way to the Nablus case, urbicide in Jenin marked the shifts in military operations to swarming and bulldozing, a new development in military doctrines that was later used in Fallujah.

Urbicide in Palestine is an ongoing story, and 2002 marked a new period of history in which Palestinian urbanity is no longer perceived as a human "habitat" but rather as the Satan nest that needs to be regularized and purified to prevent the production of other Satan terrorists. The Israeli military strategy develops, shifts and adapts with the complex Palestinian urban terrain. The 2008–2009 Israeli war on Gaza is a clear example:

> "The thing we did not count on was the bulldozer. It was a catastrophe. If the Israelis had only gone one by one inside the camp, they would never have succeeded in entering," said Mr Dama.
>
> (Goldenberg, 2002)

> 19 April 2002. The first thing that comes to mind upon entering Jenin camp is an earthquake: a large area completely leveled, a wider zone around the "epicenter" half in ruins.
>
> (Mansour, 2002: 35)

> I made a soccer field in the middle of the camp . . . I got a real kick out of every house that was demolished, because I knew that dying means nothing to them, while the loss of their house means more to them. You demolish a house and you destroy forty or fifty people for generations. If one thing does bother me about all this, it is that we didn't wipe out the whole camp.
>
> (Zadok Yehezkeli, Yediot Aharonot [Yehezkeli, 2002])

It is not surprising that because of Sharon's role in destroying and fragmenting many Palestinian cities and more precisely Palestinian refugee camp since the 1970s, his nickname is "The Bulldozer." Weizman (2007: 70) refers to this systematic destruction and the perception of the Palestinian refugee camps as embedded in Israeli policy for a very long time.

Gaza 2008/2012

The Israeli attacks on Gaza late in 2008 are another chapter in the Israeli use of urbicide as a tool to control and oppress Palestinian resistance.

Gaza was perceived by the Israelis in general and by the military elites as "one big minefield, IEDs, traps and tunnels in almost every block."

On Saturday 27 December 2008, the Israeli military attack on Gaza was launched. The attack had been meticulously planned for over six months, according to the Israeli press. The planning had two components: military and propaganda. It was based on the lessons of Israel's 2006 invasion of Lebanon, which was considered to be poorly planned and badly advertised. The Cast Lead operation employed a ground troop invasion after intensive airstrikes, which was not a common Israeli strategy when compared to the 2002 Operation Defensive Shield. The shock and awe tactic was more aggressive in terms of the number of Palestinians killed on the first day of the attack. In his article "Parsing Gains of Gaza War," New York Times correspondent Ethan Bronner cited the first day's achievement as one of the most significant of the war's gains. Israel calculated that it would be advantageous to appear to "go crazy," causing vastly disproportionate terror, a doctrine that traces back to the 1950s. "The Palestinians in Gaza got the message on the first day," Bronner wrote, "when Israeli warplanes struck numerous targets simultaneously in the middle of a Saturday morning" (cited in Chomsky, 2009; Chomsky and Pappé, 2010).

In comparison to its 2006 invasion and attacks on southern Hezbollah villages, the Israeli army began covertly preparing a masterful military campaign plan. These plans," wrote Cordesman:

> included an air attack phase, an air ground phase to further weaken Hamas and secure areas in the north, and a contingency plan to seal off the Philadelphia Corridor and the Gazan-Egyptian border. All who were asked specifically stated that the IDF did not go to war with plans to conduct a sustained occupation, to try to destroy Hamas or all its forces, or to reintroduce the Palestinian Authority and Fatah, although such contingency plans and exercises may have existed.
>
> (Cordesman, 2009: 8–9)

The bulldozer came into play again as a key Israeli military destructive machine. Instead of following road networks that were almost certainly mined and set for deliberate ambushes, the Israeli army used its armored bulldozers to smash through buildings and create alternative routes, while swarms of infantry, accompanied by bomb-sniffing dogs, were used in built-up areas.

Former Chief of the IDF General Staff, Dan Halutz, said: "We have won the war" (Collins, 2013). It seemed as if Israeli ground forces in Gaza had undergone a major cultural change in terms of decisiveness, aggressiveness, commitment to the mission, and willingness to accept casualties.

The toll of destruction was tremendous in comparison to the previously discussed cases. Urbicide here included the wanton destruction of urbanity, targeting all aspects of life. As shown in Figures 7.3a, 7.3b, 7.3c and 7.3d, the target was the everyday life structure in the Gaza strip in which complete residential neighborhoods were heavily destroyed; schools, hospitals, mosque, agricultural installations, and basic infrastructure were the targets, with an ultimate goal to win the war as quickly as possible.

Urbicide, surveillance and exception in the OPT

The many levels of Israeli surveillance and control imposed since their inception in 1948 have clear socio-economic implications for Palestinians. In particular, the previously discussed network of surveillance and control installed by Israel since its creation and intensified after the 1967 war has generated several new Palestinian spatial conditions and dimensions related to the experience of "states of exception."

These various and changeable Palestinian spatial conditions produce countless documents and images that map Palestine and foster endless mental images of the place and the people.

Consequently, analyzing or reading Palestine or the Palestinians as the condition of Palestinian geopolitical space or unified Palestinian human experience is no longer possible. Palestine after the 1948/1967 wars was dislocated, and was reproduced in new places outside Palestine. Since then it has constantly transformed space as its dimensions drastically expand and contract, and as the identities that constitute it adapt and change. Thus, this changing condition creates ever-new realities and relations that neither fit simple categories nor conform to previously encountered forms. At the same time, Palestinians are no longer categorized under the same living conditions: they are either the Palestinians who reside inside Israel or the occupied territories (*fe Al-dakhl*—interiors) or the Palestinians who reside in exile (*fey el-manfa, fey al-kharej,* or *fey Al-ghurba*).

Four interrelated states of the Palestinian spatial condition and experience of exception are identified, as presented in Figures 7.4a, 7.4b, 7.4c and 7.4d. ("State" here refers more to a state of mind, to a spatial condition, and a human experience, than a territorial boundary or geographical and sovereign area, although these latter connotations are also present.) These states are presented in chronological and scale order. This order must also be read to reflect the fact that states are interconnected and frequently renew themselves in different shapes and forms.

FIGURE 7.3A Infrastructure destruction in Gaza city during the 2012 Israeli assaults

Source: Courtesy of Yaser Qudieh

FIGURE 7.3B The governmental compound destruction in Gaza city during the 2012 Israeli assaults

Source: Courtesy of Yaser Qudieh

FIGURE 7.3C UNRWA school destruction in Gaza city during the 2012 Israeli assaults

Source: Courtesy of Yaser Qudieh

FIGURE 7.3D Refugee camp bombing in Gaza city during the 2012 Israeli assaults

Source: Courtesy of Yaser Qudieh

FIGURE 7.3E Alnu'man Mosque destruction in Gaza city during the 2008 Israeli
assaults

Source: Courtesy of Yaser Qudieh

For example, the state of exile represents the Palestinian refugees forced out of
Palestine in 1948 and 1967, but this condition of exile and refuge continues into
the present as more Palestinians leave Palestine either by force or self-imposed
exile.

The first state can be described as a state of exile and refuge. The 1948 and
1967 Israeli–Arab wars signaled: the expulsion of Palestinians; the destruction of
Palestinian cities, towns, and villages; and exile and loss of life. These conclude
the chapter that describes the disappearance of what was once Palestine. Thus,
Palestine (or *Filasteen* in Arabic) vanished from the geopolitical map of the Middle
East. A new emerging state of Israel surfaced; a new history, urbanity, and
identity had to be formulated. At the same time, novel Palestinian geo-spaces were

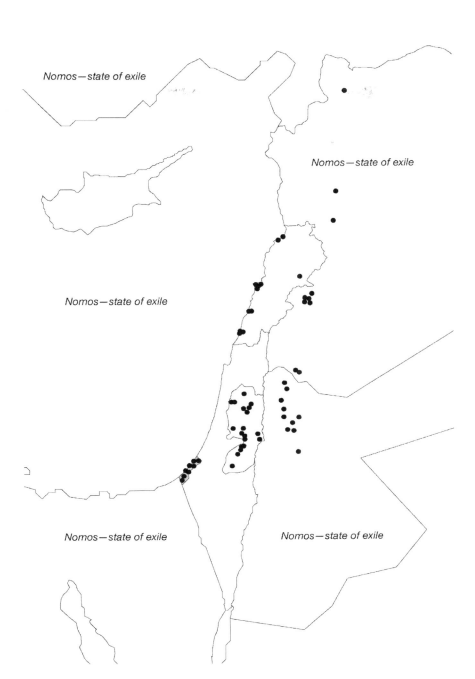

Nomos—state of exile

Nomos—state of exile

Nomos—state of exile

Nomos—state of exile

Nomos—state of exile

FIGURE 7.4A Palestinian state/space of exile

Source: Author

Palestinian space ◯

Israeli space ●

FIGURE 7.4B Palestinian state/space of paradox

Source: Author

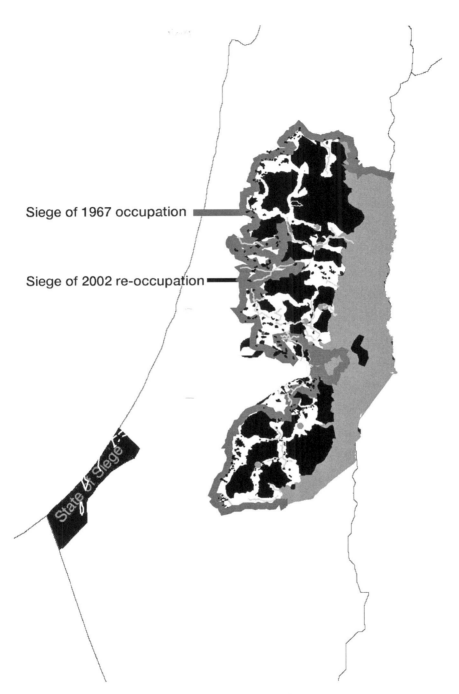

Siege of 1967 occupation

Siege of 2002 re-occupation

State of Siege

FIGURE 7.4C Palestinian state/space of siege and urbicide

Source: Author

FIGURE 7.4D Palestinian state/space of urbicide

Source: Author

constructed and physically manifested inside Palestine and in exile. Thus, Palestine became (at least for Palestinians in exile) an idea, a memory of place.

This state of exile and refuge became an existential and epistemological condition of the Palestinian experience, as a spatial and temporal state of being, belonging, and becoming, in its material and metaphorical contexts. Edward Said (Said and Mohr, 1999: 19) wrote poignantly on this state of exile when noting that "the stability of geography and the continuity of land—these have completely disappeared from my life and the life of all Palestinians."

The second state can be described as a state of paradox. This condition lies within the state of Israel itself. Palestinians who managed to remain in their homes in 1948 acquired Israeli citizenship: they are both Israelis and Palestinians. One Israeli/Palestinian describes this Palestinian experience as: "Insane. The Jewish Israelis see me as an Arab and enemy despite my papers, Arabs see me as Israeli and enemy because of my papers" (Schulz and Hammer, 2003: 79).

The third condition is appropriately labeled the state of occupation and siege, which is experienced by Palestinians residing in the West Bank and Gaza within the "lines" configured after the 1967 war. Different levels, intensities, and scales of siege can be recognized in this state, as discussed in the first part of this chapter. The mechanisms and dynamics generated from this state of siege are materialized in the contiguity/fragmentation and exclaves/enclaves produced after Oslo and the 2002 re-occupation of the OPT. After the outbreak of the second intifada in 2000, a strict Israeli military cordon was implemented in the OPT, accompanied by an accelerated process of enclaving Palestinian-built areas. This enclaving is manifest in the existing Jewish settlements (which, after a long process of formation, are now fully developed), Jewish bypass roads, and the newly constructed Israeli military checkpoints, roadblocks, road gates, and the Apartheid Wall. The Israeli settlement exclaves or islands, in spatial terms, draw the contours of the process of formation and consolidation of Jewish parcels of land in the heart of the Palestinian territoriality. The subsequent enterprise of these exclaves is to expand and multiply, as Falah (2003: 182–183) explains. The Jewish exclaves forcefully and slowly emerged within the Palestinian built environment and are connected by a network of bypass roads (and infrastructure) that serves the Jewish inhabitants of the new settlements and is forbidden to Palestinians. The spatial metaphorical reality of the Palestinian enclaves makes them appear as small pockets of land lying outside the main flows and networks that shape the territory. They are strangers in their own natural setting, yet they naturalize the presence of their conqueror.

The fourth state is the state of urbicide, the extreme condition of the state of siege. The state of urbicide represents the permanent state of invasion and strangulation taking place in many Palestinian cities and refugee camps within the state of occupation and siege.

The Palestinian body is regulated in both the "normal" state of exception (created by the 1967 Israeli occupation of the Palestinian territories) and the "extreme" state of exception (during Israeli military incursions and prolonged invasions).

It is systematically rendered vulnerable by the presence of surveillance and domination that penetrates all aspects of daily life. During invasions, curfews confine people to inside their houses, regulating the use of public space and extending to the most intimate private space, which is also invaded and redefined.

Palestinian private space has been intruded upon and targeted, not only to destroy people's sense of place and privacy, as Falah and Flint (2004) have argued, but as part of the larger Israeli–Palestinian struggle over land and water. Sovereignty over space is an important element in achieving geopolitical aims intrinsic to the longer-term policy imperative within the geopolitical colonial imaginary that guides the Israeli nation-state.

The permanent siege around many Palestinian cities since 2000, along with mobility restrictions, has made many Palestinians—especially the young generation—prisoners in their own city. Many leave the city seldom, if at all. The impact of such forcible confinement on the younger generation's perception and imagination of external spaces, cities, and the world is abstract. What for young people elsewhere are non-issues are sources of uncertainty for Palestinians. Lina Jamoul (2004) calls this phenomenon the "colonization of the mind" that results from the repeated experience of stop, search, check ID, wait for hours, have abuse hurled at you, get roughed up, and—maybe eventually—pass through. There is no other way to travel. This colonization of the mind occurs when people lack control over their own space. It becomes so naturalized that people cannot even imagine an alternative:

> A few days later I will be explaining to a Palestinian boy, who is desperate to emigrate to Syria, how we don't have to stand in line, how the soldiers don't search us, how they never turn us back. I will never forget the look on his face as I tell him we just flash our passports and are let through unhindered. "They don't stop you?" he asks, completely unbelievingly. I am ashamed to tell him that, as a foreigner, I am allowed complete free passage into every nook and cranny of his country, given that permission by an occupying military force, while he is completely prohibited from any free movement in his own country by that same occupying military force.
>
> (Jamoul, 2004: 584)

The surveillance network and restrictions on mobility also impact the young generation's dreams, which do not extend beyond visiting another Palestinian city, arranging a recreational activity, and so on. Mosa, a young student from the Gaza Strip, told me:

> I can admit that I no longer possess a dream or big expectations. Till now most of what I look forward to are small decisions that I take every year and hope I can fulfill. Because whenever I have a big dream the occupation devastates it. My only dream now is to visit the West Bank (specifically Hebron), and it seems an impossible dream to realize.
>
> (Interview with author, July 2005)

FIGURE 7.5A "In the frame"

Source: Courtesy of Amal Kaawash

FIGURE 7.5B "Are you still real?"

Source: Courtesy of Amal Kaawash

Such uncertainties and doubts are strongly reflected in the comic drawings of Amal Kawaash as shown in Figures 7.5a and 7.5b, whose work shows how Palestinian children and youths are no longer certain of anything. One image asks, "Are you still real?" while another employs the picture frame itself to evoke the infinite restrictions that Palestinians must endure.

Fragmentation of space and time

The Israeli colonial project in the Occupied Territories is articulated here as a cogwheel composed of several components that make it possible for Israel to enforce its occupation project: the Jewish settlements, the surveillance network, the demolition and destruction of Palestinian neighborhoods and houses, the military laws and so forth. The surveillance cogwheel (look back at Figure 6.1 in Chapter 6) is composed of six smaller cogs. The first is the Apartheid Wall cog, which consists of a network of barriers, including ten-foot walls topped with barbed wire and guard towers and employing motion detectors and video cameras. This Wall often prevents Palestinians from engaging in normal activities such as tending their crops, going to school or to the hospital, and visiting members of their family who happen to be on the other side of the Israeli constructed barrier. The second cog is the territorial subdivision into zones A, B or C. This zoning demonstrates that the matter of statehood is ultimately seen as one of occupation, where the fragmentation of space and time reaches a level where these very small interwoven spaces/enclaves have their own rules of movement, construction, military laws, and checkpoints. The third cog is composed of military bases and military zones that are carefully located to formulate a security and control network along the occupied Territories. The fourth cogwheel is indicated by the Israeli-only bypass roads. The fifth cogwheel consists of checkpoints and military outposts that highly hinder and control the Palestinian subject from freedom of mobility and daily life activities. The sixth cog is that of arbitrary Israeli military and administrative rules that are used during times of military invasion. These rules contribute enormously to the arbitrariness that settles into the lives of Palestinians and makes their daily routine or life projects intractable if not impossible tasks to manage. The ultimate goal of the Israeli colonial project is the slow ethnic cleansing of Palestine by encouraging voluntary transference to Palestinians whose lives have become impossible under the harsh living conditions that emerge on a daily basis, confirming Pappé's (2006) claims in this regard:

> Temporariness is now the law of the occupation . . . temporary takeover of Area A, temporary withdrawal from Area A, temporary encirclement and temporary closures, temporary transit permits, temporary revocation of transit permits, temporary enforcement of an elimination policy, temporary change in the open-fire orders . . . When the Occupier plays with time like this, everything—everything that moves, everything that lives—becomes dependent on the arbitrariness of the Occupier's decisions. The Occupier is

fully aware that he is always playing on borrowed time, in fact on stolen time, other people's time. This Occupier is an unrestrained, almost boundless sovereign, because when everything is temporary almost anything—any crime, any form of violence—is acceptable, because the temporariness seemingly grants it a license, the license of the state of emergency.

(Ophir, 2002: 60)

This multi-dimensional system of the Israeli military surveillance network generates new forms of colonialism; it is a post-modern attempt to control all dimensions of space, transforming the Palestinian Occupied Territories into the largest spatial laboratory of the twenty-first century.

The Palestinian states/spaces of exception and Agamben

The previous analysis demonstrated that Agamben's understanding of the state of exception partially explains the conditions experienced within the Palestinian states of siege and urbicide. However, his approach does not have the capacity to be the only tool to map and explain the Palestinian spaces of exception. Agamben's juridical definition of the state of exception hinders the explanation of the other forms and exceptions of Palestinians' experiences in their other states: state/space of paradox; state/space of exile/refuge; state/space of occupation/siege; and state/space of urbicide. By limiting the definition to law and juridical issues, Agamben's approach does not afford the opportunity to analyze the other forms and levels of exception that might be generated within the different state/spaces of exception; as discussed, the experience of exception is present in every aspect of the Palestinian spatial condition that goes beyond any juridical discussion: it was revealed in the Israeli military surveillance network and the reconfiguration of Palestinian spaces, the reconfiguration of the socio-cultural and economic dimensions, extending to the personal experience and perceptions of self, other, and space.

The other limitation of Agamben's state of exception is its distinction between two actors, victim versus victimizer, powerful versus powerless. Following Foucault's principle of power—that there is no such thing as two opposite classes, one with power and one without, for the simple reason that power is not a possession but an action—that analysis rejects the notion of the all-powerful sovereign and the powerless victim. Palestinians, through politics, civil and armed struggle (as will be discussed in Chapter 8), have also shaped the realities of the conflict, and their resistance has been powerful and effective as the previous sections have illustrated. It is therefore important to use other theories and methods to understand the Palestinian colonized spatial condition. For example, Foucault's theory of power and microphysics might provide us with a very interesting and powerful technique that permits deconstruction of the Israeli cogwheel of occupation (which is composed of the Jewish settlements projects, the surveillance network, the destruction and demolition exercise, the military laws, the land confiscation and others) into its distinct parts, which enables a better understanding of its mechanisms and impacts.

The intended effect of the Israeli military surveillance network, together with the long-practiced strategies it implemented, is to fragment time and space in such a way that it becomes impossible to lead a normal life. Consequently, a shift in the Palestinian modes of resistance can be observed: from non-violent resistance in the first intifada of 1987 to guerrilla-type military resistance accompanied by other modes of civil resistance in the second intifada. Resistance in the latter instance is practiced on a daily basis, in forms not necessarily readily recognizable, such as the Palestinian conception of steadfastness (*sumood*), going to school or work, bringing up children, and so on. These forms of resistance have been made possible by the spatial transformation of the Israeli surveillance and control techniques after the second intifada.

While the West Bank and Gaza Strip have been transformed into Israel's frontiers in the sense of institutional thinning, from a spatial perspective they have become hermetic ghettoes (see Gordon, 2008: 39). Palestinians, in their struggle to regain normalcy in their everyday lives, have developed survival techniques in the form of direct and indirect resistance to the Israeli exercise of power and control.

8

Palestinian resistance discourse

Palestinian cases of resistance and resilience

Resistance theories, emerging in the last several decades from neo-Marxist, neo-Gramscian, post-modern, and post-structural examinations of power struggles, have raised important ideas. The notion of resistance has received considerable attention in the recent literature on surveillance and organization studies (Thompson and Ackroyd, 1995; Webb and Palmer, 1998; Fleming and Sewell, 2002; Mann *et al.*, 2003; Hollander and Einwohner, 2004; Bigo, 2006; Bogard, 2006; Haggerty, 2006; Los, 2006; Sanchez, 2009). From the introspective metaphor of the panopticon and the "Foucauldian turn" to the expansive analogy of Deleuze's rhizome and the *surveillant assemblage* (Haggerty and Ericsson, 2000) power, resistance, control, and surveillance have all been entwined and embodied in each other in such an iterative way that they keep reproducing one other. Resistance theorists have attempted to explain why the opposition of some groups to others is politically and morally necessary in social institutions where mainstream ideologies dominate to discipline participants and social norms. Resistance in these theoretical formations is differentiated from mere opposition to authority, however; resistance is understood to contribute, in some way, to the progressive transformation of the environment by attempting to undermine "the reproduction of oppressive social structures and social relations" (Walker, 1985: 65).

Resistance is widely defined as opposition with a social and political purpose. Resistance theories attempt to explain the ways in which working class and other marginalized youth struggle against the norms or authority of schools that often seem to work against their perceived interests.

During the sixty-seven years of the Zionist colonial project in Palestine, Palestinians have developed different types of military (guerrilla type) and civil non-violent resistance. Despite the different resistance tactics employed by the Palestinians, the prevailing power relations manifest themselves in all spheres of everyday life—from a profoundly felt influence on the economic activities of Palestinians to the more physical realities on the ground, such as checkpoints, roadblocks and an often incomprehensibly applied permit system. These power relations, however, are certainly not unilateral, for they are negotiated continuously, through all kinds of pressure and resistance, and vice versa. Palestinians obviously also have power at their disposal or, in other words, they have agency. Ortner (2006) explains the resistance from a power relations change perspective, in which resistance for her is: "a form of power agency—it is a kind of complex and ambivalent acceptance of dominant categories and practices that are always changed at the very moment they are adopted" (Ortner, 2006: 144).

The discussion in this book highlights the contemporary modus of resistance post the second intifada of 2000 and the re-occupation of the Palestinian cities in 2002. This focus intends to highlight the shifts and developments in the resistance dynamics that marked a new stage in the Palestinian resistance discourse.

Knowledge and colonial power structure

Literature on Palestinian resistance discourse is mostly theoretical and based on limited anecdotal case studies, most of which are presented from a Western point of view. To explain the complex Palestinian resistance modes and link them to surveillance and the state of exception, Foucault's theory on power production demonstrates how Palestinians generated different modes of resistance to and resilience against the Israeli military exercise of power via the surveillance network. Furthermore, due to their experience of this, Palestinians survive extreme conditions of exception.

Foucault did not relegate power to the dominant class, who then preserve and wield influence in order to secure authority. Instead, power is a force that is constructed, enacted, and transmitted through the institutions, social structures, dominant rhetoric, means of communication, and physical and psychic levels that constitute life (Foucault, 1980: 174). According to Foucault, there is no "powerless" or "powerful," no two opposite classes, one with power and one without, for the simple reason that power is not a possession but an action. He draws out the inseparability of the exercise of power and the production of resistance and claims that we cannot speak of power without resistance or the potential of resistance.

Through long years of occupation, the Israeli military has developed knowledge about the OPT and its inhabitants. This knowledge has allowed Israeli military planners to install the previously discussed network of surveillance. This extreme and ubiquitous experience of power has generated a collective experience of the occupation and its impacts on Palestinian daily life. It can be said that the experience of power has reached into the very core of Palestinian individuals, touching their bodies and inserting itself in their actions and attitudes, discourses, learning processes, and everyday lives, according to Foucault's approach on this issue (Foucault, 1980: 39). It has also facilitated Palestinians' understanding of the mechanisms of the Israeli network of control, and produced a counter-knowledge to the Israeli military control and occupation practices.

Consequently, Palestinians can break through this network of surveillance, thus affirming Foucault's argument that no power exists without knowledge, every power is knowledgeable, and knowledge is one of the cogwheels.

This is evident in the several forms of resistance encountered by the Palestinian social resistance practices of survival. Palestinians unconsciously mentally map the patterns and rhythms generated by the control network, thus formulating strategies or tactics to infiltrate the particular system of control (e.g. a checkpoint or the Apartheid Wall). This knowledge can be used for empowerment, creativity, and resistance, as well as suppression. Palestinians living around the Israeli Apartheid Wall, or those for whom the Wall created an obstacle, acquired knowledge of how it operates.

They were then able to pass through without triggering the alarm system or encountering a patrolling jeep. This practice is illustrated in Avi Mograbi's (2005) documentary about the Wall and the checkpoints, and demonstrates Palestinians' in-depth knowledge of the Wall and how it works—knowledge that rivals that of the Israeli general who oversees it. One man interviewed in the documentary explains exactly how he passed through sections of the Wall several times without being caught. He knew how every element would react if he touched it, and he counted how many patrols took place each hour. This Palestinian knowledge is not merely about scientific techniques, but about how the system of surveillance operates. By trial and error, by experiencing the power of the Apartheid Wall, the checkpoint, and other elements of the surveillance system, the counter-action to break through can be developed.

Another example of knowledge and counter-knowledge is Areej Hijazi's experience of the paradox of living with the strict siege and surveillance system on a daily basis, which paradoxically enabled her to break through to Israeli cities to enjoy some normalcy:

> I go to one of the Jerusalem checkpoints and try to pass. Why, I don't know. It could be that at those times you need to do something crazy to regain some of your internal balance, and in my case the craziest thing ever is to challenge the so-called "Israeli security and checkpoints system." Success is 100 percent: each time I tried to pass, I passed not only to Jerusalem, but to Tel Aviv, Jaffa, Haifa, and Nazareth. My passport was my curly hair and the Giorgio Armani sunglasses that I bought only for the checkpoints, and guess what? I believe the $300 investment was worth it. It is so funny that I cannot see my family in Gaza for years, while I spend most of the summer swimming in Tel Aviv or having fun in Jerusalem. What a brilliant security system! In case you feel like knowing more about this issue, please let me know.
>
> (Quoted in Levey, 2008)

FIGURE 8.1 Image of Nablus kids taking classes in the street after the destruction of their school in Nablus Old Town during the 2002 Israeli invasion

Source: Courtesy of Abed Qusini

Sumood (steadfastness)

Civil resistance takes on many different forms in the OPT. In Nablus, for example, during Operation Defensive Shield in 2002, six out of the nine schools in and around Nablus Old City were subject to destruction. In an act of rejection and resistance in the face of the destruction of the city, many teachers held their classes in the street to show that the power of life is much stronger than the machine of destruction and death—see Figure 8.1. Rabab Abdul Hadi (2004) describes how schoolchildren also challenged the 100 days of curfew from July to December 2003: "Children (including my own nephew Ibrahim and nieces Widad, Noura, and Nada, who live in the eastern part, beyond Tora Bora) have been risking their lives to get to school to take their final exams."

Clearly, then, regardless of their harsh experiences of invasion, destruction, and curfews, Palestinians keep a firm grasp on education as a means to struggle against occupation. This is also evident in Irene Siegel's report from the Nablus refugee camp of A'skar:

> An 11-year-old friend of mine named Shifa' described her classroom as a tiny room that crammed in about 40 students. There were no seats; most students either stood or sat on the floor for the entire 3-hour session. Only a fraction of the usual subjects are taught, without textbooks (which either

haven't been able to be completed, or to be delivered, from Ramallah). The students often study without notebooks or pencils as well, as their families are too impoverished by the choking, endless curfew-siege to buy them.

(Siegel, 2003)

Commemoration

The remembrance of wars, of victories, and of defeats is a prime act of collective affirmation of nations. Monuments, cemeteries, and stories are constructed, and these processes of commemoration serve to construct the identity of individuals and peoples. The aim of reflecting on the function of remembrance is to present a closed cycle—the discourse on war inscribed in the collective memory in the form of monuments and commemorations. Not only are the notions of public versus private inverted but inversions start to affect other aspects and meanings of Nablus Old Town itself. This can be observed in the Palestinian martyrdom discourse that is now extended to everyday activities and social rituals. The city that is typically a celebration of life becomes the embattled arena for continual commemorations of the now unending event of death.

Places in the Old Town are converted into symbolic places that are fused with mythical meaning to provide a sense of identity in place and time. Thus, places are converted into monuments and memorial spaces that belong to the spatial aspect of memory. These places, as Lowenthal (1985, xxiii) argues, fuse history and landscape and define "sacred history" in terms of symbolic places that are shrouded with the mystique of past events. Even the names of these places and many streets have changed their names to hold new names that reflect either a martyr name or a battle name; this was strongly presented in one of the user group's mental maps.

Rebuilding and renovating can also be seen as an act of remembrance, an urgent need to memorialize. Cities are more than the sum of their buildings. A city is a tapestry of human lives and social networks that are essential to the heart and soul of the place. A disaster can tear out this social fabric, a tragedy that is comparable with the destruction of the physical infrastructure of a city. Therefore, resilience entails more than rebuilding. Recovery is a process that is larger than rebuilding buildings; social networks need to be rebuilt as well. There is a difference between the physical rebuilding of a place and the emotional/cultural rebuilding of a place. Vale and Campanella (2005) argue that recovering a wrecked city involves much more than bricks, mortar, and asphalt—or bits, bytes, and electricity. Reconstruction in post-war sites also "fundamentally" entails reconnecting severed familial, social, and religious networks of the survivors. Urban recovery occurs network by network, district by district, not just building by building. According to Campanella, it is about reconstructing the myriad social relations embedded in schools, workplaces, childcare arrangements, shops, places of worship, and places of play and recreation. Stories constructed to explain and interpret the event are an important step in the recovery process.

In Nablus Old Town, different forms of commemoration have materialized. The spontaneously generated memorials at the sites of trauma all over the Old Town are the most common pattern to remember those who were killed in these events. "Memorials are devices to articulate pain; therefore part of emotional recovery is creating physical memorials" (Vale and Campanella, 2005: 169). The established memory places, then, are not interpreted or represented by the Palestinians in a monolithic way. The polysemy of these sites reveals itself in the range of meanings attributed to them in different settings, by different narrators, and for different audiences.

The inhabitants celebrate and commemorate the tragic outcomes of the invasion and the killing of Palestinian resistance members, converting the city into a huge graveyard, a macro-space of struggle and national identity. Places where key resistance fighters were assassinated are converted symbolically into commemorative monuments. Commemoration stones inscribed with poetry of sorrow and heroism are placed on the façades of buildings; posters depicting martyrs cover almost all the Old Town's walls (see Figure 8.2).

These memorial places are numerous, and they primarily—though not entirely—consist of ordinary locations appropriated for burial of the dead during sieges or battles. But although all memory places are inevitably associated with death and mourning, not all of them are burial places. Some are alleyways where a loved one fell to a missile or a mortar, such as the corner of An Naser street with Jadet Alahanably. Other examples of such places are the tunnels where shelter was sought by the Palestinian resistance fighters during the Israeli military campaigns, such as *Hush* Aljitan and the public telephone cabin that was exploded by remote control in the Alqaryun main square (there are many other similar examples at hand). Posters of martyrs are another form of commemoration, while naming streets and neighborhoods after a martyr became a typical practice of official institutions such as the municipality, the different Palestinian political and military fractions and the inhabitants.

Though these spots became places of mourning as a result of unfortunate happenings, they have been maintained and incorporated into the larger Palestinian commemorative practices and narratives by both Old Town visitors and the inhabitants themselves. These spaces are not cordoned off or made into hallowed ground; they are used in daily routines by those who inhabit and utilize them. Here, "the language of death is spoken without embarrassment or inhibition, and death becomes at every stage intimately associated with the daily and ceremonial life" (Zonabend, 1984: 163).

Rebuilding as an act of resilience, hope, and resistance

The inhabitants of the Old Town saw the post-urbicide reconstruction projects as part of an effort to protect their cultural identity embedded in the Old Town's physical, infrastructural, spatial, and economic aspects—see Figures 8.3a and 8.3b. At the same time these projects were conceived as a means of improving living

FIGURE 8.2 Commemoration stones and poster for key Palestinian resistance martyrs
killed by the Israeli army. Caption in first stone requests passers-by to
read the *fati ah* (Ki ib Shuhada' al-Aqsa) (opening *su rah* of the Quran)
for the dead of al-Aqsa Martyrs' Brigade, followed by a list of names,
and concluding with: "When men die . . . men . . . words are rendered
mute. . . . Do not accept condolences [for the dead], and do not lower
your heads, but rather store up anger and fire a bullet in the face of
every traitor—whenever a grain falls from it, it returns to the earth to
multiply anew."

Source: Author

conditions inside the old houses by replacing the old degraded infrastructure and
installing adequate modern equipment such as toilets and kitchens. Many
interviewed people expressed satisfaction about what already had been achieved.
Nevertheless some expressed doubts about the fairness of these projects, as the
renovations carried out did not always seem to be in proportion to the real needs

FIGURE 8.3A Alsaraya building after destruction
Source: Courtesy of Abed Qusini.

or the damage. A most interesting fact was how the inhabitants perceived these projects also from a political point of view—as resistance against the Israeli military urbicidal campaign. This point came across strongly in the interviews conducted in the Old Town. Almost all respondents stressed the point that the Old Town should be renovated exactly as it was before its destruction, using the same architectural style, building material, and finishing elements. The inhabitants' struggle with both nostalgic ideas from the past and conflicting images of the future was also evident. Various nostalgic and sentimentalized recollections came to the fore. So did personal memories of the "good old days." Conflicting ideas about how the city should look in the future surfaced as well. One of the respondents stated:

FIGURE 8.3B Alsaraya building after its reconstruction by Nablus Municipality
Source: Author

"it is a war of heritage; we should sustain our cultural sites as a tool of struggle against occupation" (Saleh, interview 15 August 2005).

This type of narrative demonstrates people's political awareness and engagement as well. The rebuilding of the Old Town in particular carried emotional symbolism for the Nabulsi community, as it represents the centre of Palestinian resistance for them.

Reconstruction dynamics are also perceived to bring hope and attachment with life, despite the tremendous loss. Rebuilding cannot be done without optimism. Many people inside the Old Town have lost property that they conceived as a lifetime investment; its loss has meant for them the loss of life and a fall into despair.

"My house, I inherited from my father, it was very old and falling into decay. It is the fruit of 45 years efforts of repairing; constructing, furnishing, and they destroyed it in one hour" (Ahmed, 13 August 2005). "The loss is beyond physical material, it is the loss of the family, the loss of trees, stones that hold and tell our memories, good memories. Occupation is about oppression, humiliation and devastation" (Um Rabee, 17 August 2005).

This type of narrative demonstrates how urban devastation shatters people's lives and hope. It is true that the results of many years of investment are lost overnight, but reconstruction of buildings is also an act of reconstruction of life, which hints at a new start. Therefore, rebuilding and renovation efforts are important tools to reassure people about their future.

Mother Teresa's prayer goes as follows: "What you spend years building, someone could destroy overnight; . . . Build anyway" (Vale and Campanella, 2005: 205).

Renovation and reconstruction is conceived in this study to form an important tool for healing and recovering from urbicidal trauma and to generate an important positive moral effect. On the one hand, the scenes of devastation will be a permanent reminder of the urbicidal acts hindering the community's healing process.

New modes of Palestinian resistance

Other forms of resistance have emerged in the past ten years in the Palestinian resistance discourse. The intelligent employment of the Israeli colonial spatial strategies for oppression as a counter-strategy for resistance, such as the phenomenon of the Bab Alshams village 2013, is one to mention. As we discussed before, the Zionist colonial project in Palestine since the nineteenth century has created a complex spatial control over the Palestinians and their space. An active counter-Palestinian resistance has taken place in different forms; what is interesting about the colonial project and its counter-resistance strategies is the centrality of space (physical and/or virtual) in both. And the evolution and shifts in the Palestinian resistance demonstrate the deep understanding of the Palestinians as subject to their spatial reality and at the same time to their colonizer's spatial control dynamics that enables them to develop very interesting civil and organized resistance strategies, that in effect inspired the recent revolutions in the Arab world and extended around the globe.

It should be highlighted that other non-violent forms of Palestinian resistance exist in the form of cultural resistance that depends on the rewriting of the colonial discourse—narration, that actively engages events, discourses, and remembering practices through their multiple facets and blurred or unstable boundaries. The work of Edward Said in the question of Palestine is the strongest example for such resistance.

From spatial colonialism and oppression to "spatial" rhizomatic resistance

> *Resistance can occur via an "unpicking" of the closures of the dominant system through forms of agency which are "the activity of the contingent," such as hybridity, mimicry and "sly civility."*

(Homi, 1994: 185, 187).

Colonial and post-colonial theory is built around the concept of resistance, of resistance as subversion, or opposition, or mimicry. The work of Jeffress (2008) brings new insights to the definition of resistance that goes beyond resistance-as-subversion and resistance-as-opposition. His critique is that the discursive resistance may contribute to psychological and spiritual liberation—the decolonization of the mind—but does not necessarily lead to physical and material liberation, while for him resistance-as-opposition seeks a more concrete decolonization, yet relies on an antagonistic framework to imagine liberation for the oppressed. While post-colonial critics such as Fanon and Said recognize that liberation is more than independence from colonial power and requires the transformation of material as well as discursive realities, their oppositional paradigms fail to adequately envision a transition from colonialism to decolonization, through to a new political order. Liberation is not simply the absence of an oppressor; it is the presence of a "profoundly different construction of identity, subjectivity and human relationships" (Jeffress, 2008: 167). I agree with Jeffress's hypothesis that a new type of resistance in colonial and post-colonial context emerges— what he calls transformational resistance—which he connects to the intrinsic in Fanon's concept of decolonization—a "new humanism" that emphasizes new ways of *being, knowing and doing*, unlike the *reactive* notion of oppositional resistance that often takes the form of collective protests and social mobilization that seeks to dismantle the material structures of colonial power, or the subversive resistance in which the colonized use colonial discourse theory as a tool to deconstruct colonial knowledge and create alternative readings of the self and colonial authority. Transformational resistance is a *proactive* effort to *transform* colonizer/colonized subjectivity, colonial discourses, and material structures. Thus my thesis is built on identifying the Palestinian resistance with this type of proactive engaging and transformational resistance. Consequently, transformational resistance discourse acknowledges resistance as complicit and an agency within the oppressive logics of colonial occupation that depends on the experience and knowledge of the oppression structure to enable both the decolonization of the mind and the elaboration of a future vision for material and spiritual liberation. The Palestinian resistance discourse different forms of resistance (subversive, oppositional, and transformative) are used in parallel and on some occasions in the same time and space. It may use other forms of resistance, such as cultural, discursive and oppositional resistance; using simultaneously those different types of resistance takes it to another level that needs a different explanation. In this context it is important to highlight that transformative resistance does not only deal with the oppressed (colonized) subject; it lends itself to other agencies such as activists.

Duncombe (2002: 8) develops the thesis on political activism and resistance, for which he emphasizes the spatial dimension not only for cultural resistance but for other forms of resistance such as political action. He rightly claims that resistance can create a "free space" to challenge and transform the ideological and material hold of dominant power. Ideologically, cultural resistance creates a space for "new language, meanings, and visions of the future," something that can be noted in the different spatial resistance strategies followed by the Palestinians in the recent years.

Such "free space" from material perspective provides places of community, networking, and organizational opportunities. This spatial resistance is creative in terms of its development of spaces of negotiations that render the Palestinians as a real agency in shaping their realities and the way they weaken the colonial spaces of oppression and transform them into spaces of resistance.

Mbembe's (2003) explanation of those colonial spaces of oppression might be useful to reflect how the Palestinians could transform such colonial spaces via knowledge and counter-strategies to be spaces for resistance:

> All forms of colonial occupation create "a new set of social and spatial relations" that "seize, delimit, and assert control over a physical geographical area." The creation of such new spatial relations or "territorialization" establishes colonial "boundaries and hierarchies, zones and enclaves," "subverts existing property arrangements," "classifies people according to different categories," "extracts resources," and "manufactures large reservoirs of cultural imaginaries."
>
> (Mbembe, 2003: 25)

Hence, Palestinian spatial and transformative resistance can be explored and classified according to the techniques employed and also to its inclusion in and development of other modes of oppositional and subversive resistance. Every modus of spatial resistance being discussed, is a counter-strategy to the different Israeli colonial spatial forms of urbicide/spacio-cide by construction: control, destruction, and strangulation.

Rhezomatic resistance

I intend to call the new forms of the Palestinian (non-violent) resistance "rhezomatic"[1] because of its base of analyzing, understanding, and acting against the colonizing power structure. It is its reinvention of itself (by developing and adapting new resistance techniques) that makes it difficult to pinpoint a start or an end to it. As Deleuze and Guattari point out, "the rhizome offers some hope of bringing about a kind of 'liberation' from structures of power and dominance." Christa Bürger notes that the tree:

is meant to indicate the essence of the enemy: classical thought [which] operates dualistically and hierarchically. An extensive network of diversified, autonomous productivity, the rhizome connects diverse arenas of resistance, from language, to the arts, to activism, to everyday practices. The structure is permanently unstable, perpetually unfolding, constantly mutating, and able to adapt quickly to the rapidly changing conditions and faces of the oppressive forces it opposes. It has neither beginning nor end, but always a milieu from which it grows and which it overspills. The rhizome proceeds by variation, expansion, conquest, capture, offshoots. The rhizome pertains to a map that is always detachable, connectable, reversible, modifiable, and has multiple entryways and exits.

(Deleuze and Guattari, 1987: 23)

Israeli colonial policies play in a fluid and dual meaning that has shaped the Palestinian geo-spatial reality. The European colonialism followed spatial displacement, segregation, and separation ideology in their colonies that enabled a full dominance and exploitation of resources. The Israel colonial project has followed a similar apartheid and separation ideology, as discussed earlier, to fulfill its hidden agenda of mass displacement and ethnic cleansing, confirming Pappé's (2006) thesis. While counter-insurgents have frequently applied spatial discipline to isolate insurgents from the population in order to obtain a political solution, Israel has simply abandoned Palestinians behind walls where they live and interact without ever crossing into Israeli space yet remain under Israeli control. In other words, Israel's use of spatial methods to wall in Palestinians appears to be an attempt to enact the permanent disappearance of an unwanted population without outright ethnic cleansing, and an attempt to suppress resistance without political compromise.

The shifts that are noted in the Israeli military doctrines and the way they perceive the Palestinian territories in general and the urbanity in particular are documented in Eayl Weizman's book *Hollow Land* (2007) and can be seen post the Aqsa Intifada of 2000. This military development can be seen in the Israeli tools and techniques that are constantly changing to enforce the Israeli colonial project in Palestine. However, Palestinian space has been the center for Zionist ideology and colonial projects since its very beginnings at the end of the nineteenth century.

In an effort to disrupt and weaken the spatial aspects of the continued Israeli colonization of historic Palestine, a range of resistance practices have emerged, centered on individual and collective agency. The interesting element in these initiatives is the centrality of space that is seen, imagined, and acted on as a tool for resistance. Interestingly enough, the Israeli colonial project in Palestine was also centered on the presentation, representation, and control of this Palestinian space. These practices of "spatial resistance" act in various ways to challenge the Israeli spatial colonial regime; a recent attempt to classify such tendencies has been developed by Barclay and Qaddumi (2013) for which four modes are

highlighted: spatial analysis, advocacy, critical speculation, and physical intervention. Though such categorization can provide an interesting explanation of
Palestinian resistance modes, it could be confusing to include different initiatives
that explain different dynamics under the same umbrella. Therefore explaining
them via the rhizome concept of Deleuze and Guattari as rhizomatic resistance,
will highlight in the contemporary forms of resistance in the OPT in Bab Alshams
(tent villages movement).

(Re)colonizing: Bab Alshams

Palestinian and foreigner activists established the Palestinian tent settlement Bab
Alshams (Gate of the Sun) on 11 January 2013. A total of 250 tents, a clinic and
a village council were organized. The objectives announced were to protest about
the Israeli plan to build a Jewish settlement of 3,500 housing units on confiscated
Palestinian land (Mondoweiss, 2013) (see Figure 8.4). The village was evicted
two days later. This action has been portrayed in many media as a counter Jewish
settler's strategy to make facts on the ground, as explained in the *Guardian*: "The
Palestinian activists were borrowing a phrase and a tactic, usually associated with
Jewish settlers, who believe establishing communities means the territory will
remain theirs once structures are built" (*Guardian*, 2013).

Mimicking the colonizer discourse has been identified as subversive resistance
and has been identified as a common practice in the colonial context. Defining
the latest Palestinian resistance actions in Bab Alshams village as subversive
resistance or mimicking resistance do not do the Palestinian resistance justice or
grasp the other socio-cultural and political contexts of the Israeli colonial project
in Palestine.

I personally see the Bab Alshams and other contemporary modes of resistance
(such as the Palestinian Marathon in April 2013) as an embodiment to an earlier
call by Said (2000) in which he highlighted the need to an imaginative and creative
Palestinian resistance forms:

> The immediate task in Palestine is to establish the goal of ridding our-
> selves of the occupation, using imaginative means of struggle. That would
> necessarily involve large numbers of Palestinians intervening directly in
> the settlement process, blocking roads, preventing building materials from
> entering—in other words, isolating the settlements instead of allowing them
> . . . to isolate and surround Palestinians.
>
> (Said, 2000: 30)

Though the Palestinians in establishing and taking over this outpost and
reversing the Israeli settlers' strategy might fall under a mimicry resistance
framework, it has different techniques that take it beyond the discussion of the
discursive resistance model. It can be said that discursive resistance risks
overlooking material structures of power and privileges individual agency. The

FIGURE 8.4 Bab Alshams tent village in front of a Jewish settlement near Jerusalem
Source: Courtesy of Fadi Arouri

Palestinian counter-colonization strategy depended on this understanding of the material structure of power, and the colonial politics of space, yet it privileged and employed the collective agency as a major resistance tool. It did not only reinterpret the colonial discourse; it further lent itself to develop tactics and physical intervention towards the re-appropriation of Palestinian space that aimed at the revival of Palestinian agency as active shapers of the Palestinian reality. Deleuze and Guattari (1987) assert this argument by which creative force can be utilized for revolutionary ends while avoiding the repetition of the state-form that revolutionary struggle fights against.

The Bab Alshams village action has been followed by similar actions, such as the "return" movement inside Israel in which groups of Palestinian youngsters and families have returned to their villages of origin that had either been destroyed or their Palestinian inhabitants evacuated (such villages were declared security zones after the 1948 war): "We are no longer refugees, we returned" (the IQRITH return movement). Barclay and Qaddumi (2013) offer an interesting explanation of the significance of the Bab Alshams settlement as an act of resistance because it represents an advancement and employment of other forms of Palestinian resistance. Beyond the physical intervention in the act of construction itself, the selection of the E1 area[2] as the site for the village exhibited a level of strategic spatial analysis. The employment of legal advocacy by selecting a site where Palestinian private ownership can be proved added to complexity of this event. Therefore, a new condition is created whereby spatial resistance is enacted as a proactive strategy, directly challenging the assumptions of Palestine as a space permanently fractured by, or entirely lost to, Israeli colonization, as Barclay and Qaddumi (2013) explain it.

This latest mode of resistance moved the Palestinian resistance discourse and the anti-colonial resistance in general to another level. It followed a rhizomatic pattern for which it is neither mimetic nor hierarchical, where everything and everyone is equally, marvelously heterogeneous. The deployment of different levels and patterns of actions that connect different circles of power adds to the significance to this resistance mode (from involving social media, mobilization of local and international activities and solidarity groups, awareness, and preparation for the legal aspect). What we need to keep in mind is that, whether we are talking about the rhizome of the collective or that of an individual, both comprise a multiplicity. This multiplicity can be understood as a type of collective, assemblage, or pack. This collectivity defines the rhizome or multiplicity; the aggregate or assemblage becomes the basis for its features as a collective whole:

> A multiplicity is defined not by the elements that compose it in extension, not by the characteristics that compose it in comprehension, but by the lines and dimensions it encompasses in "intension." If you change dimensions, if you add or subtract one, you change the multiplicity. Thus, there is a borderline for each multiplicity; it is in no way a center but rather the enveloping line or farthest dimension, as a function of which it is possible to count the others, all those lines or dimensions constitute the pack at a given moment (beyond the borderline, the multiplicity changes nature).
>
> (Deleuze and Guattari, 1987: 245)

The anomalous power relations emerging from this resistance modus serve as the borderline of the multiplicity. Deleuze and Guattari (1987) describe this as an exceptional individual that alters the very nature of the collective whole—this goes beyond mere individuals. Therefore, altering the very manner of resistance techniques, strategies, and power relations in space and time enables a rupture in the colonial power structure. This corresponds to the principle of a signifying rupture against the over-signifying breaks separating structures or cutting across a single structure:

> A rhizome may be broken, shattered at a given spot, but it will start up again on one of its old lines, or on new lines . . . Every rhizome contains lines of segmentarity according to which it is stratified, territorialised, signified, attributed, etc., as well as lines of deterritorialisation down which it constantly flees.
>
> (Deleuze and Guattari, 1987: 9)

Similar to Foucault's unstable power relationships, Deleuze and Guattari's multiplicities have the potential for change, and since power relationships are simply rhizomatic multiplicities themselves, they too have this unstable nature and can be challenged in a way that can alter their very nature. If the anomaly extends past the current borderline of the multiplicity, the multiplicity changes as a whole. This does not occur simply because a line is redrawn. It extends and alters the multiplicity by adding new aspects, alliances, or individuals into the collective.

Thus, the incorporation of different tools of resistance that are shifting, changing, and developing in space and time, such as the latest " Bab Alshams" phenomenon, changes the makeup of the entire mode of resistance, and a distinctly different multiplicity emerges as a result. One might debate the multiplicity concept in spaces of oppression in which territorialized multiplicities occur due to power asymmetry. The rhizome then can be a useful tool to re-read multiplicities in resistance. While all multiplicities, whether on an individual or at a group level, constantly oscillate through phases of territorialization, deterritorialization, and reterritorialization, there are those that are strictly regulated and organized and those that are more flexible and pliable and resist structured organization. Deleuze and Guattari constantly reference a connection between the macro and micro level. The nodes of a rhizome are connected by flows, and it is this circulation that helps to hold the rhizome together. In other words, implementing different modes of resistance in different spaces and time (for example the Ni'lin weekly anti-Apartheid Wall demonstrations, the re-colonization campaigns in different locations in the OPT on a micro spatial level parallel to other resistance activities at other sites) will not only maintain the momentum of the resistance rhizome; it will help other rhizomatic resistance modes to emerge.

The 2013 Bab Alshams re-colonizing movement has been transformed into a phenomenon for which other dots on the geo-spatial map of the OPT have been assigned to further develop this experiment. When the process of resistance is completely developed and internalized, and has become self-sustaining and self–replicating, then any type of transformation of rhizomatic identity and resistance can take place. This is evident in the way the wave of Bab Alshams resonated across boundaries between groups that would be antagonistic in the context of reactive politics. For example, the political situation of Palestinians inside Israel hinders political resistance, yet the Bab Alshams rhizome has inspired and mobilized Palestinians inside Israel to develop alternative strategies of resistance that were not used before; examples are the Iqreth village return movement and the Tireh return movement. Therefore, in resistance the rhizosphere is constantly in a process of becoming, that is not a mere replication of other forms and patterns of mimesis. Overall, the modalities of this rihzomatic resistance are suggestive of the decomposition rather than seizing of centralized power, and operate through the "smoothing" or deterritorialization of the striated spaces of the colonial state power, rendering spaces "ungovernable" by the hegemonic colonial power in its colonized space and its very "free democratic" national space as well. In the rhizomes of the tent villages movement of Bab Alshams, it is possible to see the foreshadowing of another world that can be also echoed in the Tahrir, Indignados and Occupy movements in the world.

Notes

1   The rhizome is a phenomenon known for a nodal mass of roots that grows horizontally under the soil, such as a root of ginger. Breaking off one or more of a rhizome's nodes does not injure it; that's how it reproduces. Calling the social movements and resistance acts as rhezomatic here refers to a sprawling organizational structure that leverages all points of connectivity to foster growth, as explained by Joan Donovan (2012).

2   E1 (East 1) is located in the eastern part of annexed Jerusalem, which is of high political value for both the Palestinians and the Israelis. The Israeli government approved the construction of thousands of houses to connect the Jewish settlement Ma'ale Adumim. The implementation of construction plans in E1 will create an urban bloc between Ma'ale Adumim and Jerusalem, and exacerbate the isolation of East Jerusalem from the rest of the West Bank, interrupting the territorial contiguity between the northern and southern parts of the West Bank (B'tselem, 2012).

Bibliography

Abada, G., 1999. "Contextual Urban Design for Reshaping the Arabic Islamic Historical Places," Doctorate thesis, University of Stuttgart, Germany.

Abdul Hadi, R., 2003. "Appeal from Nablus: Lift the Siege off Nablus, Balata and Beit Forik," 3 January, Arabic Media Internet Network, www.amin.org/look/amin/en.tpl?Id Language=1&IdPublication=7&NrArticle=14150&NrIssue=1&NrSection=3/ [accessed June–August 2006].

Abdul Hadi, R., 2004. "Appeal from Nablus: Act Immediately to Lift the Siege off Nablus, Balata and Beit Foreek," Electronic intifada, 3 January, http://electronicintifada.net/content/act-immediately-lift-siege-nablus-balata-and-beit-foreek/1500 [accessed August 2009].

Abel, M., 1938. *Géographie de la Palestine II*, Leeds: University of Leeds Department of Semitic Languages and Literatures Library.

Abujidi, N., 2009 "The Palestinian States of Exception and Agamben," *Contemporary Arab Affairs*, 2(2): 272–291.

Abujidi, N., 2010. "Agamben and Foucault in the Occupied Palestinian Territories" in Hanafi, S. (ed.) *State of Exception and Resistance in the Arab World*, Beirut: Institute for Arab Studies, pp. 212–242.

Abujidi, N., 2011. "Post-War Social Resilience and Place Remaking" in Frerks, G. and Goldewijk, B. (eds) *Cultural Emergency in Conflict and Disaster*, Rotterdam: NAi, pp. 322–344.

Abujidi, N., 2011. "Surveillance and Spatial Flows" in Abulaban, Y., Zurieq, E. and Lyon, D. (eds) *Surveillance and Control in Israel/Palestine: Population, Territory and Power*, London and New York: Routledge, pp. 313–333.

Abujidi, N. and Verschure, H., 2006. "Urbicide as Design by Construction and Destruction Process: The Case of Nablus/Palestine," *The World Geographer*, 9(2): 126–154.

Abu-Lughod, J. L., 1991. *Changing Cities: Urban Sociology*, New York: Harper Collins.

Abu Shmais, W., 2004. "Soldiers in my House: Three Weeks to Freedom," www.najah.edu/sites/default/files/soldiers_in_my_house.pdf1268914649.pdf [accessed August 2009].

Abu Sitta, S., 2005. *The Atlas of Palestine 1948*, London: The Palestine Land Society.

Abu-Zahra, N., 2005. "Nationalism for Security? Re-examining Zionism," *The Arab World Geographer*, 8(4): 248–276.

Adams, N., 1993. "Architecture as the Target," *Journal of the Society of Architectural Historians*, 52(4) December: 389–390.

Agamben, G., 1998. *Homo Sacre: Sovereign Power and Bare Life*, Stanford, CA: Stanford University Press.

Agamben, G., 2004. "Life, a Work of Art Without an Author: The State of Exception, The Administration of Disorder and Private Life" [Interview]. *German Law Journal*, 5: 609–614.

Ahmed, N., 2011. "Gaza: A Case Study of Urban Destruction Through Military Involvement," unpublished Masters thesis in Art, Temple University, Philadelphia, PA.

Al-Dabbagh and Murad, M., 1978. *Biladuna Fitastin [Our Country, Palestine]* 10 vols, Beirut: Dar al-Tali'a.

Algazi, G. and Budeir, A., 2002. "The Transfer is Underway." *Ha'aretz*, 15 November.

Al-Nimr, I., 1976. *Tarikh jabal Nablus wal-Balqa' [History of the Nablus region]*, 4 vols, Nablus: Jam'iyyat 'Ummal al-Matabi' al-Ta'awuniyya.

Alonso, W., 1986. "The Unplanned Paths of Planning Schools," *The Public Interest*, 82: 58–71.

Altman, I., 1975. *The Environment and Social Behaviour: Privacy, Personal Space, Territory, Crowding*, Monterey, CA: Brooks/Cole.

Amnesty International, 2002. "Shielded from Scrutiny: IDF Violations in Jenin and Nablus," AI Index No. MDE 15/143/2002), www.amnesty.org/en/library/info/MDE15/143/2002 [accessed May 2003].

ARIJ (Applied Research Institute Jerusalem), 2006. "New Colonial Road To Be Constructed On Lands Of Western Ramallah Villages," www.poica.org/editor/case_studies/view.php?recordID=749 [accessed November 2006].

Assi, E., 2000. "Typological Analysis of Palestinian Traditional Court House," www.unesco.org/archi2000/pdf/assi.pdf.

Bacon, E., 1976. *Design of Cities*, New York: Penguin Books.

BADIL Resource Center, 2004a. "The Continuing Catastrophe: 1967 and Beyond," Occasional Bulletin No. 19, www.badil.org/es/recursos-en-espanol/57-press-releases-2004/1578-press-353-04 [accessed May 2003].

BADIL Resource Center, 2004b. "Estimated Initial Palestinian Refugee Population, By Year of Displacement," www.internal-displacement.org/8025708F004CE90B/(http Documents)/88D674B375875289C1257356004F8707/$file/survey-06-07+(1).pdf [accessed May 2003].

BADIL Resource Center, 2006. "Facts and Figures," www.badil.org/en/israel-and-the-nakba [accessed November 2006].

Barclay, A. and Qaddumi, D., 2013. "On Strategies of Spatial Resistance in Palestine," *Open Security; Reconciliation and Conflict*, 14 February, www.opendemocracy.net/open security/ahmad-barclay-dena-qaddumi/on-strategies-of-spatial-resistance-in-palestine [accessed June 2013].

Benevelo, L., 1967. *The Origins of Modern Town Planning*, Cambridge, MA: MIT Press.

Ben-Gurion, D., 1973. *My Talks with Arab Leaders*, New York: Okpaku Communications.

Benvenisti, M., 1970. *The Crusaders in the Holy Land, Jerusalem*, New York: Israel Universities Press.

Benvenisti, M., 2000. *Sacred Landscape: The Buried History of the Holy Land since 1948*, Berkeley, CA: University of California Press.

Berman, M., 1987a. "Life in the Shadows: The Underside of New York City," *New Internationalist*, 167.

Berman, M., 1987b. "Among the Ruins," *New Internationalist*, 178, www.newint.org/issue 178/among.htm [accessed May 2003].

Berman, M., 1996. "Falling Tower: City Life after Urbicide" in Crow, D. (ed.) *Geography and Identity: Living and Exploring Geopolitics of Identity*, Washington DC: Maisonneuve Press, pp. 172–192.

Berman, M., 2006. "*Moments of Grace: The American City in the 1950s*, by Johns, M. 2003," Book Review in *Harvard Design Magazine*, 23, Fall: 1–5.

Bernadotte, F., 1948. Progress Report of the United Nations Mediator on Palestine (UN Doc. A/648, 16 September 1948), http://unispal.un.org/UNISPAL.NSF/0/AB14D4AAFC4E 1BB985256204004F55FA [accessed June 2005].

Bevan, R., 2006. *The Destruction of Memory: Architecture at War*, Edinburgh: Reaktion Books.

B'hess, M. and O'beed, F., 2004. *The Massacre of Nablus*, Jerusalem: Alquds.

Bigo, D., 2006. "Security, Exception, Ban and Surveillance" in Lyon, D. (ed.) *Theorizing Surveillance: The Panopticon and Beyond*, Cullompton, UK: Willan.

Bishop, R. and Clancey, G., 2003. "The City as Target, or Perpetuation and Death" in Bishop, R., Phillips, J. and Yeo, W. (eds) *Postcolonial Urbanism*, New York: Routledge, pp. 63–86.

Bloch, L. B., 1961. *Feudal Society*, Chicago, IL: University of Chicago Press.

Bogard, W., 2006. "Surveillance Assemblages and Lines of Flight" in Lyon, D. (ed.) *Theorizing Surveillance: The Panopticon and Beyond*, Cullompton, UK: Willan.

Bonaiuto, M., Breakwell, G. and Canto, L., 1996. "Identity Processes and Environmental Threat: The Effects of Nationalism and Local Identity Upon Perception of Beach Pollution," *Journal of Community and Applied Social Psychology*, 6: 157–175.

Bondi, L., 1993. "Locating Identity Politics" in Keith, M. and Pile, S. (eds) *Place and the Politics of Identity*, London: Routledge, pp. 84–101.

Bonine, M. E., 1990. "Bazaar" in *Encyclopaedia Iranica*, vol. 4, London and New York: Routledge & Kegan Paul.

Bonnes, M. and Secchiaroli, G., 1995. *Environmental Psychology: A Psychosocial Introduction*, London: Sage.

Broadbent, G., 1990. *Emerging Concepts in Urban Space Design*, New York: Van Nostrand Reinhold International.

Bronstein, E., 2004. "The Nakba: An Event that Didn't Occur (Although it Had to Occur)," www.palestineremembered.com/Articles/General/Story1649.html [accessed September 2005].

B'tselem, 2002. "Operation Defensive Shield: Soldiers' Testimonies, Palestinian Testimonies," www.btselem.org/Download/200207_Defensive_Shield_Eng.pdf [accessed November 2006].

B'tselem, 2004. "Forbidden Roads: The Discriminatory West Bank Regime," www.btselem. org/download/200408_forbidden_roads_eng.pdf [accessed November 2006].

B'tselem, 2005. "Statistics on Checkpoint and Road Blocks," www.btselem.org/english/ Freedom_of_Movement/Statistics.asp [accessed November 2006].

B'tselem, 2012. "The E1 plan and its Implications for Human Rights in the West Bank," 2 December, www.btselem.org/settlements/20121202_e1_human_rights_ramifications [accessed May 2013].

Burke, G., 1971. *Towns in the Making London*, London: Edward Arnold.

Burke, J., 2001. "Homes Razed in New Israeli Attack," *The Observer*, 15 April: 21.

Butina, G., 1993. "The Art of Building Cities: Urban Structuring and Restructuring" in Hayward, R. and McGlynn, S. (eds) *Making Better Places: Urban Design Now*, Oxford: Butterworth Architecture, pp. 64–71.

Butina, G. and Bently, I., 1991. "Constructing Local And Regional Identity" in Arisitidis, A., Karaletsou, C. and Tsoukala, K. (eds), *Socio-environmental Metamorphoses* (12th International Conference proceedings of the IAPS), Chalkidikik, Greece, 11–14 July 1992.

Calame, J. and Charlesworth, E., 2002. "The Divided City as Broken Artefact," *Essay for Mediterranean: Protection of Cultural and Environmental Patrimony*, vol. 2.

Carter, H., 1983. *Introduction to Urban Historical Geography*, London: Edward Arnold.

Cashdan, E., 1983. "Territoriality among Human Foragers: Ecological Models and an Application to Four Bushmen Groups," *Current Anthropology*, 24: 47–66.

Castells, M., 1983. *The City and the Grassroots: A Cross-Cultural Theory of Urban Social Movements*, London: Edward Arnold.

Catudal, H. M., 1979. *The Exclave Problem of Western Europe*, Tuscaloosa, AL: University of Alabama Press.

Celebi, E., 1968. 1611–1682. *Narrative of Travels in Europe, Asia, and Africa, in the Seventeenth Century*, trans. R. J. von Hammer, New York: Johnson Reprint.

Cervero, R. and Wilson, A., 1994. *Planning Responsibly for Adult Education*, San Francisco, CA: Jossey-Bass.

Chomsky, N., 2009. "Exterminate all the Brutes: Gaza 2009," 19 January (revised 6 June 2009), www.chomsky.info/articles/20090119.htm [accessed May 2013].

Chomsky, N. and Pappé, I., 2010. *Gaza in Crisis: Reflections on Israel's War Against the Palestinians*, London: Penguin Group.

CIA (Central Intelligence Agency), 2006. *CIA World Factbook: Israel.* www.cia.gov/cia/publications/factbook/geos/is.html [accessed November 2006].

Clay, G., 1973. *Close Up: How to Read the American City*, New York: Praeger.

Cohen, A., 1993. *The Symbolic Construction of Community*, London: Routledge.

Cohen, A., 1994. *Self-Consciousness: An Alternative Anthropology of Identity*, London: Routledge.

Collinge, C., 1999. "Self-organization of Society by Scale: A Spatial Reworking of Regulation Theory," *Environment and Planning D: Society and Space*, 17: 557–574.

Collins, J., 2013. "A Problematic Duo? Airpower and Casualty-averse Decision-making: Israel and the Second Lebanon War," *The Journal of The Royal Canadian Military Institute*, January–February, 73(1): 10.

Connerton, P., 1989. *How Societies Remember*, Cambridge: Cambridge University Press.

Connolly, W. E., 2002. "Confessing Identity/Belonging to Difference" in Connolly, W. E. *Identity/Difference*, Expanded Edition, Ithaca, NY: Cornell University Press, p. xiii.

Conzen, M. P., 1978. "Analytical Approaches to the Urban Landscape" in Butzer, K. W. (ed.) *Dimensions of Human Geography*, Chicago, IL: The University of Chicago Department of Geography.

Conzen, M. R. G., 1958. "The Growth and Character of Whitby" in Daysh, G. H. J. (ed.) *A Survey of Whitby and the Surrounding Area*, Eton: Shakespeare Head Press, pp. 49–89.

Conzen, M. R. G., 1960. *Alnwick, Northumberland: A Study in Town-Plan Analysis*, Publication No. 27, London: Institute of British Geographers.

Conzen, M. R. G., 1981. "The Plan Analysis of an English City Centre" in Whitehand, J. W. R. (ed.) The *Urban Landscape: Historical Development and Management: Papers by M. R. G. Conzen*, Publication, No. 13, London: Institute of British Geographers.

Conzen, M. R. G., 1988. "Morphogenesis, Morphological Regions and Secular Human Agency in the Historic Townscape, as Exemplified by Ludlow" in D. Denecke and G. Shaw (eds) *Urban Historical Geography, Recent Progress in Britain and Germany*, Cambridge: Cambridge University Press, pp. 253–272.

Corbin, C., 2002. "Representation of an Imagined Past: Fairground Heritage Villages," *International Journal of Cultural Studies*, 8(3).

Cordesman, A. H., 2009. *The Gaza War: A Strategic Analysis*, Washington, DC: CSIS Center for Strategic and International Studies.

Coward, M., 2001a. "Urbicide and the Question of Community in Bosnia-Herzegovina." Unpublished thesis) submitted in partial fulfilment of the requirements for the degree of PhD in Politics, Newcastle University, UK.

Coward, M., 2001b. "Community as Heterogeneous Ensemble: Mostar and Multiculturalism," paper presented in the ISA Annual Convention, Chicago, 21–24 February.

Coward, M., 2002a. "Community as Heterogeneous Ensemble: Mostar and Multiculturalism," *Journal of Alternatives: Global, Local, Political*, 27: 29–66.

Coward, M., 2002b. "Urbicide in Bosnia," paper presented in Cities as Strategic Sites: Militarization, Anti-Globalization and Warfare Conference, Manchester, 6–9 November.

Coward, M., 2004. "Urbicide in Bosnia" in Graham S. (ed.) *Cities, War and Terrorism: Towards an Urban Geopolitics*, Oxford: Blackwell, pp. 154–171.

Coward, M., 2005. "Against Anthropocentrism: The Destruction of the Built Environment as a Distinct Form of Political Violence," paper presented at Urbicide: The Killing of Cities Workshop, Durham, UK, 24 October.

Coward, M., 2006. "Against Anthropocentrism: The Destruction of the Built Environment as a Distinct Form of Political Violence," *Review of International Studies*, 32(3): 419–437.

Coward, M., 2009. "Network-centric Violence, Critical Infrastructure and the Urbanisation of Security," *Security Dialogue*, Special Issue on Urban Insecurities, 40(4–5): 399–418.

Coward, M., 2009b. *Urbicide: The Politics of Urban Destruction*, London: Routledge.

Cowen, D., 2007. "National Soldiers and the War on Cities," *Theory and Event*, 10(2): 1–18.

Creswell, K. A. C., 1989. *A Short Account of Early Muslim Architecture*, Aldershot: Scholars Press.

Crouch, D. P., Garr, D. J. and Mundigo, A. I., 1982. *Spanish City Planning in North America*, Cambridge, MA: MIT Press.

Cullen, G., 1959. *Townscape*, London: Architectural Press.

Cullen, G., 1971. *The Concise Townscape*, New York: Van Nostrand Reinhold.

Dabbagh, M., 1965. *Biladna Falastin (Our Country Palestine)*, vol. 1, Beirut: The Arab Institute for Research and Publishing.

Dahlman, C. and Tuathail, G., 2005. "The Legacy of Ethnic Cleansing," *Political Geography*, 24(5): 569–599.

Darwish, M., 2001. "Not to Begin at the End," *Al-Ahram Weekly Online*, 10–16 May, Issue No. 533, http://weekly.ahram.org.eg/2001/533/op1.htm [accessed June 2005].

DCI/PS (Defence for Children International, Palestine Section), 2001. A Generation Denied: Israeli Violations of Palestinian Children's Rights, Jerusalem: DCI/PL, www.dci-palestine.org/sites/default/files/generationdenied.pdf [accessed February 2004].

De Cauter, L., 2004. *The Capsular Civilization: On the City in the Age of Fear*, Rotterdam: NAi.

De Certeau, M., 1984. *The Practice of Everyday Life*, trans. S. Rendall, Berkeley, CA: University of California Press.

Delaney, D. and Leitner, H., 1997. "The Political Construction of Scale," *Political Geography*, 16(2), Special Issue: Political Geography of Scale: 93–97.

Deleuze, G. and Guattari, F., 1987. *A Thousand Plateaus: Capitalism and Schizophrenia*, Minneapolis, MN and London: University of Minnesota Press.

Devine, P. Wright and Lyons, E., 1997. "Remembering Pasts and Representing Places: The Construction of National Identities in Ireland," *Journal of Environmental Psychology*, 17: 33–45.

Donor Support Group, 2002. "Physical and Institutional Damage Assessment West Bank Governorates March–May, 2002 Summary Report," Local aid coordination committee, http://pdf.usaid.gov/pdf_docs/PNACQ160.pdf [accessed February 2004].

Donovan, J., 2012. "How Occupy Birthed a Rhizome," *Waging Non Violence*, 17 September, http://wagingnonviolence.org/feature/how-occupy-birthed-a-rhizome/ [accessed May 2013].

Doumani, B., 1995. *Rediscovering Palestine: Merchants and Peasants in Jabal Nablus, 1700–1900*, Berkeley, CA: University of California Press.

Doumani, B., 2004. "Scenes from the Daily Life: the View from Nablus," *Journal of Palestine Studies*, 34(1): 1–14.

Driver, F. and Gilbert, D. (eds), 2003. *Imperial Cities: Landscape, Display and Identity*, Manchester: Manchester University Press.

Duncan, J. S., 1998. "Classics in Human Geography Revisited: J. S. Duncan, 1980: 'The Super Organic in American Cultural Geography,' Author's Response," *Human Geography*, 22(4): 571–573.

Duncombe, S. (ed.), 2002. *Cultural Resistance Reader*, London: Verso.

Dupuis, M. and Vandergeest, P., 1996. *Creating the Countryside: the Politics of Rural and Environmental Discourse*, Philadelphia, PA: Temple University Press.

Durrheim, K., 2001. "The Role of Place and Metaphor in Racial Exclusion: South Africa's Beaches as Sites of Shifting Racialisation," *Ethnic and Racial Studies*, 24: 433–450.

Durrheim, K. and Dixon, K., 2004. "Dislocating Identity: Desegregation and the Transformation of Place," *Journal of Environmental Psychology*, 24(4).

Edwards, D., 1997. *Discourse and Cognition*, London: Sage.

Edwards, D. and Potter, J., 1992. *Discursive Psychology*, London: Sage.

Edwards, L. Glaeser and Shapiro, J. M., 2001. *Cities and Warfare: The Impact of Terrorism on Urban*, Cambridge, MA: Harvard University.

Efrat, Z., 2003. "The Plan" in Weizman, E. and Seal, R. (ed) *Civilian Occupation: The Politics of Israeli Architecture*, London: Verso, pp. 60–71.

El-Fanni, I., 1999. *Nablus in the Greek and Roman Civilizations*, Nablus: Nablus Municipality Publications.

El-Fanni, I., 2007. "Shechem-Mamurta-Mabratha-Neapolis," *This Week in Palestine*, Issue No. 7, www.thisweekinpalestine.com/i107/pdfs/March%202007.pdf [accessed May 2013].

Elisséeff, N., 1980. "Physical Lay-out in the Islamic City" in Serjeant, R. B. (ed.) *The Islamic City*, Paris: Presses Universitaire de France, pp. 327–385.

Entrikin, J. N., 1989. "Introduction: The Nature of Geography in Perspective" in Entrikin, J. N. and Brunn, S. D. (eds) *Reflections on Richard Hartshorne's The Nature of Geography*, Baltimore, MD: Johns Hopkins University Press, pp. 1–15.

Entrikin, J. N., 1991. *The Betweenness of Place*, Cambridge: Polity Press.

Evans, G., 2002a. "Living in a World Heritage City: Stakeholders in the Dialectic of the Universal and Particular," *International Journal of Cultural Studies*, 8(2).

Evans, M., 2002b, "Clausewitz's Chamelean: Military Theory and the Future of War," *Quadrent Magazine Defence*, XLVI(11).

Evans, M., 2004. "Clausewitz's Chameleon: Military Theory and Practice in the early 21st Century" in Evans, M., Ryan, A. and Parkin, R. (eds) *Future Armies, Future Challenges, Land Warfare in the Information Age*, Crows Nest, NSW: Allen & Unwin, pp. 26–42.

Falah, G., 1996. "The 1948 Israeli-Palestinian War and its Aftermath: the Transformation and De-signification of Palestine's Cultural Landscape," *Annals of the Association of American Geographers*, 86(2): 256–285.

Falah, G., 2003. "Dynamics and Patterns of the Shrinking of Arab Lands in Palestine," *Political Geography*, 22: 179–209.

Falah, G and Flint, C., 2004. "Geopolitical Spaces: The Dialectic of Public and Private Spaces in the Palestine–Israel Conflict," *The Arab World Geographer*, 7: 11–134.

Falamaki, M. M., 1992. *Formation of Architecture in Iranian and Western Experiments*, Tehran: Nashr-i-Faza.

Falpan, S., 1979. *Zionism and the Palestinians*, London: Croom Helm.

Feidi, S., 2000. "The Historical and Morphological Transformation of the Urban Spaces in Old Nablus," Master's thesis. University of Jordan, Amman.

Feld, S. and Basso K. H. (eds), 1996. *Senses of Place*, Santa Fe, NM: School of American Research Press.

Fentress, J. and Wickham, C., 1992, *Social Memory: New Perspectives on the Past*, Oxford: Blackwell.

Finkelstein, N., 1995. *Image and Reality of the Israel-Palestine Conflict*, New York: Verso.

Finkelstein, N., 1998. "Securing Occupation: The Real Meaning of the Wye River Memorandum," *New Left Review*, 232: 128–139.

Fischbac, M. R., 2000. "Nablus" in Mattar, P. (ed.) *Encyclopaedia of the Palestinians*, New York: Facts on File.

Fischer H., 1999. *Collateral Damage, Crimes of War: What the Public Should Know*, New York: Norton.

Flapan, S., 1979. *Zionism and the Palestinians*, London: Croom Helm.

Fleming, P. and Sewell, G., 2002. "Looking for the Good Soldier, Švejk: Alternative Modalities of Resistance," *The Contemporary Workplace, Sociology*, 36(4): 857–873.

Floor, W. M., 1990. "Bazaar" in: *Encyclopedia Iranica*, vol. 4, London and New York: Routledge & Kegan Paul.

Forester, J., 1989. *Planning in the Face of Power*, Berkeley, CA: University of California.

Foucault, M., 1980. *Power/Knowledge: Selected Interviews and Other Writings, 1972–1977*, ed. C. Gordon, New York: Pantheon.

Foucault, M., 1984. *The Foucault Reader*, ed. P. Rabinow, New York: Pantheon.

Fowler, P., 2011. "Palestine: A Future for Its Heritage?, www.thisweekinpalestine.com/details.php?id=3352&edid=192 [accessed February 2009].

Frieldand, R. and Boden, D. (eds). 1994. *No Where/Space, Time and Modernity*, Berkeley, CA: University of California Press.

Gamboni, D., 2001. "World Heritage: Shield or Target?," *The Getty Conservation Institute Newsletter*, 16: 5–11.

Ganor, E., 2005. "Holy Land or Living Hell? Ecocide in Palestine," *Earth First!*, 25(6), www.earthfirstjournal.org/articles.php [accessed April 2006].

Giddens, A., 1979. *Central Problems in Social Theory*, Berkeley, CA: University of California.

Giddens, A., 1984. *The Constitution of Society, Outlines of the Theory of Structuration*, Cambridge: Polity Press.

Gieryn, T. F., 2000. "A Space for Place in Sociology," *Annual Review of Sociology*, 26: 463–496.

Gillis, J., 1994. *Commemorations: The Politics of National Identity*, Princeton, NJ: Princeton University Press.

Ginbar, Y., 1997. "Demolishing Peace: Israel's Policy of Mass Demolition of Palestinian Houses in the West Bank," *B'Tselem Information Sheet*, September.

Goldenberg, S., 2002. "The Lunar Landscape that was the Jenin Refugee Camp," *Guardian*, 16 April, www.guardian.co.uk/world/2002/apr/16/israel.readersyear [accessed May 2013].

Golledge, R. G. and Stimson, R., 1979. *Spatial Behaviour: A Geographic Perspective*, New York: Guilford.

Gordon, N., 2008. "From Colonization to Separation: Exploring the Structure of Israel's Occupation," *Third World Quarterly*, 29(1): 25–44.

Graham, S., 2002a. "Clean Territory: Urbicide in the West Bank," *Open Democracy*. www. opendemocracy.net/conflict-politicsverticality/article_241.jsp [accessed May 2013].

Graham, S., 2002b. "Urbanizing War/Militarizing Cities: City as Strategic Site," *Archis*, 3: 25–35.

Graham, S., 2003. "Lessons in Urbicide," *New Left Review*, 19: 53–78.

Graham, S., 2004a. "Cities as Strategic Sites: Place Annihilation and Urban Geopolitics" in Graham, S. (ed.) *Cities War and Terrorism: Towards an Urban Geopolitics*, Oxford: Blackwell, pp. 31–54.

Graham, S., 2004b. "Constructing Urbicide by Bulldoze in the Occupied Territories" in Graham, S. (ed.) *Cities War and Terrorism: Towards an Urban Geopolitics*, Oxford: Blackwell, pp. 198–214.

Graham, S., 2005. "Remembering Fallujah: Demonising Place, constructing Atrocity," *Environment and Planning D: Society and Space*, 23: 1–10.

Graham S., 2007. "War and the City," *New Left Review* 44, March–April, http://new leftreview.org/II/44/stephen-graham-war-and-the-city [accessed May 2013].

Gregory, D., 2003. "Defiled Cities," *Singapore Journal of Tropical Geography*, 24: 307–326.

Gregory, D., 2004. "Palestine and the War on Terror," *Comparative Studies of South Asia, Africa and the Middle East*, 24: 183–195.

Guardian, 2013. "Palestinian Protesters Evicted from West Bank Site," 13 January, www.guardian.co.uk/world/feedarticle/10608602 [accessed June 2013].

Gwynne, A., 2005. "It is Far From Quiet Here," *Al-Ahram Weekly On-line*, 22 September, http://weekly.ahram.org.eg/2005/728/re101.htm [accessed April 2013].

Habraken, N. J., 1998. *The Structure of the Ordinary*, Cambridge, London: MIT Press.

Habraken, N. J., 2000. *The Structure of the Ordinary*, Cambridge, MA: MIT Press.

Haggerty, K., 2006. "Tear Down the Walls: On Demolishing the Panopticon" in Lyon, D. (ed.) *Theorizing Surveillance: The Panopticon and Beyond*, Cullompton, UK: Willan.

Haggerty, K. and Ericsson, R., 2000. "The Surveillant Assemblage," *British Journal of Sociology*, 55(4): 605–622.

Hague Convention of the Protection of Cultural Property in the Event of Armed Conflict, 1956. Cited from: http://portal.unesco.org/en/ev.php-URL_ID=13637&URL_DO=DO_TOPIC&URL_SECTION=201.html [accessed April 2013].

Hakim, B. S., 1986. *Arabic-Islamic Cities, Building and Planning Principles*, London: Kegan Paul.

Halbwachs, M., 1992. *On Collective Memory*, Chicago, IL: The University of Chicago Press.

Halileh, S., 2002. "The Effects of Israel's Operation Defensive Shield on Palestinian Children Living in the West Bank," Birzeit University, Palestine: Institute of Community and Public Health, 29 June.

Halper, J., 1999. "Dismantling the Matrix of Control," SEARCH for Justice and Equality in Palestine/Israel, www.israeli-occupation.org/2009-09-11/jeff-halper-dismantling-the-matrix-of-control/.

Hanafi, S., 2004. "Targeting Space Through Biopolitics: The Israeli Colonial Project," *Palestine Report*, 18 February.

Hanafi, S., 2006. "The Spacio-cide of Palestine" in Misselwitz, P. and Rieniets, T. (eds) *City of Collisions: Jerusalem and the Principles of Conflict Urbanism*, Basel, Boston, MA, Berlin: Bikhauser-Publishers for Architecture, pp. 93–101.

Harvey, D., 1992. "From Space to Place and Back Again: Reflections on the Condition of Post-Modernity" in Bird, J., Curtis, B., Putnam T., Robertson, G. and Tickner, L. *Mapping the Futures: Local Cultures, Global Change*, London: Routledge, pp. 3–30.

Harvey, D., 1993. "Class Relations, Social Justice and the Politics of Difference" in Keith, M. and Pile, S. (eds) *Place and the Politics of Identity*, London: Routledge, pp. 22–40.

Harvey, D., 1998. "The Body as an Accumulation Strategy," *Environment and Planning D: Society and Space*, 16: 401–421.

Hass, A., 2002. "Israeli Tanks Roll across the West Bank," *Ha'aretz*, 4 April.

Hass, A., 2003a. "Operation Destroy the Data," *Ha'aretz*, 14 March, http://web.archive. org/web/20030313224244/http://news.haaretz.co.il/hasen/pages/ShArt.jhtml?itemNo= 155181 [accessed February 2004].

Hass, A., 2003b. "You Can Drive Along and Never See an Arab," *Ha'aretz*, 22 January, http://jewishvoiceforpeace.org/content/hass-you-can-drive-along-and-never-see-arab [accessed February 2004].

Hass, A., Hare, A. and Kra, B., 2001. "Four Palestinians Killed in Gaza Clashes: Violence in the Territories Continued Throughout The Two Day Holiday Period, Particularly in the Gaza Strip. The West Bank was Relatively Quiet Yesterday and Monday," *Haaretz*, 10 October, www.haaretz.com/print-edition/news/4-palestinians-killed-in-gaza-clashes-1.71534 [accessed February 2004].

Hassner, P., 2000. "Beyond War and Totalitarianism: The New Dynamics of Violence," in Prins, G. and Tromp, H. (eds) *The Future of War*, The Hague: Kluwer Law International, pp. 197–211.

Hayden, D., 1995. *The Power of Place: Urban Landscapes as Public History*. Cambridge, MA: MIT Press.

Heathcote, E., 2005. "Call this civilization?" *Financial Times*, 19 August. www.archiseek. com/content/showthread.php?t=4236 [accessed 19 August 2005].

Heidegger, M., 1997. *Kant and the Problem of Metaphysics*, Bloomington IN: Indiana University Press.

Herb, G. and Kaplan, D. (eds), 1999. *Nested Identities: Nationalism, Territory and Scale*, Lanham, MD: Rowman & Littlefield, pp. 9–30.

Herod, A., 1997. "From a Geography of Labour to a Labour of Geography," *Antipode*, 29(1): 1–31.

Herscher, A., 2005. "Modernism Urban Destruction and the History of Spatial Violence in Kosovo," unpublished paper presented at Urbicide: The Killing of Cities Workshop, Durham, UK, 24 October.

Hewitt, K., 1983. "Place Annihilation: Area Bombing and the Fate of Urban Places," *Annals of the Association of American Geographer*, 73(2): 257.

Hewitt, K, 1987. "The Social Space of Terror: Towards a Civil Interpretation of Total War," *Environment and Planning D: Society and Space*, 5(4): 445–474.

Heynen, H. and Loeckx, A., 1998. "Scenes of Ambivalence: Concluding Remarks on Architectural Patterns of Displacement," *Journal of Architectural Education*, 52(2): 100–108.

Hirschheim, R. and Newman, M., 1988. "Information Systems and User Resistance: Theory and Practice," *The Computer Journal*, 31(5): 398–408.

Hobbes, T., 1998 [1651]. *Leviathan*, Oxford: Oxford World Classics.

Hollander, J. A. and Einwohner, R. L., 2004. "Conceptualizing Resistance," *Sociological Forum*, 19(4): 533–554.

Homi, B., 1994. *The Location of Culture*, London: Routledge.

Human Rights Watch, 2002. "Israel, The Occupied West Bank and Gaza Strip, and The Palestinian Authority Territories Jenin: IDF Military Operation," 14(3), May, www.hrw. org/reports/2002/israel3/israel0502.pdf [accessed February 2004].

Hutton, H., 1993. *History as an Art of Memory*, Hanover, NH: University Press of New England.

ICOMOS (International Council on Monuments and Sites), 2002. "The Impact of War on Iraq's Cultural Heritage," cited from www.international.icomos.org/risk/2002/iraq 2002.htm [accessed February 2004].

Ignatieff, M., 1999. *The Warriors Honour: Ethnic War and the Modern Conscience,* London: Vintage.

Ismail, S. (ed.), 1982. *The Arab City: Its Character and Islamic Cultural Heritage,* Riyadh: Arab Urban Development Institute, Saudi Arabia.

ITIC (Intelligence and Terrorism Information Centre) at the Centre for Special Studies, n.d. "Nablus: The Main Infrastructure of Palestinian Terrorism," www.intelligence.org. il/eng/bu/nablus/appen_b.htm [accessed 15 July 2005].

Jackson, J. B., 1994. *A Sense of Place, a Sense of Time,* Newhaven, CT: Yale University.

Jacobi, M. and Stokolos, D., 1983. "The Role of Tradition in Group-Environment Relations" in Feimer, N. R. and Geller, E. S. (eds), *Environmental Psychology,* New York: Praeger Press, pp. 16–78.

Jameson, F., 1989. *Postmodernism,* Durham, NC: Duke University Press.

Jamoul, L., 2004. "Palestine: In Search of Dignity," *Antipode,* 36(4): 581–592.

Jaussen, A. J., 1927. "Coutumes Palestinians: Naplouse et son District," Paris: Geuthner.

Jeffress, D., 2008. *Postcolonial Resistance: Culture, Liberation and Transformation,* Toronto: University of Toronto Press.

Jones, III. J. P. and Natter, W., 1999, "Space and representation" in Buttimer A., Brunn, S. D. and Wardenga, U. (eds) *Text And Image: Social Construction of Regional Knowledges,* Leipzig: Selbstverlag Institut für Länderkunde, pp. 239–247.

Kalboune, A. 1992. *Nablus City History, 2500 BC–1918 AD,* Nablus Dar Alqalam: Kalboune.

Kaldor, M., 1999. *New and Old Wars: Organized Violence in a Global Era,* Cambridge: Polity.

Kaldor, M., 2001. "Beyond Militarism, Arms Races and Arms Control," Essay prepared for the Nobel Peace Prize Centennial Symposium, 6–8 December, www.ssrc.org/ sept11/essays/kaldor.htm [accessed May 2004].

Keith, M., and Pile, S. (eds), 1993. *Place and the Politics of Identity,* London: Routledge.

Khalidi, R., 1997. *Palestinian Identity: The Construction of Modern National Consciousness,* New York: Columbia University Press.

Khalidi, W., 1961. "Plan Dalet: Master Plan for the Conquest of Palestine," *Journal of Palestine Studies,* 18(1).

Khalidi, W., 1992. *All That Remains: The Palestinian Villages Occupied and Depopulated by Israel in 1948,* Washington, DC: Institute for Palestine Studies.

Khalidi, W., 1992. *Palestine Reborn,* London: I. B. Tauris.

Khalidi, W., 1999. *Bena'a Al-Dawala Al-Yahoudiyyah 1897–1948,* Beirut: Majallat al-Dirasat al-Felastianiyyah.

Khan Alwakalah project, www.enpi-info.eu/files/features/OPT%20-%20NABLUS%20 restoring%20the%20Old%20City_en.v.2.pdf [accessed May 2004].

Khatib, A., 1986. "Housing in Nablus: Socio-Economic Characteristics and Housing Satisfaction of three Palestinian sub-groups," PhD Dissertation, University of New York.

Khoury, N., 2004. "One Fine Curfew Day," MIFTAH.org, www.miftah.org/Display.cfm? DocId=3119&CategoryId=20 [accessed March 2005].

Kimmerling, B. and Migdal, J. S., 2003. *The Palestinian People: A History.* Cambridge, MA: Harvard University Press.

Klett, F. R. and Alpaugh D., 1976. "Environmental Learning and Large Scale Environments" in Moore, G. T. and Golledge, R. G. (eds) *Environmental Knowing: Theories, Research, and Methods,* Stroudsburg, PA: Dowden, Hutchinson & Ross, pp. 121–130.

Kostof, K., 1996. "Urban Tissue and the Character of Towns," *Urban Design International*, 1(3): 247–263.

Kostof, S., 1991. *The City Shaped*, London: Thames & Hudson.

Kropf, K., 1998. "Typological Zoning" in Petruccioli, A. (ed.) *Typological Process and Design Theory*, Cambridge, MA: MIT, pp. 127–140.

Krupat, A., 1983. "Foreword," in Radin, P., *Crashing Thunder: The Autobiography of an American Indian*, Lincoln, NE: University of Nebraska Press, pp. ix–xviii.

Lalli, M., 1992. "Urban-Related Identity: Theory, Measurement and Empirical Findings," *Journal of Environmental Psychology*, 12: 285–301.

Lane, A., 1991. "Urban Morphology," *Urban Design Quarterly*, London, April, pp. 10–14.

Larkham, P., 1987 "Urban Morphology in Poland," *Urban Morphology News Letter*.

Larkham, P., 1998. "Urban Morphology and Typology in the United Kingdom" in Petruccioli, A. (ed.) *Typological Process and Design Theory*, Cambridge, MA: MIT, pp. 159–177.

Lefebvre, H., 1974. *The Production of Space*, trans. D. Nicholson-Smith, Oxford: Blackwell.

Lefebvre, H., 1991. "The Production of Space," Oxford: Blackwell.

Levey, G., 2008. "Twilight Zone/Free Passage," *Ha'aretz*, 8 August, www.cosmos.ucc.ie/cs1064/jabowen/IPSC/php/art.php?aid=88157 [accessed 18 January 2014].

Loeckx, A., De Smet, H. and Vermeulen, P., 1996. *Resumptions, Compressions, Economy*, Antwerp: Pap.

Lofland, L., 1998. *The Public Realm. Exploring the City's Quintessential Social Territory*, New York: Aldine de Gruyter.

London Middle East Institute, 2002. "Helping to Preserve Middle Eastern Cultural Heritage," www.lmei.soas.ac.uk/writings_docs/PreservationOfTheMiddleEast.doc [accessed 22 August 2006].

Los, M., 2006. "Looking into the Future: Surveillance, Globalization and the Totalitarian Potential" in Lyon, D. (ed.) *Theorizing Surveillance: The Panopticon and Beyond*, Cullompton, UK: Willan.

Lowenthal, D., 1985. *The Past is a Foreign Country*, Cambridge: Cambridge University Press.

Lynch, K., 1960. *The Image of the City*. Cambridge, MA: MIT Press.

Lynch, K., 1972. *What Time is This Place?* Cambridge, MA: MIT Press.

Lynch, K., 1981. *Theory of Good City Form*, Cambridge, MA: MIT Press.

Lynch, K., 1991. "The Visual Shape of the Shapeless Metropolis" in: Banerjee T. and Southworth, M. (eds) *City Sense and City Design: Writings and Projects of Kevin Lynch*, Cambridge, MA: MIT Press.

Lynch, K., 2000. *The Image of the City*, Cambridge, MA: MIT Press.

Lyon, D., 2007. *Surveillance Studies: An Overview*, Oxford: Polity Press.

Magen, I., 1993. *The New Encyclopedia of Archaeological Excavation in The Holy Land: Shechem*, Jerusalem: Ariel, pp. 1354–1359.

Mann, S., Nolan, J. and Wellman, B., 2003. "Sousveillance: Inventing and Using Wearable Computing Devices for Data Collection," *Surveillance Environments, Surveillance & Society* 1(3): 331–355.

Mansour, M., 2002. "A Week in Jenin: Assessing Mental Health Needs Amid the Ruins," *Journal of Palestine Studies*, 31(4): 35–43.

Margalit, M., 2005. "The Truth Behind Formal Statistics," Israeli Committee against House Demolitions, 15 May, www.icahd.org/node/207 [accessed February 2006].

Masalha, N., 1992. *Expulsion of the Palestinians: The Concept of "Transfer" in Zionist Political Thought, 1882–1948*, Washington, DC: Institute for Palestine Studies.

Masalha, N., 1997. *A Land without a People: Israel, Transfer and the Palestinians 1949–1996*, London: Faber & Faber.

Masalha, N., 2002. "Israel's Moral Responsibility Towards the Palestinian Refugees," *Eclipse*, 15 May.

Masalha, N., 2003. *The Politics of Denial: Israel and the Palestinian Refugee Problem*, London and Sterling, VA: Pluto Press.

May, R., 1983. *The Discovery of Being*, New York: Basic Books.

Mbembe, A., 2003. "Necropolitics," *Public Culture*, 15(1): 11–40.

Mehrag, S. J., 1999. "Making it, Breaking it, and Making it Again: The Destruction and Reconstruction of War-torn Societies," MA (War Studies), Royal Military College of Canada, Kingston.

Mehrag, S. J., 2001. "Identicide and Cultural Cannibalism: Warfare's appetite for Symbolic Place," *Peace Research Journal*, 33(3): 89–98.

Mendieta E., 2004. *The Frankfurt School on Religion*, New York: Routledge.

Mills, E., 1864. *Three Month's Residence at Nablus: An Account of the Modern Samaritans*, London: AMS Press.

Misselwotz, P. and Rieniets, T. (eds), 2006. *City of Collision: Jerusalem and the Principles of Conflict Urbanism*, Basel: Birkhäuser.

Mofaz, S. H., 2002. "Operation Defensive Shield: Lessons and Aftermath," Policy #387 Washington Institute, Improving the Quality of USA Middle East Policy, 18 June, www.washingtoninstitute.org/policy-analysis/view/operation-defensive-shield-lessons-and-aftermath [accessed February 2005].

Mograbi, A. (director), 2005. *Avenge but One of My Two Eyes* (documentary), Israel/France.

Mondoweiss, 2013. "Palestinians Establish New Village: Bab al-Shams, 'Gate of the Sun'– in Occupied E1," 13 January, http://newsmotion.org/feed-story/palestinians-establish-new village%E2%80%93-bab-al-shams-%E2%80%98gatesun%E2%80%99%E2%80%93-occupied-e1 [accessed May 2013].

Morris, A. E. J., 1982. "The Changing Suq: Commercial Heart of the Islamic City," *Journal of Middle East Construction*, 7(11): 14.

Morris, B., 1989. *The Birth of the Palestinian Refugee Problem 1947–1949*, Cambridge: Cambridge University Press.

Morris, B., 1998. "Rashid Khalidi—the Palestinian identity: The Construction of Modern National Consciousness," *Journal of Israeli Studies*, 3: 266–272.

Moore, G. T., 1976. *Theory and Research on the Development of Environmental Knowing*, Stroudsburg, PA: Dowden, Hutchinson & Ross.

Moudon, A. V., 1994. "Getting to Know the Built Landscape: Typomorphology," in Frank, K. A. and Schneekloth, L. H. (eds) *Ordering Space: Types in Architecture and Design*, New York: Van Nostrand Reinhold, pp. 289–311.

Moudon, A. V., 1997. "Urban Morphology as an Emerging Interdisciplinary Field," *Urban Morphology, Journal of the International Seminar on Urban Form*, 1: 3–10.

Moudon, A. V., 1998. "The Changing Morphology of Suburban Neighbourhoods" in Petruccioli, A. (ed.) *Typological Process and Design Theory*, Cambridge, MA: MIT Press, pp. 141–157.

Mumford, L., 1945. *City Development*, New York: Harcourt, Brace.

Mumford, L., 1961. *The Culture of Cities*, New York: Harcourt, Brace.

Mumford, L., 1973. *The City in History: Its Origins, Its Transformations and Its Prospects*, Harmondsworth: Penguin Books.

Murphy, A., 2002. "The Territorial Underpinning of National Identity," *Geopolitics*, 7(2): 193–214.

Nablus Municipality website: www.nablus.org [accessed June 2013].

Naimark, N. M., 2001. *Fires of Hatred: Ethnic Cleansing in Twentieth-Century Europe*, Cambridge and London: Harvard University Press.

Nassar, N., 2006. "Colonization by Imagination: On the Palestinian Absence from the Landscape" in Misselwotz, P. and Rieniets, T. (eds) *City of Collision: Jerusalem and the Principles of Conflict Urbanism*, Basel: Birkhäuser Architecture.

Nora, P., 1996. *Realms of Memory: The Construction of the French Past*, New York: Columbia University Press.

Nordbruch, G., 2002. "Narrating Palestinian Nationalism: A Study of the New Palestinian Textbooks," Middle East Media Research Institute.

O'Hare, D., 1991. "Reconciling Tourism and Local Identity in Prague," unpublished Master's Thesis, JCUD, Oxford.

O'Neill, M. J., 1991. "Evaluation of a Conceptual Model of Architectural Legibility," *Environment and Behaviour*, 23(3): 259–284.

Ophir, A., 2002. "A Time of Occupation" in Segev, T. (ed.) *The Other Israel: Voices of Refusal and Dissent*, New York: New Press, pp. 51–66.

Oren, N., Bar-Tal, D., and David, O., 2004. "Conflict, Identity, and Ethos: The Israeli-Palestinian Case" in Lee, Y.-T., McCauley, C. R., Moghaddam, F. M. and Worchel, S. (eds) *The Psychology of Ethnic and Cultural Conflict*, Westport, CT: Praeger.

Ortner, S., 2006. *Anthropology and Social Theory: Culture, Power, and the Acting Subject*, Durham, NC: Duke University Press.

Osborne, Brian S., 1996. "Figuring Space, Marking Time: Contested Identities in Canada," *International Journal of Heritage Studies*, 1(1&2), Spring.

O'Tuathail, G. and Dahlman, C., 2006. "Post Domicide) Bosnia and Herzegovina: Homes, homeland and one million returns," *International Peacekeeping*, 13: 242–260.

Pacional, M., 2001. *Urban Geography: A Global Perspective*, London: Routledge.

Palestine Monitor, 2006a. "Fact Book 2012," www.almubadara.org/new/edetails.php?id=1769 [accessed June 2013].

Palestine Monitor, 2006b. "Gaza Facts and Figures Since the Beginning of the Invasion on 28 June 2006: Facts and Figures until 07 August," www.almubadara.org/new/edetails.php?id=1769 [accessed June 2013].

Palestinian National Information Center: http://www.palestine-info.co.uk/en/default.aspx?xyz=U6Qq7k%2BcOd%2FF7pkgJUE53N3pZngd29EpsttB6nMYWX2nJGsstEllO5nh AsV9Hej3tnX2OmWlaLuVD4WhWPEfaiDnthjss5Vp [accessed June 2013].

Papayanis, N., 2004. *Planning Paris before Haussmann*, Baltimore, MD: Johns Hopkins University Press.

Pappé, I., 1994. *The Making of the Arab–Israeli Conflict, 1947–1951*, London: B. Tauris & Co.

Pappé, I. (ed.), 1999. *The Israel/Palestine Question*, London: Routledge (Rewriting Histories Series).

Pappé, I., 2006. *The Ethnic Cleansing of Palestine*, London: One World.

PASSIA (Palestinian Academic Society For The Study of International Affairs), 2002. *The Palestine Question in Maps: 1878–2002*, Jerusalem: PASSIA.

PCBS (Palestinian Central Bureau of Statistics), 2005. "Palestinian Central Bureau of Statistics Released the Results of the Annual Report on Transportation and Communication Statistics in the Palestinian Territory," www.pcbs.gov.ps/Portals/_pcbs/Press Release/trans_comm_e.pdf [accessed June 2013].

Petruccioli, A., 1998. "Exotic, Polytheistic, Fundamentalist Typology: Gleaning in the Forms of an Introduction" in Petruccioli, A. (ed.) *Typological Process and Design Theory*, Cambridge, MA: MIT, pp. 9–18.

Pieterse, J., 2002. "Globalisation, Kitsch and Conflict: Technologies of Work, War and Politics," *Review of International Political Economy*, 9(1): 1–36.

Pirenne, H., 1936. *Economic and Social History of Medieval Europe*, London: K. Paul, Trench, Trubner & Co.

Porteous, D. and Smith, S. E., 2001. *Domicide: The Global Destruction of Home*. Montreal, QC: McGill-Queen's Press.

Proshansky, H., 1978. "The City and Self Identity," *Environment and Behaviour*, 10, 147–169.

Proshansky, H. M. and Fabian, A. K., 1986. "Psychological Aspects of the Quality of Urban Life" in Frick, D. (ed.) *The Quality of Urban Life*, Berlin: De Gruyter.

Proshansky, H., Fabian, A. K. and Kaminoff, R., 1983. "Place–identity, Physical World. Socialization of the Self," *Journal of Environmental Psychology*, 3: 57–83.

Qamhieh, K. H., 1992. "Saving the Old Town of Nablus: a Conservation Study," un-published PhD Dissertation, The Mackintosh School of Architecture, University of Glasgow.

Rabie, J., 1982. "Towards the Simulation of Urban Morphology," *Environmental and Planning, Planning and Design*, 18(1): 57–70.

Rapoport, A., 1977. *Human Aspects of Urban Form*, Oxford: Pergamon.

Reeves, P., 2000. "Action! Roll Out the Propaganda War," *The Independent*, 30 October.

Relph, E., 1976a. *Place and Placelessness*, London: Pion.

Relph, E., 1976b. "The Placelessness of Place," in Bird, J., Curtis, B., Putnam, T., Robertson, G. and Tickner, L. (eds) 1992, *Mapping the Futures: Local Cultures, Global Change*, London: Routledge.

Riedlmayer, A., 1994. "The War on People and the War on Culture," *The New Combat*, Autumn: 16–19.

Riedlmayer, A., 1995. "Killing Memory: The Targeting of Bosnia's Cultural Heritage Testimony," presented at a Hearing of the Commission on Security and Cooperation in Europe, www.google.be/search?newwindow=1&biw=1163&bih=838&q=Riedlmayer%2C+1995+%2C+killing+memory&oq=Riedlmayer%2C+1995+%2C+killing+memory&gs_l=serp.3...279433.289886.0.290135.26.22.4.0.0.0.109.1310.20j2.22.0.ernk_time combined...0...1.1.32.serp..20.6.265.oveEc790ljA [accessed February 2004].

Riedlmayer, A., 2002. "Destruction of Cultural Heritage in Bosnia-Hercegovina, 1992–1996: A Post-war Survey of Selected Municipalities," Bosnia-Herzegovina Cultural Heritage Report, Cambridge, MA.

Robinson, G. M., 1990. *Conflict and Change in the Countryside: Rural Society, Economy and Planning in the Developed World*. New York: Belhaven Press.

Rodinson, M., 1981. *The Arabs*, trans. A. Goldhammer, original French publication 1979, Chicago, IL: University of Chicago Press.

Roger, P., 1865. *Letter from Roger Pocock to Morley Roberts*, Commonwealth miscellanea, Cambridge: Cambridge University Library.

Rogers, A. P. V., 1996. *Law on the Battlefield*, Manchester: Manchester University Press.

Rogers, M. E., 1865. *Domestic Life in Palestine*, New York: Eaton & Mains.

Rossi, A., 1982. *The Architecture of the City*, Cambridge, MA: MIT Press.

Rotbard, S., 2003. "Wall and Tower (Homa Umigdal): the Mold of Israeli Architecture in Civilian occupation" in Weizman, E. and Seal, R. (eds) *Civilian Occupation: The Politics of Israeli Architecture*, London: Verso, pp. 40–56.

Rykwert, J., 2002. *The Seduction of Place*, New York: Vintage Books.

Sack, R., 1980. *Conceptions of Space in Social Thought: A Geographic Perspective*, Hong Kong: University of Minnesota Press.

Sack, R., 1983. "Human Territoriality: A Theory," *Annals, Association of American Geographers*, 73: 55, 74.

Sack, R., 1986. *Human Territoriality: Its Theory and History*, Cambridge: Cambridge University Press.

Sack, R., 1997. *Home Geographicus: A Framework for Action, Awareness, and Moral Concern*, Cambridge: Cambridge University Press.

Said, E., 1979a. *The Question of Palestine*. New York: Times Books.

Said, E., 1979b. "Zionism from the Standpoint of Its Victims," *Social Text* 1: 7–58.

Said, E., 1999. *Out of Place*, New York: Vintage Books.

Said, E., 2000. "Between Worlds" in Said, E. *Reflections on Exile*, London: Granta, pp. 554–568.

Said, E. and Mohr, J., 1999. *After the Last Sky, Palestinian Lives*, New York: Columbia University Press.

Saliba, R., 1997. "The Mental Image of Downtown Beirut 1990: A Case Study in Cognitive Mapping and Urban Form" in Davie, M. (ed.) *Beyrouth: Regards coisée*, Tours: URBAMA, Coll. Villes du Monde Arabe, No. 2, pp. 305–349.

Sanchez, A., 2009. "The Facebook Feeding Frenzy: Resistance-through-Distance and Resistance-through Persistence in the Societied Network," *Surveillance & Society*, 6(3): 275–293.

Sayer, A., 1989. "The 'New' Regional Geography and the Problems of Narrative," *Environment and Planning D.: Society and Space*, 7, 253–276.

Schama, S., 1995. *Landscape and Memory*, New York: Vintage Books.

Schnell, I., 1994. *Perceptions of Israeli Arabs: Territoriality and Identity*, Tel Aviv, Research in Ethnic Relations Series.

Schnell, I., 2001a. "Introduction: Changing Territorial Concepts in Israel," *Geo Journal*, 53(3): 213–217.

Schnell, I., 2001b. "Transformation in Territorial Concepts: From Nation Building to Concessions," *Geo Journal*, 53: 221–234.

Schîlch, A., 1982. "European Penetration and the Economic Development of Palestine, 1856–1882" in Owen, R. (ed.) *Studies in the Economic and Social History of Palestine in the 19th and 20th centuries*, Oxford: Oxford University Press, pp. 10–87.

Schulz, N., 1971. *Space and Architecture*, London: Praeger.

Schulz, N., 1980. *Genius Loci: Toward a Phenomenology of Architecture*, New York: Rizzoli.

Schulz, S. and Hammer, J., 2003. *The Palestinian Diaspora: Formation of Identities and Politics of Homeland*, London: Routledge.

Shafir, G., 1989. *Land, Labor and the Origins of the Israeli-Palestinian Conflict 1882–1999*, Cambridge: Cambridge University Press.

Shahjahan, R. A., 2012. "From 'No' to 'Yes': Postcolonial Perspectives on Resistance to Neoliberal Higher Education," *Discourse: Studies in the Cultural Politics of Education*, 35(3): 1–14.

Shaw, M., 2003. *War and Genocide: Organized Killing in Modern Society*, Cambridge: Polity Press.

Shaw, M., 2004. "New Wars of the City: 'Urbicide' and 'Genocide'" in Graham, S. (ed.), *Cities, War, and Terrorism*, Oxford: Blackwell, pp. 141–153.

Shaw, M., 2005. "New Wars of the City: Urbicide and Genocide" in Graham, S. (ed.) *Cities, War and Terrorism: Towards an Urban Geopolitics*, Oxford: Blackwell.

Sheik Hassan, I., 2005. "Charting a Palestinian Strategy of Exile: Burj El Barajneh Refugee Camp," Master's thesis, Catholic University, Leuven, Belgium.

Sheik Hassan, I. (ed.), (forthcoming) *On Urbanism and Activism: Addressing Palestinian Camps/Reconstructing Nahr El Bared*, Zürich: Park Books.

Sheik Hassan, I. and Hanafi, S., 2009. "(In)Security and Reconstruction in Post Conflict Nahr alBarid Refugee Camp," *Journal of Palestine Studies*, XL(1): 27–48.

Siegel, I., 2003. "A Report from Nablus: Sunday, September 22, 2002," http://orias.berkeley.edu/2003/peace/nablus.pdf [accessed 30 July 2010].

Simmons, S., 2001. "Urbicide and the Myth of Sarajevo," *Persian Review*, 4(6): 24–30.

Slyomovics, S., 1998. *The Object of Memory: Arab and Jew Narrate the Palestinian Village*, Philadelphia, PA: University of Pennsylvania Press.

Smith, N., 1992. "Homeless/Global: Scaling places" in Bird, J., Curtis, B., Putnam, T., Robertson, G. and Tickner, L. (eds) *Mapping the Futures: Local Cultures, Global Change*, London: Routledge, pp. 87–119.

Smith, N. and Katz, C., 1993. "Grounding the Metaphor: Towards a Specialized Politics" in Keith, M. and Pile, S. (eds) *Place and the Politics of Identity*, London: Routledge, pp. 67–83.

Soja, E., 1989. *Post-Modern Geographies: The Re-assertion of Space in Critical Social Theory*, London: Verso.

Sune, E., 2002. "What Lies Beneath: Excerpts from an Invasion," EAPPI, 1 November, http://eappi.org/en/news/eareports/r.html?tx_ttnews%5Btt_news%5D=11048&tx_tt news%5BbackPid%5D=4837&cHash=bjhoqcwthzxlm [accessed February 2004].

Tamari, S., 1981. "The Palestinians in the West Bank and Gaza: The Sociology of Dependency" in Khalil, N. and Zureik, E. (eds) *The Sociology of the Palestinians*, London: Groom Helm, 82–111.

Taylor, S., 2003. "A Place for the Future? Residence and Continuity in Women's Narratives of Their Lives," *Narrative Inquiry*, 13: 193–215.

Tehranian, M., 1998. "Globalization, Localism, and Islamism: Migration, Identity and World System Developments," *International Political Science Review*, 19(3): 418–440.

Thompson, P. and Ackroyd, S., 1995. "All Quiet on the Workplace Front: A Critique of Recent Trends," *British Industrial Sociology, Sociology* 29: 615–635.

Trancik, R., 1986. *Finding Lost Space: Theories of Urban Design*. New York: Van Nostrand Reinhold.

Tristram, H. B., 1866. *Routes In The Holy Land*, London: The Society for Promoting Christian Knowledge.

Tuan, Y., 1977. *"Space and Place": The Perspective of Experience*, Minneapolis, MN: University of Minnesota Press.

Tuan, Y., 1980. "Rootedness Versus Sense of Place," *Landscape*, 24: 3–8.

Tuan, Y., 1991. "Language and the Making of Place: A Narrative-Descriptive Approach," *Annals of the American Association of Geographers*, 81(4): 686.

Twiggers-Ross, C. L. and Uzzell, D. L., 1996. "Place and Identity Process," *Journal of Environmental Psychology*, 16, 205–220.

UNESCO (United Nations Educational, Scientific and Cultural Organization), 2003. "Draft UNESCO Declaration Concerning the Intentional Destruction of Cultural Heritage," General Conference proceedings, 32nd session, Paris, http://unesdoc.unesco.org/images/0013/001307/130780e.pdf [accessed June 2004].

UNESCO, 2009. *Inventory of Cultural and Natural Heritage sites of Potential Outstanding Universal Value in Palestine*. Ramallah: Palestinian Department of Antiquities and Cultural Heritage.

United Nations, 2012. *World Urbanization Prospects: The 2011 Revision: Methodology*, New York: Department of Economic and Social Affairs Population Division.

United Nations Secretary General, 2002. *Report of the Secretary-General Prepared Pursuant to General Assembly Resolution ES-10/10*, New York: United Nations.

UNOCHA (United Nations Office for the Coordination of Humanitarian Affairs), 2002. "Humanitarian Update Occupied Palestinian Territories 01 October 2002," http://relief web.int/report/israel/ocha-humanitarian-update-occupied-palestinian-territories-01-oct-2002 [accessed June 2004].

UNOCHA, 2003. "Occupied Palestinian Territory Humanitarian Update, 01 September–15 October 2003," http://reliefweb.int/report/occupied-palestinian-territory/ocha-humanitarian-update-occupied-palestinian-territories-1 [accessed June 2004].

UNOCHA, 2004. "Initial Report: The Humanitarian Consequences of the IDF Operation in the Old City of Nablus," www.bethlehemmedia.net/nablus_report.pdf [accessed February 2006].

UNOCHA, 2005a. "UNOCHA Records 605 Closure Barriers in the West Bank," *Electronic Intifada*, 4 May, http://electronicintifada.net/cgibin/artman/exec/view.cgi/11/3817 [accessed February 2006].

UNOCHA, 2005b. "Cost of Conflict: Nablus after Five Years of Conflict," December, www.ochaopt.org/documents/opt_cashwork_ocha_costconflict_dec_2005.pdf [accessed February 2006].

UNRWA (United Nations Relief and Works Agency for Palestine Refugees), 2005. "Map of UNRWA's Area of Operations," http://reliefweb.int/map/occupied-palestinian-territory/unrwa-area-operations-2005 [accessed February 2006].

Unsal, B., 1959. *Turkish Islamic Architecture*, London: D. N. Vilbe.

USAF (United States Air Force), 1998. "USAF Intelligence Targeting Guide," www.fas.org/irp/doddir/usaf/afpam14-210/part20.htm [accessed February 2006].

Vale, L. and Campanella, T. (eds), 2005. *The Resilient City: How Modern Cities Recover from Disaster*, Oxford: Oxford University Press.

Verhaert, I., 2006. "Urbicide in Beirut 1975–2006," unpublished Master Thesis, Catholic University of Leuven, Leuven.

Virilio, P., 2002. *Ground Zero*, trans. C. Turner, London and New York: Verso.

Walker, J., 1985. "Rebels with our Applause: A Critique of Resistance Theory" in "Paul Willis's ethnography of schooling," *Journal of Education*, 167: 63–83.

Webb, M. and Palmer, G., 1998. "Evading Surveillance and Making Time: An Ethnographic View of the Japanese Floor in Britain," *British Journal of Industrial Relations*, 36(4): 611–627.

Weiss, E., 2006. "Eitam: Expel Palestinians, Dismiss Arab MKs." *Ynet News*, www.ynetnews.com/articles/0,7340,L-3302275,00.html [accessed February 2007].

Weizman, C., 2001. "A Brief Biography and Quotes," *Palestine Remembered.com*, www.palestineremembered.com/Acre/Famous-Zionist-Quotes/Story645.html [accessed April 2006].

Weizman, E., 2003. "Politics of Verticality" in Weizman, E. and Segal, R. (eds) *Territories, Islands, Camps and Other States of Utopia*, Cologne: Verlag der Buchhandlung Walther Kînig, pp. 65–112.

Weizman, E., 2004a. "Builders and Warriors: Military Operations as Urban Planning," Site, 2 November, www.wooloo.org/Terror/weizman.html [accessed April 2006].

Weizman, E., 2004b. "Strategic Points, Flexible Lines, Tense Surfaces and Political Volumes: Ariel Sharon and the Geometry of Occupation" in *Cities, War, and Terrorism: Towards an Urban Geopolitics*, Malden, MA: Blackwell, pp. 172–191.

Weizman, E., 2007. *Hollow Land: Israel's Architecture of Occupation*, London, New York: Verso.

Weizman, E., 2011. The *Least of All Possible Evils: Humanitarian Violence from Arendt to Gaza*, London and New York: Verso.

Weizman, E. and Segal, R., 2003. "Introduction 5. The Mountain: Principles of Building in Heights, & 6. The Battle for the Hills" in Weizman, E. and Segal, R. (eds) *Civilian Occupation: The Politics of Israeli Architecture*, London: Verso, pp. 19–26 and 80–108.

Whitehand, J. W. R., 1981. "The Background to the Urban Morphogenetic Tradition" in Whitehand, J. W. R. (ed.) The *Urban Landscape: Historical Development and Management: Papers by M. R. G. Conzen*. Institute of British Geographers, Special Publication, No. 13, London: Academic Press: 1–24.

Wilson, A. L., 2000. "Professional Practice in the 'Modern' World" in Mott, V. W. and Daley, B. J. (eds), *New Horizons in Continuing Professional Education*. San Francisco, CA: Jossey-Bass.

Wilson, A. L, 2001. "Place, Power, and Planning in Continuing Professional Education" in Cervero, R. M., Wilson, A. L. & Associates (eds) *Power, Practice: The Struggle for Knowledge and Power in Society*, San Francisco, CA: Jossey-Bass.

Wilson, J. A., 1969. *Egyptian Rituals and Incantations in Ancient Near Eastern Texts Relating to the Old Testament*, third edition with supplement, ed. J. B. Pritchard. Princeton, NJ: Princeton University.

Wood P., 2004. "Fixing the Problem of Fallujah," 7 November, http://news.bbc.co.uk/2/hi/middle_east/3989639.stm [accessed March 2005].

Woolf, G., 1992. "The Unity and Diversity of Romanization," *JRA* 5: 349–352.

Wright, G. Ernest, 1965. *Shechem: The Biography of a Biblical City*, London: Gerald Duckworth & Co.

Yaakov, S. and Levine, E. (eds), 1974. *Political Dictionary of the Middle East in the 20th Century*. New York: Quadrangle.

Yehezkeli, T., 2002. "We Made Them a Stadium in the Middle of the Camp," *Yedi'ot Aharonot*, 31 May.

Yiftachel, O., 2002. "Territory as the Kernel of the Nation: Space, Time, and Nationalism in Israel/Palestine," *Geopolitics*, 7(2): 215–248.

Yiftachel, O., 2004. "Contradictions and Dialectics: Reshaping Political Space in Israel/Palestine: An Indirect Response to Lina Jamoul," *Antipode* 36(4): 607–613.

Yiftachel, O., 2006. *Ethnocracy: Land and Identity Politics in Israel/Palestine*, Philadelphia, PA: University of Pennsylvania Press.

Zonabend, F., 1984. *The Enduring Memory: Time and History in a French Village*, trans. A. Forster, Manchester: Manchester University Press.

Index

Page numbers in *italics* refers to an illustration/figure